THE UNBELIEVABLE PLIGHT OF MRS. WRIGHT

WRITTEN BY Dr. Diana Wright
ND, MBA, BSN, RN

For more information, contact Dr. Wright:
dwright@therightsolutions.com
www.DrDianaWright.com

First paperback edition, July 2019. Published by Kharis Publishing, imprint of Kharis Media LLC.

All Kharis Publishing products are available at special quantity discounts for bulk purchase for sales promotions, premiums, fund-raising, or educational needs. For details, contact:

Kharis Media LLC
Tel: 1-479-599-8657
support@kharispublishing.com
www.kharispublishing.com

Dedicated to the memory of Jennifer Claire Allen Anderson
May 27, 1969 to June 2, 2017

BRIEF TABLE OF CONTENTS

DETAILED TABLE OF CONTENTS

PEOPLE IN THE BOOK

Listed in order of appearance.
(TRS refers to TRS Healthcare, originally The Right Solutions)

Part 1

Leon Johnson – My paternal grandfather

Lena Graves – Former girlfriend of Leon's and sister-in-law of Leone's

James, Michael, Herbert – my paternal grandmother's siblings

Leone Lyndall/Buddy – My paternal grandmother

Alma Rebecca – Leone's mother, my great-grandmother

Miss Annie – Leone's father's girlfriend

Leon Jr. "Fox" – My father

Jerilyn "Jeri" – My paternal aunt

Sherman "Red" – My paternal aunt

Carolyn – My paternal aunt

Alma "Tirr" – My paternal aunt

Frances – Leon's second wife

Henry Floyd Fearn – My maternal grandfather

Mary Alma Worthington Fearn – My maternal great-grandmother, Henry's mother

Merton Melvin Fearn – My maternal great-grandfather, Henry's father

Arland – Henry's brother, my maternal great uncle

Blanche – Henry's sibling, my maternal great

Edmund – Henry's brother, my maternal great uncle

Mary Elizabeth – Henry's sister, my maternal great aunt

Eugene – Henry's brother, my maternal great uncle

Josephine – Henry's sister, my maternal great aunt

Lydia – Henry's sister, my maternal great aunt

Lacy – Nellie's younger sister, my maternal great aunt

Hazel – Nellie's older sister, my maternal great aunt

Blanche – Nellie's older sister, my maternal great aunt

Nellie Dean Rowe – Henry's wife, my maternal grandmother

Brooks – My maternal uncle

Neva Jean – My mother

Howard – My maternal uncle

Donald – My maternal uncle

Maxine Jo – My maternal aunt

Sandy – Jerilyn's son, my paternal cousin

Leon III "Sonny" – My oldest brother

Gary – My older brother

Diane/Dian/Diana – Me

Mark – My younger brother

Part 2

Lena Mae – My father's love affair

Toby – My next-door neighbor boy in Kilgore, Texas

    Kitty and Arthur Brown – Toby's parents

    Lance – Toby's brother

Mrs. Freeman – My first-grade teacher

Maggie Beth – Girl in my first-grade class

Jan – Carolyn's best friend, my cousin

Bernice – Carolyn's other best friend

Brad – Jan's son

Derrick – Mark's childhood friend

    Pa Robinson – Derrick's grandfather, Mark's adopted father

    Nanny – Pa's wife, Derrick's grandmother

Brent Kingston – My fifth-grade crush

Mrs. Carpenter – My fifth-grade teacher

    Trisha Ryan – My first lifelong, best friend

    Texada – Trisha's grandmother

    Sarah – Trisha's mother

    Courtney – Trisha's father

    Troy – Trisha's older brother

Shawn – Neighbor boy in Shreveport

Christina – Shawn's sister, neighbor girl in Shreveport

Kelly – Shawn's sister, neighbor girl in Shreveport

Mr. Hall – Our Shreveport family doctor who was a pharmacist

Dena Kay - My cousin, Uncle Don's daughter

June Nelson – My childhood best friend, grandma's neighbor

    Mrs. Gillis – June's grandmother

    Heather Mattie Lois – June's mother

    Chad – June's older brother

Cecil McCune – My sixth-grade teacher

Kimberly – Tall girl in my sixth-grade class

Luther Smith – Eighth-grade quarterback, my boyfriend in tenth grade, later my first husband

Eric – My uncle Sherman's best friend, a reporter for the Shreveport Times newspaper

Brian Mont – My uncle Sherman's best friend

Audrey – Sherman's wife, my aunt

Graves – Sherman's son, my cousin

Dodie Fox/Mrs. Fox – Landlady of the Shreveport duplex when I was 12

Uncle E.F. – My aunt Tirr's husband, my uncle

Margaret "Dirl" – Leon's sister

Dorothy Gipson – My seventh-grade best friend

Chris – Dorothy's brother

Shane – My boyfriend when I was 15

Lily Beaver – One of the girls in my eighth-grade class who mama beat up, my friend

Damon – Lily's little brother

Mr. Naser – Arabic slumlord, our landlord on College Street

Barnes Family – Upstairs apartment dwellers on College Street

Wendy and Jane – The Barnes' daughters, my best friends in ninth grade

Carrie – My ninth-grade best friend

Tara – My best friend in ninth-grade

Joey – My boyfriend in tenth-grade, Scot's friend

Logan – Haughton, Louisiana Chief of Police's son

Mary – Luther's mother

Emma – My freshmen year of college roommate and friend

Dana – My first daughter, Luther is her father

Harper – Worked in the college financial office, friends in college

Meme and Papa – Luther's grandmother and grandfather

Liam – Luther's friend

Olivia – My college friend who was 32 at the time, divorced mother

James – Luther and I's neighbor in Monroe, later moved in with Scot and I in Ruston

Miss Anne Elizabeth – Old lady that Mama took care of in a big house

Miss Evelyn Avery – Anne Elizabeth's daughter

Charlotte Avery Evelyn – Anne Elizabeth's granddaughter

Oliver – Miss Anne's great grandson that had a crush on me, lawyer

Evelyn Avery – Miss Anne's great-granddaughter, Frank's sister

Jimmy Wingo – Our garage apartment neighbor when I moved back in with Mama

Bryan – My cousin who visited in Monroe when I went back to college

Dr. Hall – My pediatrician for Dana in Monroe

Mason – Trisha's husband

Amelia – Luther's girlfriend/affair

Jake – Neighbor in the trailer park

Isabella – Jake's daughter

Alex – My best friend when living in the trailer

Mia – My next-door neighbor at the new trailer, my best friend

Don – A friend I met in Beginning Experience, a Catholic program

Donna – Don's daughter

David Wright – My present husband

Part 3

Melanie Aichele (Wright) – My first daughter with David

Stacy, Angie, Kerry, and Amy -

David's nieces

Rosemary – David's sister

Pauline – David's mother

Arlis – David's father

Megan – The first RN that I worked with

Sofia – Our Greek neighbor on Patton St

Bridget - My single elderly neighbor on Patton St, Marianna's best friend

Joan – My friend who moved into Bridget's house after she died

Carol Kaye – Nursing school friend

Ella, Madison, and Scarlet – nursing school friends

       Ethan – Madison's cheating husband

       Daniel – Ella's cheating husband

Tessie – Pa Robinson's granddaughter

Betty Grace – Head nurse of the ICU at Riverside Hospital in Bossier City

Victoria – The RN I worked with on my first night shift at Riverside

Grace – A nurse at Riverside

Julia "Julie" Faught (Wright) – My second daughter with David, my third daughter and youngest child

Aiden – LPN at Riverside

Matthew – Unmarried pharmacist friend

Dr. Jenkins – My doctor that delivered Melanie and Julia

Layla – Unit Director of the L&D unit at Riverside

Nora – My roommate in the hospital when I had Julia

Paula – David's sister

Robert – Paula's husband

Dr. Hannah Evans – Cardiologist I worked with at Riverside

Dr. Simmons – ER doctor at Riverside

Michelle – Mark's wife

Kevin – Mark's son, my nephew

Dr. Bryant – A plastic surgeon who performed my breast augmentation procedure

Dr. Evans – Owner of the Doctor's Hospital in Shreveport

Dorothy Washington – Nurse aid that worked at Doctor's Hospital

Henry Charles – Dr. Evan's son, the Hospital Administrator

Kim – Gary's wife

       Ali – Kim's daughter, my niece

Dr. Barry Richardson – Former Dean of Centenary College's Frost School of Business; my interviewer for the Centenary College MBA program

Piper – Luther's wife's mother-in-law; dropped off designer clothing on my back porch

Tom Bickham – My best friend; a hospital administrator at Bossier General Hospital

Joseph Turner – My friend; the assistant administrator at Doctor's

Hospital

Dr. Wong – Neurologist that was attempting to sexually assault me at Doctor's Hospital

Daniel – Director of Outpatient Respiratory Therapy and Prosthetics at the Shreveport VA

Jackson – RN at Shreveport VA

Sam – Assistant administrator at the VA

A TV Host – Television host of Primetime

John Noles – Political campaign manager for Edwin Edwards (former Louisiana Governor); a friend; social worker at the Shreveport VA

Owen – Started Tritek Medical Staffing as a respiratory therapy agency

Aubrey – Owen's wife

Lillian – Girl that showed up at my house in Springlake at age 16

Abdul – A crazy old, rich Arab man who Owen visited

Johnathan – Ali's older brother; Gary and Kim's son; my nephew

Sue – Sonny's wife

Rod – My carpenter for our house in Siloam Springs on Highway 68

Mrs. Natalie Harris – Julia's sixth grade teacher and cheerleading coach

Dylan – Dana's criminal love interest in Dallas

Part 4

Anthony – Friend from Insurance school who rented a desk at my first

TRS office

Art Morris – President of Arkansas State Bank; my banker friend

Walter Gray – Local Siloam Springs businessman who helped with competitor analysis for TRS

Carrie – Nurse who worked the first shift for The Right Solutions; staffed by Anthony

Kelly – Staffed LPNs and CNAs in nursing homes 1997

Renee – Staffing coordinator for Columbia Hospitals

Pat, Rick, Chris, Nettie Anders, and Debra Dormont – Nurses from 1997

Cherrie – Injured nurse who ended up working for TRS for many years

Joe Carter – Man eating with Senator Stratton Taylor at a restaurant in 1997 that I saved from cardiac arrest with DON instructions

Senator Stratton Taylor – Oklahoma Senator 1982-2006; eating with Joe Carter when he went into cardiac arrest

Jane – Hardworking nurse who supported her husband's racing and two sons

Father Ricci – Catholic priest who convinced Melanie to run for Queen Concordia

Camila – Mom of one of Julia's ball team members; kept Julia while I was sick; caterer for Melanie's and Aunt Julie's weddings

Isaac – TRS CFO, 1998; worked for TRS for many years; close friend

Jack – CPA I hired in 1998

Robin – CNA I hired in 1998; presently a TRS recruiter

Luna – TRS nurse that drove a motorcycle and had a bulldog, 1998

Jenny – RN who worked as much as she could, 1998

Mike – RN who convinced me to enter travel nursing

Tom – TRS nurse, 1998

Garth – TRS LPN nurse, 1999 (later married Mary and I attended the wedding)

Lori – TRS ICU nurse, 1999

Gloria – TRS nurse, 1999

Lynda – Friend from the middle school; rewrote paperwork for travel nursing, 1999

Joshua Andrew "Josh" Graves – Dana's husband

Nathan and Hazel – CNAs running an agency out of Harrison

Ivy – Partner with Nathan and Hazel

Kathy – LPN from Harrison; employee of TRS; stole the concept and everything from TRS in 2001

Traca – Vice President of TRS in 1999; left with Kathy

Ruby, Selene, and Tina – Nurses who attempted a murder-for-hire scheme

Jonathan Barnett – David and I's close friend in Siloam Springs; contractor for my second building

Elaine – TRS recruiter, 2001

Bo – TRS software programmer; presently IT Director

Jack and Goldenchild – TRS CRTT and RN, 2000

Donna – TRS RN, 2001

Sophie – TRS RN, 2001

Mary – Clerk for TRS; left with Kathy to start a competing agency

Stella – Kathy's assistant

Leah – Left with Kathy to start a competing agency; former accounting manager

Michelle – Corporate lawyer hired for the Harrison lawsuit; added more law suits on TRS

Joe – Julia's boyfriend senior year of high school

Johnny – TRS RN, 2002

Beverly – TRS RN, 2002

Amy – Trisha's oldest child, lived with me until she married Chad (Husband Chad)

Virginia – TRS recruiter, 2002; presently a TRS Recruiter Team Lead

Lincoln Baker – My second attorney that helped me with the Georgian Court case

James Barnett – Jonathan Barnett's brother

> **Marilyn** – James' wife
> **Abby** – James and Marilyn's daughter; my street in Siloam Springs is named after her

Isabella – Dana's second child; died shortly after being brought home from the hospital

Vicky – TRS RN, 2003

Ryan – Chief Sales Officer at TRS, 2001-2018

Alexander – Dana's oldest child

Aaron – Dana's foster child who had a severe case of hemophilia

John Boozman – Arkansas Representative 2001-2011; Senator 2011-present (2019); nominated me for businessman of the year, 2004

Maxine – TRS LPN, 2004 (husband Barry)

Cara – TRS L&D/MedSurg/ER nurse, 2004

Sheryl – TRS nurse, 2004

Clint – Melanie's husband

Taylor – Julia's husband

Julie – David's sister (husband Bob)

Jimmie Bilby – TRS employee since 2000; presently CoNexus CEO

Chad – Amy's husband

Doris – TRS ICU nurse, 2005

Dr. Dave Smith – TRS nurse who had his PHD, 2005

Brenda – TRS RN, 2006

Ann – TRS RN in Alaska, 2006

Chrissy – TRS RN, 2006

Sean – Tontitown Fire Chief

Alice – Shane's wife; hired in credentials

Maureen – My assistant at TRS; presently Director of Human Resources

Alan Beauleiu – President and speaker for ITR Economics; one of the country's foremost economists

Jeri – Former Chief Financial Officer for TRS; stole over $1 million from TRS

Vicky and Loy Hoskins – Other victims of Jeri's theft

Joanie – Nurse friend

Elizabeth – My first granddaughter; Dana's daughter

Jessica – TRS RN, 2006

Part 5

Courtney – TRS recruiter that was hurt in a motorcycle accident during a Cozumel company cruise, 2007

Jan – TRS employee and RN, 2007-present day (2019)

Sawyer – Melanie's oldest child

Jack – Dana's third child

Sheppard – Julia's oldest child

Carson – Ali's first child

Beau – Melanie's second child

Summit – Julia's second child

Bill – TRS LPN, 2008

Lily – TRS nurse, 2009

Markus – TRS RN, 2009

Steve – TRS nurse, 2009

Hunter – Graphic designer for TRS, 2009

Patti – TRS nurse, 2010

Anita – TRS recruiter, 2010-present day (2019)

Abby – TRS RN, 2010

Joe Shadowen – TRS recruiting manager, 2010

Jerry – TRS employee, 2010

Nicholas Webb – TRS LPN to RN

p

Kelly Fletcher – TRS LPN to RN

Caleb – TRS assistant manager, presently COO at TRS

Dr. Jonathan Parker – Doctor I went to in May 2012

Dr. Rogers – Doctor that found the ovarian tumor in my colon wall

Bonus Content

Words of Wisdom
Forgiveness is a walk in faith every day.
We need to say every day, "I forgive everyone, everything, I can, I will, and I do." Then the Father will forgive us.

Words of Wisdom and *Rules of Business* look like this. I wrote these in as lessons learned from the stories I share. Each and every one of these is important to me. I hope you take them to heart and apply them to your life, no matter what your role or calling is.

TRS Story:

Robin the Recruiter

Robin, a CNA, worked at various nursing homes. One day she injured her back at the nursing home, so I went and got her. I drove her to the ER and stayed with her while she waited to be seen. She was treated and released. The insurance I had at the time requested that I bring her in-house to work...

TRS Stories look like this. These are funny, special, or just plain weird stories of in-house employees working in my office. Each story is true and usually about how they started working for me or something funny that happened to them.

Nurse Story:
Debra

Debra's story is sad. At 42, she had three daughters, ages 16, 14, and 12. One day she was scheduled to work in the Emergency Room in Tulsa, when she called off to say she was having chest pain. Her girls drove her to the family doctor. There she was made to wait her turn in the waiting room. She deteriorated. The girls threw her back in the car to drive to the Emergency...

TRS Nurse Stories look like this. These are funny, special, or just plain weird stories about REAL nurses that have worked for me. Each story is true and was recorded by actual TRS recruiters or myself.

Cancer Scare:
Stage 0

It was at the end of the Queen Concordia race that I went for my annual pap smear. It was positive for pre-cancerous cells of non-HPV origin. I was 40. I have been tested over 10 times. I have always been non-HPV positive, but the MDs kept testing me, as they refused to believe my cancer could be a gene. It was cancer Stage 0...

Cancer Scares look like this. These are instances where I knew cancer was looming on the horizon. Each passage foreshadows my final diagnosis.

THE UNBELIEVABLE PLIGHT OF MRS. WRIGHT

PREFACE

L ong ago now, when I was in my mid-twenties, and already an experienced and proficient nurse, I saw my future in a graph. It was 1985; I was attending a seminar given by the Joint Commission of Hospital Accreditation (JCAHO) when the speaker put up a visual aid—a demographic analysis of the future of nursing. One line of the graph followed the baby boomer population as they aged. The other line predicted the declining number of nurses. The two lines intersected in the year 2000— when the baby boomers would increasingly be in need of medical care.

As if a flash bulb had gone off in that dimly lit room, I immediately knew what I had to do. Work, study, plan, work, strategize, work, get certified, go back to school, work, and oh yes, did I mention, work?

I had fifteen years to catch that wave. Fifteen years to figure out a business model. Fifteen years to make my mark.

When I make up my mind to do something, it gets done. I have known exactly where I was going since I was six years old. I do not wake up in the morning wondering what my life will hold. I know exactly where I am going and have a plan to get there. I am never lost in life. I never wondered who I was or what my sexual identity was. Many people do not have a basic navigational plan for how to get from Point A to Point B in their lives or in work. I always had a plan A, plan B, and back-up plan C. People follow leaders who are not lost. I was a servant leader, often doing the hardest jobs myself and teaching others how to do their jobs.

Nursing, more than most other professions, is about people. We welcome you into the world and we hold your hand as you leave. We are intimate with blood, urine, skin, breath, and fecal matter. We insert needles, remove catheters, cuff arms, and read charts. No matter how far technology advances, there will always be a need for a nurse's human touch. We traffic daily in pain, joy, and everything in between. We form close bonds both with the patients we care for in their beds and with our fellow health care workers as we pass in the hospital corridors. Nursing is an art and a science. We are privileged to be with people in some of their most intimate and difficult moments.

For all these reasons and more, I have always found the name "nurse" degrading. Why must a profession be called something that women do with their babies and breasts? In my career as a nurse, a hospital administrator, and as the founder and owner of a thriving healthcare business, I have always strived to bring dignity and professionalism to patient care.

That is why when I started my own business I always called it a "healthcare" business. When I founded The Right Solutions, on November 1, 1996, I had $18,000 in cash and a $50,000 credit line. Today, the company has an annual growth rate of nearly 205% and is one of Staffing Industry Analysts' fastest-growing staffing firms. In 2005, we became only the sixth Healthcare Staffing Company to be certified by JCAHO and have received a rating of 100% ever since. TRS Healthcare, owned by me, a Registered Nurse, is the only privately-owned nursing staffing agency in the United States of my size. The year 2000 has come and gone and I certainly caught my wave. At times the going has been rough, but I survived by having a plan and working my plan. I've always kept my hand firmly on my navigational rudder and righted my course. Among my many accomplishments and awards, I was recognized as Arkansas Best Nurse of the Year (2015), Arkansas Business Executive of the Year (2008), and Businessman of the Year (2004) presented by President George W. Bush.

I am most proud of my Doctorate in Naturopathy, which I attained at the age of 61. I was able to put aside my medical prejudices and open my acceptance to a different type of medicine. For years I had only believed in allopathic medicine, which is the chemical drugs of man. I had to open up my mind to accept the natural ways of God. In the words of Dr. Ralf Kleef, "there should not be chemical drugs versus natural medicine, but only good medicine versus bad medicine."

THE UNBELIEVABLE PLIGHT OF MRS. WRIGHT

Your story is yours to tell. You can't make apologies for your truth; how you felt, the way something impacted you is your history now.

Frank Whalen

THE UNBELIEVABLE PLIGHT OF MRS. WRIGHT

INTRODUCTION

This is my story.

To understand where I ended up, I need to tell you how I came about in the first place.

I have overcome domestic and spousal abuse, poverty, hunger, lack of education, and being a divorced mother with a small child to become a valued, wealthy, highly educated, self-made millionaire, owner and president of a nationwide travel nurse company that is one of the largest in the US. I have grown my company from running it myself to where it is today.

I have no high school degree, but I have completed my GED, graduated in May 15, 1981, with a four-year nursing degree: Bachelor of Science (BSN) in Nursing. I became a Registered Nurse in 1982. I have a Master of Business (MBA) Degree I obtained May 4, 1991. Along the way, I worked hard, resulting in many awards and certificates.

At the age of 60, I went back to school to obtain by Doctor of Naturopathic Medicine. I completed my doctorate and have explored homeopathic and naturopathic medicines to help other people ever since.

This is my story.

PART ONE

Life Before I was Born

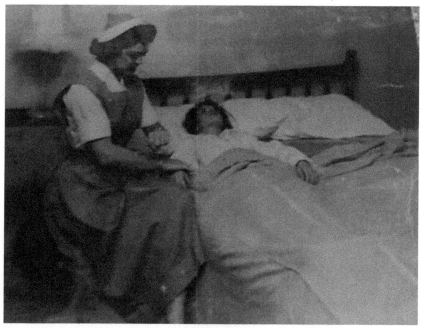

My Aunt Carolyn Johnson working as a nurse

1893-1940's

My Paternal Side

My grandfather was a successful businessman with multiple prospering businesses in his lifetime. He was my father's father, born Leon Johnson Sr. in 1893.

Leon was in love with a young woman named Lena, who was not in love with him. Instead, she was in love with a young man by the name of James Graves. James had three younger siblings, the youngest being Leone, the only girl. Leone Lyndall was just 16 years old when her mother Alma Rebecca suddenly died from an illness no one understood, at the young age of 39. It was probably ovarian cancer.

Leone and her three brothers, 1912

Leone's father began dating another lady he intended to marry named Miss Annie. With James married to Lena, Leon Johnson, my grandfather, decided he would marry Leone, so that he could at least be in the same family as Lena. Besides, as he would say, "Leon and Leone belonged together". He convinced Leone that he truly loved her, so she climbed out of her bedroom window on Christmas Eve and they were married by the justice of peace on Christmas morning. Leon was secretly delighted at the thought of his father-in-law and new brother-in-law waking up on Christmas morning with their only little girl gone.

My grandfather was a strategist. He reasoned everything out and took steps to make his desired outcome true. But he was also vindictive and unforgiving. I would love to say that my grandfather grew to love my grandmother very much, but it simply is not true. He was contemptuous and hateful, sleeping in separate twin beds all their married life. While he was unloving towards her, he managed to father five children in eight years while working day and night, aiming to work himself out of poverty. He established himself as an entrepreneur. He had three auburn-haired children with blue eyes: Leon Jr, "Fox", Jerilyn "Jeri", and Sherman "Red". Carolyn had reddish brown hair with blue eyes and Alma, "Tirr", was a black-haired child with lavender eyes. Tirr was very beautiful.

According to a newspaper article written about Leon in 1928 from Chronicles of Shreveport and Caddo Parish:

*Leon Johnson Sr.,
my grandfather*

Mr. Johnson received a high school education, graduating with high honors. His father had planned to make a school teacher of him, but that profession was the one most of all distasteful to Leon. So, his father told him he would have to go to work. Consequently, the young boy went to work at $30 per month. He remained here until he went back to Longstreet to work for L. T. Holmes. Here he worked for the same salary he received in Logansport but at the end of one year he set his own price. At the end of the second year with Mr. Holmes, Leon was found in full charge of the store, buying, bookkeeping, handling cotton, managing the gin and, in fact, doing all kinds of things, working early and late.

Upon the opening of the World War, he felt it his duty to volunteer, which he proceeded to do. He was sent to Tulane and given three months training there and sent across as a private. The armistice was signed just after he landed "Over There," so he was sent up into the Army of Occupation at Coblenz where he remained in full charge of a Government Post Exchange, after which he returned to the United States and resumed his old job with Mr. Holmes. Remaining with this one year, he decided that it was time to get out for himself.

At the time he left Mr. Holmes he had saved about $1,500, and came to Shreveport. He went to the Hicks Company and asked for credit to go into a little grocery business. Mr. Hicks authorized his branch in Homer (the place Mr. Leon decided was the best oil boom point in which to locate a grocery) to extend Mr. Johnson credit. So, his first little Cash-and-Carry Store opened for business. This was operated for seven months, Mr. Leon doing practically all the work himself, averaging 17 hours work per day, living on leftovers mostly. When the oil boom broke out in Haynesville he opened a large grocery there which was the best the town had ever had. Business began to grow and the store in Homer was sold at a nice profit and efforts were concentrated in Haynesville.

A very large business was done with the oil field people, often delivering tons of groceries to the oil fields when the roads were so bad and muddy that it took as high as ten pairs of mules to draw one load of groceries.

Several times when the weather was so very bad, Leon was afraid to send his men to the fields with these

My grandfather's store

35

loads, so he took a negro and went himself. It took as long as 15 hours to make a trip four miles with a load of groceries to the oil field and come back, on several occasions, with icicles hanging all over his clothes. He endured all this because he saw he was getting nearer and nearer the goal he had set for himself, but he did not, of course, move his family out there. After about two years the oil business began to get dry, he sold out and went to El Dorado, Arkansas, during that boom, and to Smackover, Arkansas, about the same time.

To get his bearing, he purchased the meat and poultry market and coffee department of the Big Chain; ran this two year then opened a delicatessen on Line avenue. Succeeding with this he built a two-story brick store on Gladstone Boulevard and opened the finest and most complete grocery in Shreveport. Last year did

Leone Graves Johnson

a business near $400,000 cash groceries; while this year the business is going at the rate of half a million per year. The store has cold storage and operates its own bakery. The drawing card to his store is the parking space of two large lots. Mr. Johnson's success is due to hard work and perseverance. He owns an attractive brick home at 539 Forest Avenue. "Cash for everything" is one of Mr. Johnson's mottoes.

There are four children in the home--Leon, Jr., Alma, Jerilyn and Carolyn.

Leon was one of the first grocery store owners to put carts

36

in his store in 1930. Until that time, the customer would enter the store with a list and the shop owners would run around the store gathering the customer's items and bring them back to the front counter. Leon found that when shoppers had freedom to browse, they bought more. The new concept at his stores brought curiosity and that drew shoppers who enjoyed the experience of pushing their own shopping carts around in his big store.

In 1929, amid the worst stock market crash in history, my grandfather left my grandmother with five young children. Carolyn, their fourth, was born with a severe cleft palate that required 21 surgeries to repair. My grandmother was left to devote her life to trying to find a way to give Carolyn a life worth living. Carolyn was 21 before she received her final surgery.

Leon moved above his store in a small office apartment for a period. Then he built himself a large beautiful home and found himself a new wife, Frances. They added clothing stores, fur shops, a movie theater, pharmacy and liquor stores. He continued to prosper until his death.

Leon felt very strongly that he should support his family. He provided Leone with a generous alimony payment of $300.00 per month in 1929 (about $4,300 per month in 2018). This amount would remain the same for her entire life, which, in 1930, provided her with enough money to have a maid, gardener, and chauffeur. All her children went to boarding schools so Carolyn could have the surgery she needed.

My grandfather was so adamant that his former wife be taken care until the day of her death that in his will he had

an actuary estimate my grandmother's death date and her money was set aside before anyone else got a share of his estate. I remember the actuary calling Leone's house. He discussed with her how long he thought she was going to live. My

Jeri, Carolyn, Tirr, and Fox Johnson

37

grandmother replied to him," I know you think you know how long I'm going to live, but have you asked God yet?"

Leon Johnson Sr. in chair; Leon Johnson Jr. standing

Leon sent his children to boarding school. The boys were seven years apart and attended Kemper Military School. My fifteen-year-old father, Fox, had been there for years when his younger brother showed up at the tender age of just eight years old. Sherman was a sensitive child who missed his mother very much. The boys were exposed to a military maneuver at school where the instructors pretended to blow up the bridge. These two brothers, along with some friends, decided to steal chemicals from their father's (Leon) store to blow up the bridge. Fox thought this would be the very thing they needed to send Sherman home to his Mother, Leone. When the boys blew up the bridge, Kemper expelled both boys permanently. This was not the outcome Fox had hoped for. He was trying to send Sherman home, not himself. This was the beginning of many such schemes of grandeur that would fall far short of Fox's expectations.

Leon sent his daughters, Alma and Jerelyn, to San Antonio, Texas to attend Our Lady of Guadalupe Boarding School. As fate would have it, Carolyn, the youngest daughter, went to Saint Louis for another surgery to try once again in the 1930's to repair her cleft palate. They had tried metal implants, bone grafts, skin grafts and all had failed. The child was now nine years old, could not eat, and could not talk because of her missing pallet in the roof of

Alma Rebecca Johnson Neely "Tirr"
and Leone Johnson "Buddy"

38

Jan Courtney, my cousin

her mouth. Leone was desperate to find a solution for Carolyn, so she could have a normal life. They had waited for the esteemed surgeon to operate on Carolyn for months. Now that they were in Saint Louis, where Carolyn was required to stay. Carolyn had to be in the hospital for several months.

When the boys had managed to get themselves thrown out of boarding school, Fox could not take care of Sherman because he was too irresponsible. Leon would not take care of the boys because he was too busy. So, Leon did the only thing he could do: he took his 14-year-old daughter Alma out of boarding school. Leon brought her home to run Leone's house and babysit Sherman until Leone could come back home with Carolyn from the hospital in Saint Louis.

From that point on, all of the Johnson children went to school like other children, graduating from Byrd High School. They lived on Forrest Street in the lovely red brick home Leone shared with Leon. It was just a block from the high school. After graduation,

Leon Johnson

Widely-Known Local Retired Grocer Dies

Leon Johnson, 711 E. Ridge Dr., a longtime wholesale and retail groceryman here, died at 3 a.m. today at the Physicians and Surgeons Hospital following a brief illness.

A native of Longstreet, Mr. Johnson had resided here since 1921 and was retired from the grocery business at the time of his death.

HE ESTABLISHED the first neighborhood shopping center and theater here and opened the first supermarket in the city. He also operated the first cold storage for furs here and owned Morrison Cafeteria here and also in Lafayette and Alexandria at one time.

He was a charter member of the Shreveport Gun Club, a member of the Joppa Masonic Lodge for 50 years and a member of Noel Memorial Methodist Church. He was a veteran of World War I, having served as a sergeant in the Army.

FUNERAL SERVICES will be held at 2 p.m. Tuesday at the Osborn Funeral Home Chapel with Dr. James W. Middleton, pastor of the First Baptist Church, officiating. Burial will be in Forest Park Cemetery.

Survivors include two sons, Leon Johnson Jr. of Moss Point, Miss., and Sherman G. Johnson of Shreveport; two daughters, Mrs. Thomas Courtney Jr. of Shreveport and Mrs. E. F. Neely of Benton; two brothers, Leroy Johnson of Houma and Lutz Johnson of Denver, Colo.; three sisters, Mrs. J. M. Warren and Miss Ernestine Johnson, both of Shreveport.

Fox went to Kilgore Junior College where he met his wife, while Tirr and Carolyn went to business school to be secretaries. Jeri got married at seventeen. Red became a gun smith and lock smith.

At the time of my parents' wedding in 1943, all of the adult and teenage children were still living with Leone in her home. All were still living off the $300 alimony payment and child support provided by Leon. This still paid for maid and chauffeur services.

My Maternal Family

Henry Floyd Fearn was born in 1895. He grew up with his mother Mary Alma Worthington Fearn, who married Merton Melvin Fearn. Mary Alma had eight children: Henry who was the oldest, Arland, Blanche, Edmund, Mary Elizabeth (who died at age four of appendicitis), Eugene, Josephine, and Lydia. Henry was a horseman in World War I.

Nellie Dean Rowe was born the sixth of seven children, the youngest being Lacy. Hazel was three years older than Nellie. Hazel was her next older sister, she named the new baby for the girl that lived down the street, "Nellie Dean". Her sisters were Blanche, Lacy, and Hazel.

Henry met Nellie while she was living in Wichita, Kansas working in a sanitorium for mentally handicapped children. He was an oil field carpenter at the time. They married shortly after they met and had five children: Brooks, Neva Jean (my mother), Howard, Donald, and Maxine Jo (named for Henry's sister).

*Nellie Rowe Fearn
and her sister Hazel Rowe*

A Life Changing Death

The oldest child of Henry and Nellie was Brooks, then 18 months later Neva Jean (Mama) was born. Brooks was a beautiful, blue-eyed, blond, big, strong boy who was sweet-tempered and kind. He was smart and won many school awards. Mama was different than Brooks in every way. She had very dark skin, like her father's mother and green eyes. She was a nasty-tempered child from her birth. Whatever joy Brooks gave Grandma, Mama stole away.

Howard, Neva Jean, and Brooks Fearn

When Brooks was 10 years old he came home from school sick. He began to have difficulty breathing. There were no close neighbors to help her and Grandma could not carry Brooks to town several miles away on foot. She had her other four small children and couldn't leave them. She sent Mama to run to town to get the doctor. There were several things wrong with this plan. First, Mama never understood urgency or timeliness. Second, Mama had no sense of direction. Thirdly, Mama got sidetracked on just about everything and could never finish anything in her life. Today we know she had ADHD, but back in the 1930's she was just naughty. But besides Mama's personality defects, the doctor was not home as there was an epidemic of diphtheria in the school at the time. He was busy attempting to save several of the children's lives by performing tracheotomies. Most of the children in that rural Kansas town died of diphtheria anyway despite his best efforts. Only six out of 12 children in Brooks' fourth grade class survived.

Eight-year-old Mama came back hours later with no doctor and by that time Brooks had died in his mother's arms. She tried to relate her misadventure to her mother who whipped her and accused her of killing her brother. Mama in true Mama fashion would later accuse her own mother of killing Brooks by not having enough guts to slice open his throat to give him a tracheotomy. Some old wounds can never be healed.

Mama's Family

The Fearn family was an uneducated, poor, white trash, oil-field family who were brawlers and fighters. Mama's family did not smoke. Every one of them, except Howard, were as mean as a snake with Mama being the meanest one of them all. Her whole family feared her, and no one liked her except for her father, Henry Fearn, who adored her. She adored him too.

My grandmother, Nellie Dean Rowe Fearn, was a hard woman who doled out harsh physical discipline with no notice and no explanation of what was not done to her liking. Grandma pounded upon my brothers and myself any chance she could.

Grandma Fearn could barely stand to be in the same room with Mama. She didn't approve of anything Mama did: her cursing, poor housekeeping, inability to cook, chain smoking of cigarettes, or her physical cruelty to her children (which Grandma was too blind to see came from her). Mama was a woman who never backed down from a confrontation. In fact, she usually caused most of them. She loved to curse, smoke, and fight. She was perpetually unhappy, with a low frustration level, common in people with selective low intelligence and poor self-esteem. My mother was not dumb, she just had big gaps in her thought processes. She had absolutely no common sense.

Grandma Fearn didn't like anything about Mama. I really couldn't blame her, Mama always smelled bad from the cigarettes which she never put out. Mama had a cigarette holder like Cruella Deville. Mama thought she was so glamorous holding her cigarette extended in the holder. Mama never ever was without a lit cigarette. She even slept with a cigarette burning in an ash tray all night long. I know because I was in the

Words of Wisdom

Common sense is a gift from God; a lack of common sense is a really bad thing.

bed next to her, and next to me was Mark, my younger brother. In addition to her being smelly and verbally nasty with a mean temper, Mama was lazy. The laziness drove my hard-working Grandma over the edge against Mama. And then, of course, there was Brooks death, which Grandma always felt was all Mama's fault.

1943

Mama and Fox

My father's family was not truly wealthy, per se, but his father had made money. Mama thought she had hit the jackpot when she married Fox! She was a student when she met Fox at Kilgore Junior College. She was more than happy to marry this handsome young man from a wealthy family, even if he was a complete loser.

Mama and Fox were married on an Air Force base with no family present, August 3, 1943. Fox was due to ship out to World War II the next morning as a fighter pilot. They had one night together. Fox sent Mama to live with his mother and siblings. There Mama lived for four years waiting on her husband to return. She did her best to cause chaos at every turn.

Mama was happy living with her mother-in-law, Leone, who was the sweetest-tempered, kindest woman you would ever meet. Leone Lyndall Graves Johnson was a hard worker so Mama, who was a "guest" for four years, could laze around smoking cigarettes. She fit right in as all Fox's family smoked. She loved sniping at her new sister-in laws. They were everything Mama was not. The Johnson's were genteel. They were calm and fun loving with hardly ever a bad word to say about anyone. My aunts were all about 5'2" with hourglass figures. They were very thin with high intelligence. Mama had an apple shaped body with huge breasts, a round tummy, and skinny legs. She was thin as a newlywed. The rationed war groceries continued to ensure that none of them gained any weight, but she still towered over her sisters-in-law with her flawed figure. Their figures alone were reason enough for Mama to hate Fox's sisters.

Life was a lot of fun for Mama, living with four young

people her age and her sweet Mother-in-law. Mama sat around doing nothing except smoking cigarettes and everything was great until Jerilyn's husband came back for a visit from the war and got her pregnant. Soon there was a new baby in the house for everyone to enjoy. Mama was green with envy. Unfortunately, envy and jealousy were the feelings that made Mama so unreasonable and impossible to live with. Mama was insanely jealous of the baby. Why didn't she have a baby (her husband had not been home in two years for a visit, but that was beside the point!). Fortunately, she did not take her anger out on the baby, as she liked her. She just made everyone around her suffer. By the time Fox got home from the war, the Johnson's were more than ready to get Mama in her own home.

Sandy, the new baby, grew up in a house of young adults who called Leone Mother. Sandy, at just over a year old, took to calling Leone "Muddy", as she couldn't say Mother. "I'll be your Buddy, but I won't be your Muddy", my Grandmother said. So, Buddy she became to everyone from that day forward.

As soon as Fox came home, Mama promptly got pregnant. Soon Sonny was born. Over the next 17 years they had four children: Sonny, (Leon III) was the oldest, second, Gary, third, Diane, and lastly, Mark.

When Fox came home from the war, Buddy split her lot on Forrest Street where she lived. Fox built Mama the home of her dreams. But she was miserable living next door to her in-laws. Fox was trying to be an entrepreneur like Leon, but while he had a photographic memory he lacked the ability to carry out what he read. He could quote any passage out of any book he read, by page number and exact text, but he could not read directions, pick up a screwdriver, and turn a screw. He could not execute a plan. He also was distracted by anything he considered fun and had no will power. Drinking, women, prospecting, treasure hunts, pawn shops, basically anything to have a good time distracted him. In that arena, Fox and Mama were a perfect match. Both shirked responsibility while pursuing what felt good for them at the time. Neither of them ever considered the consequences of their actions and how they would affect other people. They never gave a second thought on how any of their actions would ever affect their future or their children's future.

Fox Johnson, my father and Neva Jean Fearn Johnson, my mother

THE UNBELIEVABLE PLIGHT OF MRS. WRIGHT

PART TWO

Little Red Hen

THE UNBELIEVABLE PLIGHT OF MRS. WRIGHT

1958

The Divorce

It was 1958 when Fox was traveling throughout the south selling insurance. My parents had been married seventeen years. He and Mama were living in Little Rock, Arkansas. I was 17 months old when my mother discovered that my father was having an affair with a 17-year-old girl, Lena Mae. (Yes, the same name as my grandfather's love interest, I am not making this up.) He spent the rest of his free time in bars when he was on the road where he met Lena Mae. Lena Mae had already given birth to two little boys when she met my father. Her mother had custody of those children. This left Lena Mae and Fox a lot of time to enjoy each other's company. My mother was 39-years-old and pregnant with my younger brother, Mark.

When Mama found out about the affair, she became convinced that Fox was a chronic philanderer. Mama was furious! This was her first time to have a true cause for her anger. Now she had a real reason. She used this to her full advantage.

Mama's mouth was a toilet and she fouled everyone that met her. No one could curse like Mama! Mama always used to say she could make a sailor blush, as if cursing in every sentence of every discussion somehow made you more prestigious. Cursing and screaming, fueled by Fox's drinking, and both chain-smoked. They battled for almost a week with every sentence out of their mouths sprinkled with curse words. They drank pot after pot of coffee, so they could be sure to be alert in caffeine overdoses to attack each other with more hurtful verbal attacks. She flew into him so often with her physical attacks, she finally had him worked up enough that he hit her.

Diana, Gary, Cynthia, Sonny, Jan, and Sandy,
The Johnson Grandchildren

Mama was not a small woman. She was 5'7" and weighed about 180. When she attacked she raised her arms over her head to make herself look larger, like a bear, then would run toward the chosen victim screaming in rage. She was scary. Fox, on the other hand, was a small man. He was 5'8" with curly auburn hair, startling blue eyes, and weighted about 145 pounds.

When Fox finally hit Mama back, it hit a nerve in Sonny. He was only thirteen and just starting to enter puberty. Sonny had listened to the nastiness of the fight for days. Sonny is a happy fun-loving person who was always the most popular kid in school and a good athlete. Mama screamed at Sonny for help. Sonny was always everyone's knight in shining armor. He was the protector of the family. He always tried to protect me from Mama and Gary's chronic abuse. Sonny tried to keep Mama on an even keel. But this battle was something no thirteen-year-old boy should have ever been exposed to, much less involved in. Sonny was no match for Fox's strength fueled by his anger and caffeine. He did the only thing a child protecting his Mama could do. Sonny ran and got his shotgun.

Fox knew his oldest son could shoot. He had taught him himself. Fox was obsessed with guns and the old west. He had practiced his quick draw so many times that a couple of years earlier he had shot himself in the leg when he discharged his gun prematurely. He pulled the trigger and it discharged in the leg without ever getting the gun out of the holster. Sonny backed Fox out of the house that day and told him if he ever came back he would shoot him. Sonny didn't have to worry about it, Fox never came back. Besides Fox had another family to go to. Lena Mae was pregnant too.

When Mama raged for a week at Fox, she never considered that he might leave although she screamed that at him for hours. She never considered how she would support her children. Mama didn't have a job. In fact, she had never worked a day in her life.

She never considered forgiveness or love. To the day she died, she never thought she played any role in any of her actions. In her mind, she was a victim that had done nothing to cause the divorce. Up until the day he died, she cursed him on an hourly basis. She wanted revenge and blood, she wanted to hate.

When he walked out that door, she was devastated. She could not believe he abandoned her. She never took a shred of ownership for his involvement with another woman even though she extolled for hours her hatred of sex and men.

Here she was in Little Rock, Arkansas, in a home she could not afford, with children she did not know how to support and pregnant at age forty. She did the only thing she knew she could do. She moved back in with her mother-in-law. Leone was the only person kind enough to care for her and her children. But by now Buddy's alimony was getting harder and harder to live on. Gone was the chauffeur and the yard man came only once a month. Mother did the only thing she could do. She sent me to live with my Grandma Fearn at the age of 21 months. I would stay there until after Mama had her new baby and could get back on her feet. Her plan was to go to school and get a job.

<u>1959</u>

My Earliest Memory and How it Impacted My Life

My earliest memory is when I was 26 months old. I was living at my Grandma Fearn's house while my younger brother was carried to full term and eventually born on June 14, 1957. Grandma was destitute when her husband died, as she had never held a job during her marriage. They were so poor that they had never owned a home. When my Grandfather died in 1954, of liver failure, they had purchased a lot with some out buildings on the lot. They were basically tiny storage sheds with no bathrooms that my grandmother and Aunt Maxine lived in.

My uncle Howard was a chemical engineer and unmarried. He had a good job with Exxon (called Esso in those days). He decided to build his mother a three-bedroom, one bath, tiny, little, cheap house, around 700 square feet. There were no frills at all. The floors were linoleum. There was no trim anywhere in the house. The cabinets were the cheapest available. The layout was terrible for a custom-built home. The living room was narrow and long forcing you to sit on the couch facing one direction, while the TV was on the left of the couch, so you had to turn your head to see it. Forget about seeing the television if you were seated in the last seat from the TV.

The kitchen was so tiny that there was no place to eat. By the time I was born, my uncle had enclosed the porch to hold Grandma's small dining table which was awkward as you had to step down to the porch. But at least there was room for the table and her sewing machine, so she could sew. Grandma was an excellent seamstress.

On a late June afternoon, Grandma had a handyman working on the trim around the front door. Still a baby, I was

Diane Johnson, 8 months

completely potty-trained, but my speech was still difficult to completely understand. I was talking to the handyman. I was standing in the front flower bed just a few feet from the man when I saw a frog. "Grandma, Grandma, I peed a poggy in the powerbed!", I bubbled excitedly. Grandma tore out of the house running quickly, grabbed me up by one arm, and began hitting me in the middle of my back as hard as she could. She knocked the air out of me. The handyman started yelling, "What are you doing? Are you crazy? She didn't pee in the flower bed she saw a frog!" He was so upset by the violence of the outburst he gathered his tools and left without finishing the door trim.

Words of Wisdom

Grandmothers should never hit grandchildren. Children learn lifelong lessons from cruelty and grandmothers.

Believe it or not, this was a defining moment in my life. I felt unjustly abused. At two years old, I knew my grandmother should not be hitting me. I knew I did nothing wrong.

At that moment I became a champion for the underdog. Nothing can make me angrier quicker than injustice. I began looking for ways to make life better for people unjustly treated. I have hired many unqualified people and taught them how to earn a six-figure income. I have made friends of the lowest economic levels and given opportunities to those who have none, all because of the words of this one handyman.

The House on 701 Thomas Street

Mama finally got over her initial shock of the divorce and the delivery of the new baby, Mark. She decided to move to Kilgore, Texas where I already had been staying with Grandma for six months. I remember the day we went to see the shack. It seemed large with a good floor plan. The kitchen and dining room were large, with a living room. There were three bedrooms with one full and one-half bath off the dining room. The house was cold and drafty. There was no way to get warm in the winter. Something in the house was always broken with no man around to repair it.

The house was just down the street from the Kilgore Middle and High School where both of my older brothers would go to school. At two and a half I took off running across the yard, when suddenly a rock hit me at the base of my neck that knocked my face into the dirt. Again, I lost my breath. This was how I met Toby, the next-door neighbor boy who was five.

Toby's parents were Kitty and Arthur Brown and they were as country as country can be. Arthur was a huge man who wore overalls all the time and Kitty wore snap up

Diane Johnson, Age 2

the front housedresses that looked like night gowns. She was short but heavy. They had a baby named Lance that was exactly the same age as Mark. The reason that the Browns were all so large was that Kitty cooked all the time. Any time of the day or night she had wonderful smells coming from her house. The minute one meal was over the kitchen was cleaned up and she went right into the next meal. Kitty cooked fabulously delicious meals that were all ended by dessert. When the boys were older, the Browns bought their boys Shetland ponies and kept the horses inside the house. One of ponies was so smart he could open the back-screen door to enter and leave at will.

This constant cooking was such a contrast to Mama's cooking. Mama only had about three meals she regularly cooked. If anything got eaten too quickly she just stopped making it or buying it. We had peanut butter but no jelly, and most of the time no bread. We never had any condiment except mustard because Mama loved mustard, so no mayonnaise or ketchup. There was never a drop of milk in the house, and very seldom eggs. Mama was allergic to milk and eggs. Remember everything was about Mama.

Mama served the same thing for breakfast every day. Each child got a cup of coffee with about 1/3 cup of powdered milk and 1/3 cup of sugar. The coffee was a mixture very much like syrup. As a child I loved it. If we had bread, she would make burned toast which we dipped in the coffee syrup. We had a toaster, but, somehow, Mama always managed to burn the toast. One day when I was about three, my brother Gary told Mama, "don't forget to burn the toast I am beginning to like it that way." Since then, I have always liked very, very dark toasted bread.

If we got lunch that day: lunch was often a bowl of corn meal mush, which was a little corn meal cooked like a hot cereal (polenta), a peanut butter fold over, or a cheese and mustard fold over with such a sharp taste that I hated it as a preschooler. But supper was the main event. Mama's meals had a reputation in the neighborhood, just not a good one.

First, there was meatloaf surprise. It started out with about two pounds of hamburger meat then Mama opened the refrigerator and threw anything that had not been eaten from the week or two before, the corn meal mush, canned peaches, leftover soup, corn, green beans, bread (not crumbs, just big pieces) literally anything she could find. She then put it in a cast iron, Dutch oven and put it in the oven until the edges were burned and it was still raw in the middle. She would scoop it out from the sides. It was served as the entire entree. Sometimes she served baked potatoes with it if she felt there was not enough bread in the meatloaf surprise. Mama put as little time into cooking as absolutely possible and burned almost everything. Mama would start a meal then wander off and start some art project or read and forget all about supper cooking.

Meatloaf surprise was served reheated until it was gone. This usually lasted close to a week with the kids unable to eat much of it. My teen age brothers ate it better than I did as a preschooler, but Mark just cried.

Second was chicken noodle soup. Mama would take a whole chicken and throw it in a pot of water with black peppercorns and boil it until the meat fell off the bones. No onion or any other spice or even salt was used. When she felt the chicken was "done" she took a large spoon and stirred like crazy until the meat, bones, skin, and cartilage were swirling in the broth, which she did not remove, then she would add a bag of egg noodles. This was not too bad the first night except you had to pick out all the bones and skin and gristle. But by the second or third night the soup was exactly like paste, with the egg noodles completely deteriorated in a gelatinous mass of bone, fat, and gristle mess. The preschoolers didn't mind this as bad as the teenagers. This meal also lasted close to a week before it finally got so disgusting she would throw it into the next week's meatloaf.

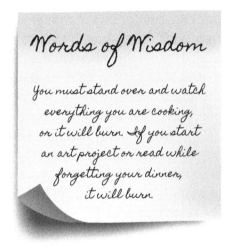

Words of Wisdom

You must stand over and watch everything you are cooking, or it will burn. If you start an art project or read while forgetting your dinner, it will burn.

Third was Mama's spaghetti. Somehow, she managed to make this pretty good. But it went too fast as all the kids ate it. That did not make her happy, so she usually fell back on meatloaf surprise or chicken noodle soup for the meal of the week. I suspect she really liked her spaghetti and felt a sense of accomplishment, which is why she even bothered to cook it every few weeks.

Because she didn't work, Mama relied on the generosity

of her brother, father-in-law, and her sisters-in-law for financial support. I never knew of a time when she applied for any type of government assistance of any kind. Fox sent no child support or alimony, as he was a deadbeat dad. Whenever Mama received any money from anyone, she had a priority list of how the money should be spent. First came her cigarettes, several novels for her entertainment, then she retrieved whatever she could from the pawn shops, paid the rent, bought food and the utilities were last. Mama had an unusual way of paying bills. She never paid anything until the landlord was beating on the door or the utilities were turned off. Every month the rent was late, and the utilities were turned off. I remember Thomas Street being very, very cold. I think that in reality it was cold for about five months a year. The rest of the time it was actually quite nice or hot, but I don't remember that, but it was East Texas.

Occasionally, the food became a crisis which interestingly occurred when summer came. Then Mama would ship the older boys off to Buddy in Shreveport, Louisiana. Mark and I would go to Mama's sister Maxine in Mineola, Texas. As Maxine came from the same family as Mama she was the same type of child abuser only on a much, much more mentally normal level. Maxine would not yell, but then things would build up. She would go crazy about something that I had no control over.

One Sunday I was ready for church ahead of the boys. She sent me out to sit on the porch telling me not to get dirty. I was eight at the time. I was sitting there holding my hands together when a bird flew overhead and pooped on my head. She tore me up both verbally and physically while pulling my head under the faucet pulling my one-inch short hair. Again, I knew I did nothing wrong, which furthered my fury over injustice.

Mama's Getting a "Job"

Mama decided she had to get a job, but she had no skills. First, she decided to go to Secretarial School which she hated. She graduated and never worked as a secretary. Then she went to Beauty School and got her license. This was a disaster for me. She decided she was going to practice on me. Every single Sunday she would practice cutting my hair in the bathroom. Throughout my preschool days, I had shorter hair than any of my brothers, except Sonny who was wearing a crew cut in the early 1960's. Mama had a real talent for being unable to cut two single hairs the same length. I looked like a lawn mower had hit my head. My hair was about one half to one inch long all over my scalp which made me stand out like a sore thumb while all the other little girls who had long, beautiful hair. I wore this hair style until I was in second grade when I started begging for my hair to grow out. As an adult I have never worn short hair willingly.

Mama never worked as a beautician. After beauty school, she decided to go to college and finish her degree. She pursued paralegal training, which she dropped out. She trained as an assistant to a financial advisor, but never graduated either. I do not know for sure, but I suspect that Fox's father was paying for all the training. I have no idea what she was always studying as she did not graduate from college until I was in my mid-twenties (it was a degree in Religion). I do know that she dropped out of nursing school when I started nursing school. All in all, Mama was always going to school pursuing a career that she never actually worked.

Anyway, Mama was never home with us kids. When Mark was a tiny baby we had Margeen, a very young black lady who kept us. Mother said she had to fire Margeen because she bounced Mark so hard when she was feeding him that he could not keep the formula down. I remember sitting under the kitchen table at Margeen's feet while she fed Mark eating a ketchup and bread "sandwich". Margeen was kinder to us than Mama.

After

Words of Wisdom

If you're going to spend the time and the money to get a degree, make sure it is something you want to do with your life, and you can earn a living for your children. Think through the entire duties of the job. Example: If you own a gym you must wash towels, if you don't enjoy washing towels, don't buy a gym.

Margeen, Mama stayed home with us more. Mark had a terrible delay in walking but not in cursing. Mark's first word was, "Shit!!!", which he said clearly and often. Followed by several other curse words that he went around saying: "Shit, Hell, Damn, Shit". He couldn't say much more that was clearly understood until he was well over three. Mama thought this was hilarious.

When Mark was about two and I was four, Buddy had given Mark a bomber jacket that looked just like Little Joe Cartwright from Bonanza. While we didn't have TV, we visited our Grandma Fearn on Sunday's, mostly this was so my mother would have someone new to fight with. Mark and I would watch The Cartwright's on TV. I loved Mark's jacket. I had a second hand, red, fuzzy, fur jacket that Mark loved. We always wanted to wear each other's jacket but that was expressly forbidden! If I was caught holding his jacket I got a whipping. Mama chose the stupidest things to be rigid about.

But the lure of Little Joe's jacket was too much for me and Mama wanted us to disappear. She certainly believed in the Old Mother Hubbard Nursery Rhyme, and if we got in her way, caused her any work, or disturbed her hobbies, she "whipped them up soundly and put them to bed". I had already learned to clear out and stay out.

One afternoon, in an effort to get away from her perpetual wrath, I took Mark away from the house and immediately exchanged jackets with Mark. He loved to feel the fur on my jacket, while I became a cowboy in his. I had Mark stand on the neighbor's porch while I practiced running up and down the stairs on my imaginary horse, pretending to be Little Joe. Mark was content to pet the fur. As I raced down the five stairs, Mark decided he should try to race down the stairs also. He tripped and fell, cutting a large laceration across his forehead. Blood was everywhere. We were wearing the wrong coats! This was a beating for sure. He was crying so loudly! I was so scared that I jerked off the Little Joe jacket and threw it on the ground. I ran to find Mama. At barely four, I was so completely scared by the blood, pain, and fear of a beating that I could not remember the word for cut, or injury, or any word to describe what had happened to Mark. I could just scream, "Mark, and grrraaahhh!"

Mama grabbed him up in her arms and ran out on the front porch. It was just after 3:00 in the afternoon. Sonny was up the street walking home from school. Mama had Mark wrapped up in a towel with blood still pouring when she screamed for Sonny to run. Mama was never one to function in a crisis, so Sonny threw his books down and raced about a fourth mile home. He grabbed the keys and drove Mama to the doctor's office to get Mark stitched up. Gary and I were left at home alone. Sonny's books were never recovered.

Poor Mark was exhausted from his ordeal as they had to stitch up his head with six stitches, which is a lot for a little two-year-old boy. He cried and cried, then suddenly was not there! The whole family looked under every bed, the bathrooms, and every closet. Mama thought he might have run away since he got hurt but it was getting dark. A little two-year-old boy wouldn't normally run away at dark after a terrible injury requiring stitches. There was a creek at both ends of the street. We were all getting frantic. The police and neighbors were called, and the search began. I was told to stay in the house, alone, in case he came back. By this time the search had gone on for a couple of hours. There was still no sign of Mark. I needed to go to the bathroom. Imagine my surprise when I went in the half bath and found Mark asleep sitting on the toilet, with his head resting on his knees. When the door was open the toilet was behind the bathroom door so while everyone had glanced in the bathroom no one had looked on the toilet.

Mama's Favorite

Mama had a soft spot for Mark. She preferred him over the other boys and me. He was quiet, delayed in talking and walking. He cried a lot. Actually, Mark cried all the time. He just never could understand why Mama was so mean half the time for no reason, and kind the rest of the time. It hurt his feelings so bad, he just cried more. Because he cried so much, he would cry himself to sleep several times a day. Everything made Mark cry. I made up my mind that I would try everything not to make Mark cry.

I cried at the daily abuse Mama called discipline without

a shred of teaching what a child could do to "mind". Several times I asked what I did wrong, trying to learn what was making her so angry so I could learn how to avoid making her mad. She considered the questions insolence. She would not answer me. She would slap me as hard as she could in the face, making my small ears ring after I had already received a "spanking". I was three when I realized I would receive a spanking every day no matter what I did or did not do. I quickly learned that I could be sound asleep in the middle of the night and beaten awake for some imagined wrong. No behavior I did or did not do could prevent the abuse.

I just began hiding from her. I would hide in her closet. There was a very large box in her closet that was filled with old clothes, so I would bury down in the clothes, cover up my head, and day dream. I do not remember ever going to sleep but I remember spending every free moment trying to figure out how to develop a plan out of this miserable little life. Mama never looked for me. She was content for me to be out of her sight and out of her mind.

When I did not hide in the closet I hid under the bed. Mark and I hid there a lot. It was a great place to hide when Gary was home as he couldn't fit under the low bed. Gary delighted in doing things to Mark and me. It is a wonder we survived his abuse. I really don't think we would have if it had not been for Sonny who was bigger and smarter than Gary. He threatened Gary with his life if he hurt us.

1961

Gary, My Older Brother

Gary was abnormal. He was exactly like Mama. He was negative, loved to abuse animals and people smaller than himself, and smoke. He thought injuries were the funniest thing in the world. Gary literally got all the worst personality traits of both of our parents. Gary would grow up to be an alcoholic and drug abuser, the second most negative person I had ever met, and the most sadistic abuser. Gary would make poor decisions all his life fueled by his addictions, and his unbridled temper. Gary was a bully and like all bullies he only attacked until someone fought him back. Then Gary would crumble and cry just like a baby. He was exactly like Mama in a male-exaggerated way. He was a nightmare.

At 12 years old, Gary was a force to be reckoned with. I was only four. He murdered small animals in front of Mark and me. He stuck firecrackers up the rectums of turtles and watched them explode, laughing hysterically. He cut heads off cats and chickens while he laughed.

Mark and I went to bed together in the big double bed we shared with Mama. He put on monster masks then beat on the window to awaken Mark and me. Gary would hide when Mama came to see why we were screaming so hysterically at the boogie man. Finally, one day, I figured out it was Gary. He had on the mask and beat on the window; I told him in my best fearless voice a four-year-old can muster,

Gary Johnson, my brother

"I know that's you Gary. I'm going to tell Mama". I don't remember him beating on the window much after that as I refused to scream and cry but just stood him down, yelling his name. But try as I might to convince Mark it was Gary, the two-year-old continued to cry every time Gary pulled any of his nonsense on us.

Mama made Gary babysit a lot. For an unemployed mother, she was seldom at home, which was a good thing, as Mama being home was a sure sign that it was going to be a nasty, bad day. Maybe she was going to school of some kind. I really do not know where she was.

Gary had to babysit because Sonny had a job. For Gary, babysitting meant tying me and Mark with our hands behind our back and throwing us on the bed to stay all day. Sometimes Sonny came home and untied us. When summer came, Gary decided to stake Mark outside to a tree with belts buckled around the trunk of the tree whenever Mother was gone. I never knew why he didn't tie me outside, but he never did. He terrorized me by throwing knives at my doll he placed on the top of the doorframe. I jumped up and down as the knives came whizzing by above my head. Gary always untied Mark just before Mama got home. She never believed me over Gary, ever. Mark never said a word, he just cried.

Mama loved to smoke. She smoked 24 hours a day, every day. It never occurred to her to protect her children from a lit cigarette. She would go to kiss me while the cigarette in her mouth would burn into my face. If she helped with getting dressed or bathing, the cigarette was burning holes all over my body. If I cried too much, she would slap me in the face for crying and "give me something to cry about". My older brothers started calling me Cry-ann, instead of Diane. No matter how much I cried, Mark literally cried from morning to night from the abuse.

I never got to go to Kindergarten, because in 1962 Kindergarten cost money and we didn't have any money for school. Or any money for anything else either. Shoes were out of the question, except in the cold wintertime then I had one pair. Six to seven months of the year we went barefoot with the bottoms

Diane Johnson

of our feet becoming tough as shoe leather. As time went on, utilities were rarely turned on. Gary and Sonny both smoked and cigarettes came before anything else. Mama said you couldn't keep yourself clean if you didn't keep the water turned on. She always kept the water turned on. We took cold showers unless it was really cold then Mama would have us stand naked in a basin the middle of the kitchen, boil water on the stove (if the gas was still on) and pour water over us.

1962

The Little Red Hen

I entertained myself by learning to read. I had started to read at the end of my fourth year and by first grade I had read every picture book in the library. Mama loved to read. She would go to the library when she didn't have money to buy her own novels. We went to the library frequently. My absolute favorite book was The Little Red Hen. In the story the little red hen finds a grain of wheat and asks for help from the other farmyard animals to plant it, but none of them volunteer. At each later stage (harvest, threshing, milling the wheat into flour, and baking the flour into bread), the little red hen again asks for help from the other animals, but again she gets no assistance.

Finally, the Little Red Hen has completed her task. She asks who will help her eat the bread. This time, all the previous non-participants eagerly volunteer. She declines their help, stating that no one aided her in the preparation work. Thus, the hen eats it, with her chicks, leaving none for anyone else.

I always thought of myself as "the little red hen" because my hair was reddish brown, about the same as in the story book. At four years old, I was already forming my initiative to work hard and be as different from Mama as possible.

Poverty

Money was becoming more and more scarce as the relatives got tired of supporting us. My grandfather and my uncle were the only ones still sending money regularly, except Buddy, who sent allowance each week for me and the boys. Sonny and Gary got $2.00. Mark and I got a dime a piece per week.

One day when I was five and Mark was three the allowance had come, and Gary gave me and Mark our dime, plus one of his dollars. He sent us to the store to buy bread. He

Words of Wisdom

The moral of this story is that those who say no to work offer no contribution to the production do not deserve to enjoy the product: "if any would not work, neither should he eat."

told us we could spend our money on candy. The only problem is that the store was over a mile away across a state highway where the traffic drove at 70 miles per hour. Mark still could not run unless I was pulling him every step of the way. We were in front of the last house on Thomas Street, about a fourth of a mile away from home, when, suddenly, a pack of big dogs

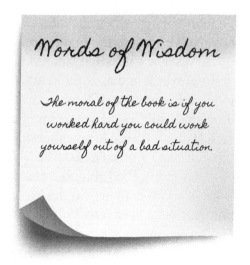

Words of Wisdom

The moral of the book is if you worked hard you could work yourself out of a bad situation.

were running right towards us. I grabbed Mark, pulling him as he could not run, half dragging him. I pushed him to the back side of the screen door of the house. I kicked the door while clutching the screen door tight to keep it closed behind the two of us. The large dogs growled, barked, sniffed us, and then wandered over the porch. One jumped against the screen terrorizing us, making us scream. Then, as quickly as they came, the dogs just ran off the way they came. My heart was beating wildly, but I cowboyed up. We continued to the store to get Gary his bread. Failure to follow his order could have caused problems worse than a pack of big dogs.

When we got to the store, I had my dime and Mark had his. There was a little boy in the front of the store with a stick. Mark shouted out, "I want to buy your stick for a dime." The little boy eagerly handed it over. I could have killed Mark. He bought a stick. Unfortunately, this would foreshadow many other incidences in the future. Like the day after Christmas when Mark sold his brand-new bike, that his aunts got him, for a dollar. We never saw that bike again. Mark bought all kinds of useless things with his allowance. One time he bought a baby turtle, another time a rock.

Mama's Attacks

When Mama was not attacking her children physically, she

Words of Wisdom

When you're being criticized or attacked verbally, always consider the source. Look at the person making the allegations and the negative comments. Decide for yourself if that person is worth listening to or not, most of the time you will decide they are not. I was able to do this at five years old. I looked at my mother and decided she was an unworthy source of non-valuable criticism that wasn't worthy of taking into my soul. I rejected her evaluation of me.

I was able to decide at five years old, that my internal Holy Spirit was a much stronger guiding light than a mentally deranged tyrant. I would look at her and block out all the negativity that she would say to me. I knew I was valuable.

was cursing them with verbal attacks. To me she said," your eyes are the color of shit" and called me a, "shit-ass split ass girl". To the boys she said, "I'd trade two of you for one girl any day". Me too! For a while, I thought there really was an option to trade the older brothers off for a sister. That would have been really exciting to have a sister to play with.

My Younger Brother Mark

Mark and I usually did not fight at all. If he wanted something, I just gave it to him, so when I wanted something, he would just give it to me. The things Mark wanted were a nice

Words of Wisdom

This refusal to accept others' criticism is the exact reason why, in my business, I never put faith in any outside consultants, surveyors, or any other supposed "experts". All these people only see what you tell them or what they are shown. This is very much like a Christmas package sitting under the tree. When you look at Christmas package all you see are the wrapping and the bows. No one has any idea what's really inside. When a consultant comes into your business all he sees is what the company has given to him. He doesn't see deeper into your "center". He also stumbles through his own biases and limited knowledge base to come up with feedback to charge money for information that you already knew yourself. The same is true with psychiatrists, psychologists, and most people working in social services. Be careful when you engage "experts" and decide to rely on outside services because they may not be valuable.

Remember, mothers are supposed to be experts over the lives of their children, but that is not always the case.

stick, a ball, a big rock, or a bird's egg. I always wanted candy or something good to eat. I really suffered from the terrible food we had to eat every day. Whenever we got candy or a treat, usually at Grandma's house, he would take a bite or two and then hand it to me saying, "you like it more than I do." That was true love.

Card Games

Violence in a home is not normal, but when you have grown up in it, it is your normal. Abuse is handed down; Mama beat an older boy, who in return beat the younger child, who then beat an animal. Then people wonder why it all happened.

Mama and Gary fought everyone else in the house. Gary fought Sonny and always lost. He was younger, but he just couldn't help trying every few days or so. Gary actually fought everyone because he was the most like Mama. Gary loved fighting me. I found out that revenge is a dish best served cold and in secret. He would beat me up. I would watch his every move, usually to get out of his way, and when he least expected it, I would retaliate. Eight years older he was stronger, but like Mama, had selective intelligence.

One way I retaliated was learning how to beat Gary at the card game known as War (or Battle) by the time I turned five. I had worked hard on learning the math needed to win this game and it paid off big time. In a home with no TV, no games, and no electricity (hence no radio), there was very little to do, so we played cards. Gary was obsessed with War. He wanted to play it every chance he got. Sonny was tired of it, so Gary made me play. Not playing was not an option. I played or suffered the consequences. I decided I would learn how to beat this thirteen-year-old bully. I started winning every time we played. The first time he was shocked in disbelief. The second time he was convinced I had hidden cards. He searched and counted every card. By the fifth or sixth day, he was raging mad. I beat him until he no longer wanted to play with me. Mama always sided with Gary on everything, so I was surprised when she said to him, "if you can't beat her stop playing with her, that will teach her." My plan had worked beautifully!

<u>1963</u>

The Wet Sucker-A Lesson

There was a little girl next door that lived there for a very short time, about two months. She was a year younger than I was. I loved her!

One day she licked a wet sucker and hit me 100 times saying "I Love You" with each slap. I stood there confused as she hit me but said the endearing words, "I Love You". I finally got so furious that I went home. I never played with her again.

This was a powerful message for me as I was able to realize as a six-year-old that people can use sweet words with mean actions.

Words of Wisdom

Most people don't have a plan; they are just living from moment to moment, always have a plan for every scenario in your life and you will be miles ahead of everyone else.

Words of Wisdom

Many times, when someone is recounting a story, I silently ask myself if they are telling me the truth. I always ask myself if this "is the truth or a lie".

Words of Wisdom

You can't play straight with crooked people.

First Grade, Lunch, and Illness

When I arrived in Mrs. Freeman's first grade class I spent recess looking at every book in her library. I had already read them all. Having very little in my head up to that time, along with a semi-photographic memory, I remembered everything in detail. Mrs. Freeman said she had never had a little girl who had already read every book she had. She had me stand up in front of the class recounting the plot to several Dick and Jane readers. The whole class was quite impressed that I could read. Mrs. Freeman went to the second-grade class to get me some other books to read.

I loved first grade! I loved my teacher; she was so kind. The children were too young to be ugly to each other. Then there were the cafeteria lunches! I still had my coffee for breakfast every morning with an occasional piece of toast, but the smells coming from the cafeteria drove me wild with anticipation for lunch every day. I was hungry most of the time, as a small child with irregular meals and poor-quality food. The lunches were delicious and served with chocolate milk! My favorite day was Friday, when they had hamburgers, chips, and cookies. I mean it just did not get any better than that! I always selected Cheetos, my absolute favorite. I ate them real slow, letting the Cheeto melt in my mouth, savoring every bite of cheesiness.

That year I got every disease I was exposed to. I picked up strep throat, ear infections, coughs, colds, chicken pox, flu, and any other illness that came along. I am sure that living in a freezing cold house, full of cigarette smoke, with improper coats, no shoes, a lack of food, and NO medical care contributed significantly to this. I got sick in October and did not get to go back to first grade until after my birthday in April. Every time I got well and went back to school for a day, I caught something else.

On November 22, 1963, our young president, John Kennedy, was shot and killed in Dallas about one hour away from where we lived. Our Uncle Howard had bought us a television set. The TV ran the coverage all day, on a day I was too sick with chicken pox to do anything but sit and watch the TV coverage. I was very impressed with the First Lady, Jacqueline, climbing out of a moving car with a shooter trying to get her. They say now that she was retrieving part of his skull. That day I made up my mind I wanted to be beautiful and daring like the President's wife. I wanted to dress impeccably with every hair in place. But I didn't want to marry a young man who would get himself killed. No, I wanted love when I grew up. I wanted it to last forever.

Christmas

Children who are poverty stricken look forward to presents more than other children. It was our first grade Christmas Party, with each child bringing a gift and every child receiving a present. I could not wait. Presents were extremely rare. Mama would occasionally buy us something, but she didn't have the discipline to save it for the actual occasion. She always gave it to us unwrapped whenever she got it. You might get something in October with nothing under the Christmas tree to which she would promptly say, "Remember, I got you a pair of shoes in October - that was your Christmas present". But the boys always had things under the tree, and Mark usually had several. I really do not think I ever received a birthday or Christmas gift, on the actual day, from Mama.

It was with great anticipation I looked forward to my number being called, but I had number 27 out of a class of 31. By the time my number was called, there were just a few not-so-well wrapped presents left. I excitedly unwrapped my present and it was a plastic bag of pooh! I was humiliated and ashamed. My cheeks burned. I said nothing, trying to hide the horrible bag of dark brown liquid in a recycled plastic bag. Maggie Beth, the sweetest little girl in the class, who was as poor as I was, came up, all out of breath and asked, "Do you like my present? I made it all by myself for you!" Still barely able to breathe I whispered, "What is it?" Maggie Beth happily replied, "Chocolate pudding, silly!" I thanked her, even though I left my first grade Christmas Party with terrible disappointment, as I slipped Maggie Beth's chocolate pudding in the trash. Even in the first grade, a girl must have some dignity; there was no way I was going to eat that!

1964

Life Decisions Made

Sitting at home day after day, trying to be quiet and stay out of Mama's hair, while waiting for a beating that was sure to come, sick or well, was very nerve-wracking. It was also very cold in the house. I remember one day I was sitting in the freezing house wrapped in a blanket, six years old

Words of Wisdom

Always be nice to everyone about everything. You never know when it will come back to you.

and angry over the circumstances of my life. There literally was nothing in the house to eat, I was freezing and the only place to even gain a little warmth was leaning back against the radiator that barely put out any heat. The longer I sat there the madder I got; it was Friday, hamburger day at school and I was missing it. I was starving. I did not dare disturb Mama for fear of being whipped with a coat hanger. I decided right there and then that I would figure out a way to earn enough money when I grew up that I could afford Cheetos every single day! I started thinking right then how my life was going to be different from my families. I wondered, "Why do some people have money and other people do not?" I had to

Diane Johnson at age 6

figure this question out to be successful, so at six years old I began a quest for the knowledge of why some people were rich, and some were not. I decided right then and there I would be one of those rich people. That day, I also decided that I wanted to be young with my children, not old like Mama. Where and how I drug up the magic number of 27, I will never know, but I decided that I would have all girls, before I turned 27. Oh, and I was only having girl children, no boys. I was able to have three girls by 26. No, my life was going to be completely different from Mama's.

I looked at Mama still sitting in the kitchen working on her second pot of coffee at noon. Abused children try to observe what is going on around them and stay a step ahead of the abuser, so they can get out of the way, to prevent as many beatings as possible. I watched her constantly, trying to anticipate her every move to stay out of her way. She hadn't been up moving all day. She had a new book to read. She was still in her robe and her hair wasn't combed. The ash tray was filled. Just looking at her made me feel sick to my stomach. There was nothing about her I wanted to emulate. I didn't want to be fat, ungroomed, smoke cigarettes, be poor, be unemployed, or be abusive to my children. I think being poor was the biggest thing I didn't want to be anymore. I didn't want to be cold, or yelled at, or hurt, or hungry. My life was going to be different.

I realized at that moment that I did not like Mama's choices for her life which were creating negative consequences for my life. I realized that if I made choices completely different from the choices Mama made, my life would turn out all right. So that established my barometer for decision making and the path for my life. From that early age of six years old, I would ask myself, "What would Mama do in this situation?" And then I would do exactly the opposite. This worked every time.

It is interesting that we children were skinny and underfed while Mama was fat. How can she be overweight with nothing to eat? She had to be eating something.

I have thought about the decisions made that fateful day when I was six years old and how they forever changed my life. One of the biggest disappointments in my life when I grew up and had enough money to buy them, was that I no longer liked Cheetos. Besides, they are not good for you.

Words of Wisdom

Learn to emulate behavior that you want to be like and eliminate behavior that you don't like.

If I hadn't known how to read and do math, I would have had to repeat the first grade. The way it was, I was still ahead of everyone else when I finally made it back to school in the spring.

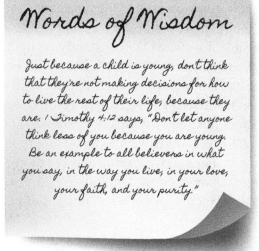

Words of Wisdom

Just because a child is young, don't think that they're not making decisions for how to live the rest of their life, because they are. 1 Timothy 4:12 says, "Don't let anyone think less of you because you are young. Be an example to all believers in what you say, in the way you live, in your love, your faith, and your purity."

Learning How to Cook

Mama usually did as little as possible. She cooked when she had to and never cleaned. She was lazy. ***That is LAZY!*** She never asked us to clean during the week, but on Saturday she would get a belt and beat everyone, especially me, for making such a mess. Mama thought that as a girl, I had more responsibility for cleaning than any of the boys did. Mama would make me make all the beds and clean up after the boys even though I was just a tiny little girl.

Saturdays were always a nightmare. She would follow behind me like a slave master striking me with the belt she always wore around her neck, while I was trying my best to clean whatever it was she wanted cleaned. The whole time she was screaming verbal aggression about how terrible I cleaned and how ugly I was compared to the boys. All the boys were large framed while I was tiny. Sonny had the exact same coloring as me with brown eyes and brown hair, but Mama wanted a big, blonde, blue eyed girl and I was tiny with cinnamon reddish-brown hair and eyes. I was her biggest disappointment to date she would say.

Mama expected me to do more domestic chores at the age of six than she expected from my brothers who were 14 and 17. She had unrealistic expectations for a girl of my age. I suffered from her ignorance. It never dawned on her that she could actually help, and the cleaning would go faster if she did. Saturdays were her day to heap abuse on me. Mark never had to clean because he was the baby.

One Saturday, Mama was not at home. All the kids were home, but she was gone. I had never cooked a meal before, but that week at school they had served hotdogs split down the middle stuffed with cheese and I had both ingredients. We also had potatoes which I baked. The boys went crazy over my meal. They bragged and asked for seconds, they couldn't believe that they had something to eat that wasn't burned, actually was prepared well and tasted very good. I don't think Mama had cooked a meal in 25 years that wasn't burned. From those first accolades on the meal I prepared, I became the full-time family cook from age six.

One day, in desperation, because we had nothing to eat,

except cheese and condiments, I invented a new creation. When I say we had nothing to cook, I mean the cabinets were literally bare. There was nothing in the freezer, no food anywhere in the house. I took the one onion we had,

Sonny and Diane Johnson

chopped it, and put it in the bottom of a pan. I topped it with a few pickles, found some ketchup packets one of the older boys brought home, added them, topped the whole pan with mustard and cheese, then baked it. My hamburger surprise was without meat or bun. Again, the boys thought it was the best thing they had ever eaten. These were very desperate times.

Food Thieves

Mark and I were regular food thieves. Up until I was nine I never thought about anyone owning food. I just saw a garden, a tree with fruit, or even once an oil spill with dead fish and I drug it home. Believe it or not, we tried to eat the dead fish, but they tasted exactly like petroleum, so we had to throw them out.

Whatever we drug home, Mama never questioned where we got it, she just prepared it and served it. This was so unusual for her because she did not feed us regularly, never breakfast, occasionally lunch, yet always dinner. But when we brought home stolen food, she would stop what she was doing. She would cook or prepare it and we would eat whatever it was. Because this was so out of character for her, it encouraged us to scavenge for more food.

One time, Mark and I brought home a basket of turnips we dug out of a neighbor's garden. He caught us digging up his turnips and asked what we were doing. I was six and Mark was four at the time. I told him we were hungry, and we were getting something to eat. The man just stood there and watched while I dug up turnips putting them in my old sand bucket. Mark still hardly talked. I thought the turnips boiled with salt were delicious. Interestingly, it was winter; Mama thought I was too sick to go to first grade, but she had no problem with me running around the neighborhood scavenging for food.

Learning From a Cookbook

When I was eight, I graduated from cooking only what I had seen cooked to reading the cookbook. One day, I got very confused with trying to read the cook book's abbreviations while I was trying to make a fresh pear cake. Mark and I had stolen the pears from a neighbor's tree. He probably didn't mind because we had picked them for days. I am sure if he didn't like it he would have told us. I came home with bushels of pears. I decided they were like apples because they were hard as a rock. I decided I would grate them up and make a cake. I found an apple cake recipe and started trying to make the pears into an apple cake. Of course, we never had eggs, or milk, or butter, but I had spices and pears. I put in a cup of salt instead of sugar. Unfortunately, the cup of salt didn't work out!

Mama canned the rest of the pears. It was a good thing because two winters later we had no food at all for about two weeks, until we remembered we had the canned pears under Mama's bed. We ate those until we got money to buy groceries; of course, it took sending Mark and me to my Aunt Maxine's for the family to decide to give more money to Mama.

In 1963, when I was six years old, was a pivotal year for me as so many life decisions that changed the course of my life were made that year. I had a lot of time on my hands to think, reason, and wait to get older to act.

<u>1967</u>

Moving to Shreveport

Third grade had just ended and I was nine years old. Mama finally got a job at the Army Ammunition Plant in Louisiana making ammunition for the Vietnam War. (It was very odd how she reconciled making bullets for the Vietnam War to kill young men with her beliefs.)

We moved to Shreveport and said goodbye to East Texas for good. Mama rented a nice house on the bus line. Mark and I shared a room like we'd done all of our life. Gary had his own room. He was seventeen. Mama had her own room. We had always slept with Mama before because there wasn't space. Mama worked 3 pm -11 pm, so she was gone by the time we got out of school. For a while there was black lady who stayed with us until 5:00 pm, then she left. Gary worked in the evening at Brookshire's, a grocery. Mark, a second grader, and I, a 4th grader, were left alone together.

Gary would come in between 8:00 to 11:00 at night. I managed our dinner, so Mark and I would watch TV, waiting on Gary. Mark would usually fall asleep before bedtime. I would be tasked with the chore of undressing him and getting him to bed. Even though he was just seven, he was bigger than I was. He was my responsibility to get him to bed, so I did.

I put my foot down with Mama and refused to let her cut my hair anymore. I started growing out my hair. I must have had some support from my aunts because I am sure that my mother would have never quit cutting it all off without someone saying something. I started looking like a normal little girl in the fourth grade, instead of a girl with the same haircut as her brother. Mama always liked our hair cut the same because people thought we were twins. She had pretty much lost interest in hair-cutting by then. Mama was getting out of the hair-cutting phase as she was busy with her new job at the ammunition plant.

My Aunt Carolyn

Where we lived was close to a bayou, so Mark and I would go down to play in the water. Some black boys were about our same age. They would play down by the Bayou and in no time, we were all fast friends. We would meet up after school, as none of us were monitored by adults. There we would have real adventures like Huck Finn and Tom Sawyer. We had a wonderful time, until somehow my grandfather found out about it and strictly forbid it. He said no little white girl should be running around with a band of boys. I was so upset, but, in retrospect, I know he was doing his best to protect me.

I always felt kindness towards my grandfather Leone. I think I was probably the person who understood him best because in a lot of ways I am like my grandfather in business. In an effort to monitor my behavior better, my Aunt, Carolyn, started coming to get me and Mark to spend the night with her and our grandmother, Buddy. She brought us to Buddy's house to spend the night. Carolyn had recently given up her apartment and moved back in with her mother. At Buddy's, we would eat ham, tomato, and lettuce sandwiches with mayonnaise and dance the twist. Carolyn was young, in her late thirties, with no husband or children. She was beautiful, inside and out.

Carolyn's best friend was my 22-year-old cousin, Jan. Carolyn also had another best friend, Bernice, and two boyfriends. Her friends would flock to Buddy's house, where Carolyn would go out to dinner with the old or new boyfriend. Everyone seemed so happy with the dancing, music, and fun clothes.

One day, Carolyn told me to go take a bath as she was taking me to see my grandfather. I spent too long in the bathroom causing her to get angry. I had never seen her angry before. From then on, things were not the same. Carolyn quit her job of 18 years. She seldom got dressed. She stopped eating and was admitted to the hospital. I always made her laugh, so my cousin was to pick me up one day, so I could cheer her up. I got dressed and waited but Cynthia never came.

In August of 1967, when I was 10 years old, my beautiful Aunt Carolyn died of ovarian cancer; she weighed 40 pounds. Mama told me she died of stomach cancer, she kept up that lie until the day she died. I never was told it was ovarian cancer until Jan, my cousin, told me. Mama felt it was important to lie so that I would not have sexual thoughts. Knowing I had a history of ovarian cancer would have been so helpful later in life.

That night, after Carolyn's funeral, I was all alone laying in my bed thinking about Carolyn, when she appeared to me in the flesh. Carolyn was a Catholic. The only non-protestant in the whole family. She told me to go get her rosary, describing the exact location. Carolyn said to become Catholic. I went and got her rosary. I became Catholic at my first opportunity. I told Mama about seeing Carolyn in a white dress very similar to a wedding dress. Mama said that was exactly what she was wearing in the coffin. I was not allowed to go to the funeral because the family thought that a child of ten was too young to attend a funeral for her aunt.

I did not know it at the time, but that same day Carolyn appeared to my cousin Jan. Carolyn definitely was not ready to die at such an early age. Jan had just had a baby boy, Brad, while Carolyn, not having any children of her own, loved the new baby. Right after appearing to me in Shreveport, Carolyn sat next to Jan in Dallas. Carolyn spent the entire day with Jan as Carolyn held Jan's baby

Carolyn Johnson

Brad. She talked with Jan for the last time. Jan and I both saw Carolyn in the flesh. I was ten, but Jan was 22; this was not just a manifestation of a child's broken heart. We both saw her wearing her funeral dress in a manifestation of the flesh.

When Carolyn died, my brother, Gary, moved in with my grandmother Buddy. He never came back to Mama's. This was a red-letter day for me because now instead of two abusers to deal with, I just had one, Mama. As long as Mama was working, she was somewhat reasonable because she was tired when she got home. The time away from the house forced her to focus her spare time on her smoking, reading, sewing, and painting. Unfortunately, all chores usually done by parents such as cooking, cleaning, and child care were either left undone or I did them. I started picking up more and more of the parental responsibilities.

Lifetime Friends

While I was finding long-term friends to be my family, so

was Mark. Mark found a boy to befriend named Derrick. Derrick was trouble on two feet. He lived with his grandparents because his mother was a drug addict who entertained many male friends for money and drugs.

Derrick took Mark home to his grandparents. Mark never left. For his entire life Mark regarded Pa Robinson, Derrick's grandfather, as his father. Pa was a drunk but a great car repair mechanic. Pa took Mark fishing, hunting, taught him to work on cars and repair everything around the house. They never separated. Nanny, Pa's wife, always had something to eat cooked. She kept a big pot of beans and cornbread on the stove for the boys all the time. Derrick would move in and out, but Mark was always there with Pa and his wife, Nanny. Derrick and Mark did not get along too well after the first few years. Derrick was getting wilder and wilder much like his mother had. But Mark stayed with his Robinson family. Years later when Pa was dying it was not his children or grandchildren who cooked him something to eat and came up to the hospital to hand feed him. It was Mark. He stayed by his bedside day and night until he died. Then Mark took care of Nanny until she died.

THE UNBELIEVABLE PLIGHT OF MRS. WRIGHT

PART THREE

Trying to Grow Up and Mama's Episodes

1968

The Move

When I was 10 and going into the fifth grade, Mama decided to move closer to Buddy. Gary and I were charged with finding a place to live. I took the bus to Buddy's and walked several blocks to Creswell Elementary School where there was a house for rent right across the street. Mama had been moved to day shifts, so she left for work about 5:30 AM in the morning and came home about 5:00 PM. Since Mark and I were third and fifth graders without anyone to get us up for school, we were frequently late to school. It got so bad, the principal made it a habit to walk across the street and get us out of bed. We rushed out the door every morning disheveled with our messy hair and no breakfast. Often our first drink of the day was from the water fountain at morning recess.

Fifth grade was wonderful! There was a beautiful blonde boy named Brent Kingston that I just loved to stare at. Mrs. Carpenter was my teacher. I met my first lifelong, best friend Trisha Ryan. Trisha was from a divorced family too, but she had a Dad that loved her. He had visitation with her on Sundays. He would take her to her grandmother's house, Texada, where he lived. I had only seen my father once, at Buddy's house when I was six years old. Fox was drunk and scratched my face with his whiskers. He breathed terrible alcoholic breath in my face. All in all, he terrified me.

Trisha and I became inseparable. We had a lot in common. Her mother, Sarah, was very strange, possibly stranger than Mama. Although they had a two-bedroom house her mother made them sleep on a palate on the floor in the living room. Trisha was not allowed to have company at all. We sneaked around because her mother was at work. Her mother was even older than mine. Sarah had Trisha after the age of 40. She had a grown half-brother that she couldn't remember ever living with. When Courtney (Trisha's father) fell head over heels at the age of 30, for Sarah, who was 40, he got her pregnant. They decided to get married. Sarah's son, Troy, was a young teenager. Troy and Courtney loved each other as a father and son. When Courtney and Sarah divorced, Trisha was a year old. Courtney took Troy with him and moved to his mother's house where he finished raising Troy alone.

Sarah was very demanding of Trisha. Even in the fifth grade, Trisha had to have something cooked for supper for her mother when she got home. Often it was tuna salad sandwiches. We had a lot in common. We both had single parents and had to prepare supper. But she had a Dad!

Courtney decided it was easier to take care of Trisha if she had a friend along, so he started taking me when he took Trisha. Courtney was the only father I ever knew.

The Lunch

During this time Mama had surprising bouts of normality. One day she told me to bring a friend home for lunch. At lunch time that day, I brought a friend home. I was scared to death because our house always looked like a bomb had gone off. Everything was everywhere covered with roaches and filth. Usually, every dirty dish in the house was sitting out on the kitchen counter waiting until the dreaded Saturday washing. Mama had not changed on that fearsome abuse. So I picked a second-best friend that I felt I could afford to lose if things went poorly, as they usually did with Mama.

I still remember the meal like it was yesterday! Mama fried red snapper, had baked potatoes, salad with dressing, and baked a homemade chocolate cake! Everything was delicious! Nothing

Words of Wisdom

Children whose home lives are chaos, with a filthy home, abuse, or any other home secret don't normally have other children over to their homes. These children know they are living a secret life without ever having to be told and normally will not bring any other children home to see their secrets.

was burned! She was dressed, with her makeup on and her hair fixed. The living room, kitchen, and bathroom were cleaned up. The table was set. Everything was beautiful and perfect! I could not believe it! It was as if I had walked into Beaver Cleaver's life. I have no idea what caused Mama to cook this wonderful meal for me and my second-best friend, but it never happened again.

Shawn, Christina, and Kelly

Down the street from us were another set of grandparents raising three small children whose mother had died of a gunshot wound under suspicious circumstances. Shawn was eight, Christina was five, and the baby, Kelly, was a year old. In the summer of 1968, when I was eleven, Shawn built a zip line in his backyard. He had it start from the concrete picnic table and end across the yard. When I took the hand grip in my hands and started off the hard table, the zip line built by a child, snapped. I fell, hitting my back on the hard edge of the picnic table. I had never hurt so bad in my life! And I had been hurt a lot. I ran crying home. As my mother was not home, I laid on the couch for the rest of the day trying to get the pain to stop. The pain never did stop. From that day on until I was 55 years old, it always hurt. I was told later that my back had been broken at three vertebras and calcified.

Mama would never consider taking one of her children to the doctor. If my brother or I ever needed to go to the doctor, we had to tell one of the aunts. They took us to the doctor and my grandfather paid for the visit. I consider myself very blessed that I was not taken to the hospital for a broken back in 1969. If I had surgery, chances are that I could have possibly wound up in a wheel chair for the rest of my life. Even though my back always hurt, I learned to deal with the pain and always kept going. I didn't let the pain slow me down or interfere with working hard and enjoying life. I just dealt with it as a part of life.

Summer

At the beginning of summer, I decided that Mark and I needed to clean house. It was Saturday, about 10:00 in the morning, and Mama was working overtime that day. I did what

Mama always did I got a belt, hung it around my neck and yelled at Mark, "Get up right now and help me clean up the house!" Mark responded by shooting me in the eye at a very close range with his sling shot. I didn't even have time to blink. The rock hit me in the eye, lacerating my cornea. I could not see at all out of the eye. Mama was working at the Ammunition Plant in Minden, LA about 30 miles away, with no car because she carpooled. (It is interesting to reflect on it now, that no matter how much Mama worked "overtime" on Saturday our lifestyle never did improve).

I did the only thing I could think of: I went and put on my nicest dress that Grandma had made me and ran down to the pharmacy to the pharmacist, Mr. Hall. He was our doctor. Whenever we were sick, we went to him and he fixed us up. I knew I could not call Buddy who lived two blocks away, because she didn't have a car. Mr. Hall called the Ammunition plant. They said they were going to find Mama and somehow get her home. Mr. Hall sat me at the soda fountain and made me a coke float and a hamburger, but I couldn't eat it. About 3:00, Mama came to get me and took me to the ER. I had to wear a patch for about six weeks and, by that time, the other eye was so strained, that I couldn't see out of either eye. Nobody thought to get me glasses.

Mark did not go with me, which was uncharacteristic because we never separated. He had stayed home. I guess what Mama said was true, "if you love a man he runs away when you need him". After that I began to withdraw a little from Mark. I think that day also did something to Mark; he was so distraught after shooting me in the eye, he jumped off a tire swing he had hung slicing open his knee open, just about the time we got home from the ER. But Mama said he "would just have to suffer because one kid in the ER was all she was going to do in one day". This coined a phrase I use all the time with my daughters and seventeen grandchildren, "Stop that! I do not feel like going to the ER today". That always worked with the girls but the other day one of the grandsons asked me, "Why don't you want to go to the ER today?" I replied with the only answer a three-year-old could understand, "Because it is closed, don't jump off that again".

Learning to Sew

Because of the care my eye needed, that summer I was sent to my Grandma's house in Kilgore, Texas. My cousin, Dena Kay, who was fifteen, was there. Dena was my Uncle Don's daughter, and everyone talked about what a hard life she had because her mother had run off and left her and her brothers with their Dad. Dena Kay was a chain smoker who had been smoking since she was eight. We spent all of our free time at Grandma's hiding, so Dena Kay could smoke. Dena Kay thought that I was really delayed on learning to smoke. She was quite concerned about me fitting in with the other smokers. She feared that I would not be popular in middle school if I was not a smoker. Unfortunately for Dena Kay, she was not the best articulator. She made about as much sense as most of the things that Mama said. I decided right there I was not going to be popular in middle school because I was not going to fit in with the smokers, because I would NEVER SMOKE!!! That was the first time I had encountered a closet smoker, but it surely would not be my last.

Grandma took Dena Kay and I to the fabric store to let us pick out any fabric we wanted and a pattern to learn how to sew. I loved blue. It was my favorite color, but Mama would have made ugly remarks about it because brown was her favorite color. I got brown cotton with tiny white flowers to make her happy. I sat down and read the pattern from front to back. I looked at the pictures of how the fabric went together. At ten, I was able to figure out the pattern quickly and cut my own fabric out. I was able to sew up my own shorts outfit. The top was a long top with puffed sleeves and a zipper. The only thing Grandma had to do on my outfit was put in the zipper. To this day, I still cannot put in a zipper without basting it in first. Poor Dena Kay could not figure out how to sew. I figured out that she wasn't bright, even if she was fifteen years old, which was quite an accomplishment in itself at the time, or so I thought.

The best thing about being at my Grandma's house was that my best friend June lived next door to my Grandma. June was a year older than me and so pretty. She had dark-blond, perfect, straight hair and big blue eyes. She was tall and thin. Just the type

Words of Wisdom

There is talking around a smoke hole in business that only smokers know, so a good rule in business is if you are not going to smoke and hang out with smokers, you have to have friends that are smokers to report back to you their discussions. Some of my best friends have smoked, but to this day I do not smoke, and I never hung out around a smoke hole.

of girl Mama always said she wanted instead of the brown-eyed, little, tiny girl she got. June's mother left her and her brother with her Grandma, Mrs. Gillis, when June was born. June and I had played together all of our life. June saw her mother on holidays. We were excited because it was almost July Fourth and her mother would be coming home for a visit. June's mother, Heather, was a dancer in Dallas, and we were both impressed with her because she was so pretty and young. Heather was only 27, with a beautiful figure, dressed in high heels and shiny clothes. Mama said that Heather made her "living on her back" (whatever that meant) and "wore cocktail dresses".

June had a Doberman Pincer named King that was the biggest dog I had ever seen in my life. June could do anything with that dog. The dog would even let June ride on his back. June really loved that dog. She loved to roam the oil fields of East Texas with her big dog by her side. June would always say we don't have to worry about a thing because King would never let anyone hurt her.

Chad was June's twelve-year-old brother. He was handsome and played baseball. Chad never spoke to me. He was just way too cool to talk to a girl two years younger than he was. Mrs. Gillis invited me to go see Chad play baseball because he was "really something". Chad played on two teams. He was the star player on both teams. Mrs. Gillis said he really had a future in baseball. As soon as June and I got to the baseball field she yelled at me to follow her. Overlooking the baseball field was a World War II watch tower. The watch towers were built for the purpose of watching for enemy attacks and fires. The watch towers were only built to last 20 years and by 1968 the 1940's tower was in disrepair.

We climbed the tall, rickety, wooden stairs to the wooden platform above. I was scared as the stairs creaked and I thought they swayed. June reassured me. June said that she came to two of Chad's ball games a week. She always watched them from the top of the tower. We had a wonderful view of the whole ball field and the surrounding area. We stayed up there the entire time racing around and around the open-air room until Chad's ballgame was over. Mrs. Gillis was finally ready to go home. When I hugged June goodbye that summer evening, I didn't know that would be the last time I would ever see June. I went back to Shreveport the next morning. The next week, at her brother Chad's next ball game, when beautiful June ran across the watch tower floor, the floor gave way, and June crashed fifty feet to her death. The saddest thing to me was that she died before she got to see her mama, Heather, for the July Fourth holiday she had looked forward to. Chad never played baseball again. King spent the rest of his days sitting on Mrs. Gillis' front porch waiting for June to come back.

I've often wondered why the tower floor gave way that night, with just one, little, thin girl running across the floor. Four days earlier, when two little girls had run all over the floor, going from one view to the next, the tower floor did not give way. For some reason God spared me; I felt a deep sense of loss and guilt about June's death for years. I always felt that it could have been me too; I still do. I have never stopped thinking of June Nelson.

Sixth Grade with Mr. McCune

That fall, when I was in sixth grade, my beautiful brother Sonny had to go to Vietnam. I started sixth grade with my teacher, Cecil McCune. He was a beautiful young man who looked a lot like Sonny. I would stare at him and think about my brother. Later, this beautiful man and his family would live on the same street that I lived on in Broadmoor. Our class was very interesting because we were located in an outbuilding, so anytime the office needed Mr. McCune, he would have to walk to the main building, which took some time. There was a tall girl named Kimberly in our class, who was an exhibitionist. Kimberly would do a strip tease dance in front of the class, taking off her dress whenever Mr. McCune left for the office. The boys went crazy. I would entertain myself by playing a game I made up from Alice in Wonderland that I called, "off with their heads". I would critique each child in class to decide if they were worthy to live or should I declare, "off with their heads?" After a good round of "off with their heads", played silently to myself, I would then play my other favorite game, "why are they so rich?" I would go through the class one by one. I would mentally discuss what their parents did for a living. It didn't take long to see the correlation of a college degree and higher earning potential. I definitely made up my mind to get a college degree. "When I grow up I'll never be poor again", I though. That would be a promise I would keep.

That same year, at age eleven, I realized how much money Mama was throwing away every month because she could not pay the bills on time. I realized the utility company charged an additional premium to have the utilities turned back on. The landlord also charged late fees. She lost everything she pawned. I sat down with her paycheck and created a budget that appeared to be adequate to cover the bills. But to cover the bills you first had to pay the bills. Then spend what was left over on the things Mama wanted. Mama and I began to develop more and more issues and divergence with regard to responsibility. I would try to convince Mama to pay the rent. She would ignore me. She continued to buy her cigarettes, novels, material, and patterns that she never sewed. Our house had become a library of used paperback novels,

89

old material, and old patterns. We argued constantly, which she tolerated only to a point. At the point that rational discussion on how we had to pay the rent became tiresome to her, she retreated into her true nature and began abuse by whipping me with whatever object she could lay hands on. Her favorite was a wire coat hanger, often leaving a trail of blood and scars down my legs which I have to this day. You would think this behavior would have turned me into a cowering, frightened child but instead it made me angry. I began to draw strength from that anger. The more anger I internalized, the more I was determined to try to change her for her own good. When she was calm, I tried to talk calmly to her and reason with her. I convinced her to turn the money completely over to me, which she eventually did. I set out to try and get the finances in order. We fought constantly over money. She constantly sabotaged me by refusing to adhere to the budget. By this time, I was eleven and I was doing all the cooking, grocery shopping, budgeting, bill-paying, babysitting, and cleaning for us.

1969

Sewing and Healing

I was so grateful to my Grandma for teaching me to sew before June died. Mama spent half of all the money she ever got on brown material and patterns that she did not sew into the brown clothes she wanted. We had closets of brown material, dressers of brown material, boxes of patterns and trims, brown zippers, brown buttons, and brown lace. We had so much brown material it took up all the space; the house was cluttered with it as it piled on top of every piece of furniture, spilling out of closets packed to the top, until finally it was just stacked in boxes on the floor.

But while we had boxes of brown material, we never had shoes, except for the one pair that we got when school started. The shoes had to last the whole school year until the next summer. By summer, they were two sizes too small and falling apart, as the shoes had been worn every day of winter.

I came home from Grandma's in the dark depression of losing June. I convinced Mama to buy me a pattern. I promptly started sewing therapy to help me get over losing June. I went through Mama's material and made myself the same dress in about three different brown fabrics. Mama bought me another pattern and I did the same thing. I worked all summer on making myself a complete wardrobe for school. It was good therapy to sit and sew as fast as I could while thinking about June. By the time summer was done, I started middle school with a full wardrobe of my own hand-sewn clothes.

All the dresses I made were very low cut. I only had two patterns and they were what they were, I wasn't good at alterations... yet. As I was under-endowed I did not see this lack of cleavage in a low top as a problem. There literally was nothing to see. At least that was what I thought. The quarterback of the eighth grade was Luther, an older man. He was tall and beautiful, the size of a full-grown man, with blue eyes and blonde hair. In eighth grade he was over 6 foot tall and weighed about 175 pounds. He was the best ball player because he was the size of a grown man and all the other boys were little. He stood every day leaning against my locker, refusing to look at me or acknowledge I was there, or let me into my locker to get my books. He was the most popular boy in school and the most beautiful. For months, I was late for class, got in trouble, and never told on him. I decided right there in the seventh grade at twelve years old, that I would marry him, and so I did.

Later after we were married he said he blocked my access to my locker every day in junior high, just to look down my low-cut dress. I guess those hand-sewn clothes really weren't very good for me. Neither was Luther, he was exactly like Mama.

Grocery Shopping

We didn't have a car. Cars cost too much money. I rode the bus whenever we needed something. We also didn't have a phone, or anything else most people had at the time even though Mama was still working.

Mama had long given up grocery shopping. It was completely my responsibility. Besides, I was doing most of the cooking, so I needed to pick out what to buy. That way I would know what was available to cook. Besides, if Mama cooked we reverted back to her three staple meals of meatloaf surprise, chicken slop soup, and spaghetti.

Words of Wisdom

A child gravitates towards the familiar even if it is negative

Going to the grocery was a struggle. To buy groceries I had to walk to the grocery that was close to the house and carry the bags back home. I could only carry two large brown paper bags at one time, so I had to go the grocery a couple of times a week. Mama still had things that were not allowed in the house like ketchup, mayonnaise, jelly, condiments, and milk.

I planned the menu, wrote out a list, poured over the specials, and bought the cheapest food possible. Bread was a staple in the house now because I planned meals and bought what I needed to cook them. I was trying to keep track of the total cost in my head, but invariably I would get to the counter and not have enough money. I would have the humiliating task of trying to figure out what I could live without because I had my menus planned. One ingredient off and I could not make the meal I had envisioned.

It was a nightmare trying to get enough food to last a week that was tasty, nutritious, and healthy. Almost every day my most valiant efforts of staying within a food budget would get derailed when one of Mark's friends would show up unexpectedly to eat. I would get furious, but Mama would say, "We are going to feed this boy; he doesn't have anything at his house." While it was one of the few logical things she ever said, it made cooking and planning difficult. I secretly think my difficulties pleased Mama a great deal; she seemed to think, "See she can't do any better than I can!"

But even at twelve, I did everything better than Mama, like cooking. By the time I was nine, I was proficient in cooking. I could read recipes, and long gone were the days when I was eight and stumbled over the measurements, often mixing up tablespoons and teaspoons. Mama didn't like to be disturbed when she was reading and would get violent, but if she was sewing you could talk to her. I would ask her things like how to tell the difference in the tablespoons and teaspoons when I cooked. She would tell me the answers.

She could be really helpful if you knew when the right time to ask was. Poor Mark just never understood how to get along with Mama, and he was her favorite! I had learned long ago to scream bloody murder before she started hitting me, which she did a lot more often than she did with Mark. I even had her convinced that girls hurt more than boys, so you didn't have to beat them as much or as hard.

But Mark tried to "man up" and not cry. He held it all in, so she beat him senseless. I was always too traumatized by the constant beating and screaming to have a conversation with him about what to do to help himself. Besides Mark and I did not talk much at all. The only question he ever asked me was, "what are we going to do today?" Because my mind never took a minute off, I always had Plan A, B, and C. Plans work. I would tell him what the plan was, and he never once said he didn't want to do the plan, he would just nod and go along.

Talking to Mark

During all the conversations Mark and I ever had, I was talking non-stop and he was nodding. He never really participated in the conversation; it was kind of like thinking, except saying it out loud to someone else. I think the cruelty was much harder on Mark than it was on me (if that is possible). He was more severely traumatized by it and has suffered depression all of his life. He was a sweet, sensitive child that did not deserve to be mistreated. The abuse really affected our self-worth.

I think it could have caused depression in me as well, but I found anger a much more useful emotion than depression. Anger motivated me. It was not an all-time destructive and negative state worthy of suppression. My anger framed a positive force that fueled my ambitions and my creativity. Anger moved me toward what I wanted. Anger fueled my optimism, creative brainstorming, and problem solving by focusing my mind and my moods in highly refined ways. Anger is the polar opposite of fear, sadness, disgust, and anxiety—feelings that prompted avoidance and solitude. When I got mad, it propelled me toward challenges I may have otherwise fled.

Words of Wisdom

I would have a plan A, B, and backup plan C, if A and B both fail because others will not go along with them. You must have plan C. That way you always know what you're doing, where you're going, and what to do when you get there. I spent every moment of my life working a plan. This was highly successful for me.

Coat Hanger Weapons

As we got older, the abuse got more violent. Anytime Mama hit me with something it just "disappeared". The belts disappeared, electrical cords disappeared, along with just about anything else that was a handy weapon. Mama had a real short attention span. She couldn't keep up with anything anyway, with the house in such disarray she never missed anything that "disappeared". But I

Words of Wisdom

Don't get sad, get mad! Anger motivates and gets things done. Sometimes, its delightful to be furiously angry and furiously successful. Depression often lays around and does nothing. Remember the best revenge is living well!

couldn't get rid of the hangers, you had to have coat hangers. All we had were wire coat hangers. I think Grandma must have known about the beatings with the coat hangers, because she always crocheted around all the hangers. There were always plenty of coat hangers that were plain wire.

It was about this time that Mama no longer just whipped

us with the coat hangers, she straightened out the curved end and jabbed them into our legs causing puncture wounds that streamed with blood. Can you imagine a mother knowingly attempting to cause her child tetanus, a deadly disease, by puncture wound? She knew that we were not immunized because she almost never took us to the doctor.

Our Uncle Sherman's two best friends were Eric and Brian Mont. Eric was a reporter for the Shreveport Times newspaper. Eric visited Buddy regularly. I frequently saw him in her home as a little child. Brian married very late in life; they were both close to forty. My Uncle Sherman married my Aunt Audrey and they had a son named Graves. Brian married a young woman in her twenties and they had two small children. This lovely, young Mrs. Mont stepped on her son's rusty truck in the front yard when she went to get the paper one morning and developed tetanus (lockjaw). She died a horrible death, leaving Brian to raise a one-year old baby girl and a three-year-old little boy by himself.

We were very aware of the deadly effects of tetanus. God protected us from tetanus. I jumped off a garage work bench at a friend's house. A nail perforated all the way through my shoe into my foot. Aunt Tirr was horrified and took me to get a tetanus shot. Mark fell on a metal flowerbed landscape edging, cutting an "L" shape from his little finger to his thumb. Mama wouldn't look at it, but I insisted he have stitches, so she took him to get the stitches and a tetanus shot. It doesn't even seem real to reflect on as an adult. My mother was attempting to murder me by giving me tetanus.

Mark and I never thought about telling Buddy or the aunts about the abuse. We thought it was normal and every little kid was beat that hard. Mama said it was good for our character.

Moving to 2701 Highland

At the end of sixth grade, the house we were living in was chosen for demolition and we had to move out by June 1, 1969. So once again I was charged with finding us a place to live. After all, I was twelve and fully capable of making all decisions for the family. Mama had started to revert to very childlike behavior when she was not furiously still beating us both. She would ask if she could go shopping. I would tell her we would have to wait a little while until we got more money. I had learned you didn't tell her, "No". That was sure to cause a fight, but she had gotten used to waiting for money to come in, so she would accept that as an answer. I started learning how to talk her down from her manic-depressive mood swings. Mama wasn't your typical manic depressive, she was manic or angry. When she was manic she was furiously working on some useless project that never turned out and usually only got partly finished. When she was angry she fought with anyone and everyone. There was no escape. She fought with the family, she railed curses against Fox, she fought the neighbors, clerks, and anyone who ever thought about being her friend. Mama did not have friends. She felt anyone who liked her enough to be her friend had to have something wrong with them, so she would start her fury and drive them away.

I went out and found us a duplex to live in. It was a shack. The landlady was named Dodie Fox. Mrs. Fox was a tiny woman about 4'8" and acted very severe. She lived alone, as her husband had recently died. Part of her living was the rent we were about to try to pay. I negotiated a deal with Mrs. Fox to pay her $45.00 a month for the rent. The duplex was what they call in Louisiana "a shotgun shack", meaning you could shoot a shotgun through the front door and it would go straight out the back door. There were only four rooms. From the front door, there was the living room and a dining room we used as a bedroom for Mark, but Mama put her sewing in there (meaning it was a mess). Next was the kitchen with just enough room for the table to jut out into the hall, but we could squeeze around it, the bathroom, and, finally, one bedroom for Mama and me to share. Mark had always slept with Mama. I had moved out of the community bed years earlier as I stayed too angry with her to sleep in a bed next to her. I put a double bed and a twin bed in the bedroom in case Mark wanted to sleep in the twin bed near us. I wound up sleeping in the twin bed while Mark and Mama slept in the full bed.

As fortune would have it, the man who had previously rented from Mrs. Fox was an electrician. He had wired the electricity to the front utility pole so there was just a minimum bill every month. Oh, Glory! The adults all thought this was just the way it should be; Mrs. Fox told us about it. Mama was happy, but I was thrilled! The money to be saved from leaching electricity from the city allowed me to purchase a water cooler. We had never had any air conditioning, so this was a big improvement in life to have some air circulating in the water cooler. Later that winter, I received some Christmas money from my Grandfather to buy clothes for school. I spent it on an air conditioner for the bedroom, so we could sleep in comfort the next summer with our free electricity.

Moving to a one-bedroom shotgun duplex was not comfortable. It was very cramped and cluttered. We still had all the same furniture, that, at one time had been very nice (furniture Mama had when Fox left her). The furniture had been moved so many times and was so old that our shack just looked dilapidated and depressing. I was always trying to clean up the house. I was figuring out that if you cleaned as you went, instead of waiting for the dreaded Saturday cleaning day, and Mama's "house screaming", then it wasn't as bad.

Grandma had given Mama an old, light gray rug for our living room. Mama's favorite color for any house was gray. (I hate gray; it is my least favorite color.) The rug was nicer than the worn-out hardwood floors. It was covered with dark stains. As I was now doing all the cleaning, cooking, washing, and bills, I decided to try and clean the gray rug. But I didn't know how to clean a rug, had no rug cleaner, had no experience, and Google didn't exist. I went and looked in the kitchen shelves for inspiration and found a tub of wood floor wax. It was old and hard, but I poured some hot water on it and it softened up. I got a rag, my elbow grease, and started to work on the light gray rug. By the time I got through with the rug, it was dark gray with none of the spots showing and looked brand new. The rug looked fantastic. I was surprised how a "new" dark gray rug made the dilapidated room look more cheerful and calm.

Washing clothes also fell to me to do. We didn't have a washer or dryer, so I would put the clothes in the bathtub, add detergent and walk on them. I would drain them, rinse twice, walking on them even more. Then wring out as much water as I could by hand. I would then haul the heavy wet clothes outside and hang them on the line to dry.

1970

The Layoffs and Episodes

As the Vietnam War was drawing to a close, ammunition was not needed as much as it had previously been needed. The Plant started shortening the hours of the workers and then laying them off, forcing them to go on unemployment for a while, then hiring them back and laying them off again. Mama's behavior had been better the last several years since she started her job. The insecurity of not knowing if she would have work drew out all the old crazy behaviors and some new ones too. She started becoming more and more paranoid and psychotic with manic episodes. She would run through the house accusing me of hiding something from her. She could never articulate what it was she wanted, just screaming at the top of her lungs, "Why are you doing this to me? Where did you put it? Why are you hiding it from me?" I would run all over the house pulling out drawers and shuffling through the contents with no idea of what she wanted. I knew better than to talk to her during this manic phase because then she would escalate. She would start pummeling me with her fists and whatever she could find until she drew blood. Then she would exhaust herself screaming some more curse words while lying down smoking and cursing and smoking and cursing.

One weekend she began an extremely long episode. She had painted the bathroom in this shack deep lavender and she was looking for a picture of a flower that she had seen somewhere but couldn't remember what the flower was called or where it was. We searched amidst cursing and screaming and begging and pleading then beatings then cursing, around and around we went until she finally found the picture of the Iris she had been looking for imprinted on a hand towel she'd gotten out of an oatmeal box. Mama then sat in the bathtub for two days painting the Iris on the wall, in the only bathroom we had. I was afraid to go into the bathroom for fear of throwing her back into another episode, but she was completely over her two-day tirade and happily painting away. For two days if I needed to pee, I had to do it with Mama sitting in the bathtub.

We stopped seeing much of Mark, he was always off learning how to be a man with Pa Robinson. The crazier Mama got, the more Pa needed Mark to do.

I finally figured out I needed to stay more with Buddy. She was lonely and really needed me. Besides it was almost a mile closer to the middle school and just one block away from Trisha.

Middle School

Middle school is hard for any girl. When you have no nice clothes, no shoes, wear the cheapest black glasses, and have bad hair, middle school gets impossible. Trisha didn't care. She never judged me. We walked to school every day. It was a two-and-a-half-mile walk. I had bus money but no clothes. I walked to and from school with Trisha and skipped lunch to have the 35 cents for the bus both ways and the 50 cents from the lunch. Each week, by walking to school and skipping lunch, I had six dollars saved up by the end of the week. I would take the bus downtown, find a cheap outfit on sale, put it on layaway and pay weekly on whatever I had on layaway. These were my first store bought clothes. My taste in clothing usually ran to anything with sequins, lace, or beading of any kind with bright colors. Mama would have a fit and say I picked out cocktail dresses. But since she was not paying for it, I just wore what I wanted. I kept clothes and shoes on layaway at all times paying it off with my bus and lunch money.

Walking though Broadmoor was a magical experience for me. Trisha and I would look at the fine old homes. I told her I am moving to Broadmoor one day. Trisha never laughed at any of my grand schemes because we were going to do them all together, like sharing our kids. We were both quite concerned that our children would not have aunts. I had no sisters and Trisha had no sisters, so the children would have no aunts. (It never occurred to us that our spouses' sisters might be our kids' aunts). I was the most concerned about this because my aunts were so important to me.

We took a blood oath one day when we both fell down a culvert while manhandling Trisha's bike down the four-foot drop into the concrete culvert. We were trying to take a shortcut home. The culvert cut off about a half mile that we would have to walk if we used the streets. We did this every day there was no rain which wasn't very often in Louisiana. Anyway, we both scraped ourselves up. We took our bloody knees and tightly pressed them together in a blood oath that we would be each other's childrens' aunts. I still honor that blood oath today. I regard Trisha's daughters as my nieces. I love them more than I could have ever thought possible when I imagined them at twelve.

Aunt Tirr

The happiest times of middle school was when I would walk out the front door and my favorite aunt would be sitting there in her new Cadillac. My Aunt Tirr was beautiful! She was such a contrast to Mama. She was kind and sweet. She was beautiful with coal black hair and lavender blue eyes. She always looked like she had stepped off of a magazine cover. She was funny and instead of saying, "Oh, my Goodness!" She always said, "Well, bless my magnolia blossoms!"

When she was in town she would come pick me up and take me to Buddy's house. There we would have a tea party drinking hot spice tea out of demitasse cups while holding out our pinkie fingers. Sometimes she would take me out to eat a snack at a cafe. We would always laugh and talk about silly things.

Tirr was married to my Uncle E.F. My Grandfather Leon's sister was Dirl, a nickname for Darling Girl as her parents didn't name her until she was ten when they let her choose her own name. She chose Margaret. My grandfather was 5'3" and Dirl was 6'1". The year I was born, Dirl, age 48, was dating E.F., age 56, and brought him to Christmas dinner at Buddy's house. The family thought they might get married as Dirl, a school teacher, had never been married.

As a favor to Dirl, E.F. hired Tirr to come work for him. She had recently graduated from secretarial school. He was in the oil business. The first week Tirr was employed, E.F. had to go to

100

Dallas on business. As was the custom in Buddy's family, Tirr said, "Be careful on the highway!" When he showed up for work on Monday, he asked her to go fishing on Friday. Tirr had to run around all over downtown Shreveport to find a pair of pants to wear fishing because neither she nor her sisters owned a pair of pants. Friday afternoon E.F. presented her with a two-karat diamond ring. He said that he knew she loved him because no one had ever been concerned

My Aunt Tirr on her wedding day

enough about him to say be careful on the highway! Tirr called her sister Jerilyn and borrowed her brand-new suit. They went to Waskom, Texas and got married the next day. After the wedding, he gave her a beautiful diamond watch that she left to me when she died of breast cancer[1] at the age of 57, along with a lovely picture of magnolia blossoms that always hung over her couch to remind me of our times together when she said, "Well, bless my magnolia blossoms!"

I always wondered what Dirl thought.

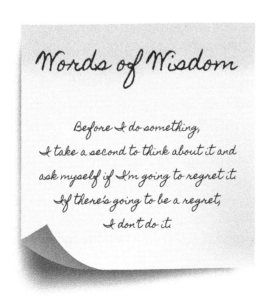

Words of Wisdom

Before I do something, I take a second to think about it and ask myself if I'm going to regret it. If there's going to be a regret, I don't do it.

My Best Friend Dorothy

My new best friend in seventh grade was a delightful girl named Dorothy Gipson. She lived off Highland Street about three blocks from where I lived. Dorothy was a gentle spirit with beautiful, <u>flowing red hair</u>. I loved

1   My biggest regret was talking her into taking chemotherapy until she died

being with her and her brother Chris. Dorothy was never allowed to go anywhere without Chris. Dorothy was sheltered from the world by her parents. Her father was overly concerned about her. She was not allowed to leave the house except with her parents. The boys did not have the same restrictions that Dorothy had. I was not used to any restrictions. Across the street from Dorothy's parents' home was a fairly large apartment complex with a large incinerator that burned all summer. Dorothy and I were convinced that the only reason it would burn in the summer like that would be to burn bodies and evidence. We spent our time there forcing Chris to accompany us over to the old building while sneaking around trying to catch someone burning evidence. This was so much fun! Dorothy was a wonderfully fun, sweet girl.[2]

I was always surrounded by boys. I had all boy cousins close to my age, and there never seemed to be as many girls on my block as there were boys; I was constantly surrounded by boys. I began to pray every day, that God would never send me boys. I did not want any boys! I wanted three girls. I named them, Antonia Leone (after my grandmother Buddy), Carolyn Jean (after my aunt and Mama), and Melanie from Gone with the Wind, my favorite novel and character of all time.

I know God hears the prayers and longings of little children because every day, from that time on, I lifted up my desire for three girls to God. And I received them.

I didn't get Antonia (thank you, God) and I didn't get Carolyn, but I got my Melanie and she is the sweetest and most peaceful person, just like in the novel. Actually, Melanie has my personality and is more like me than the other girls. I guess I could have been less of a bitch if I had been treated as kindly as I treated Melanie.

Trying to Grow Up

I had babysat since I was twelve. I always had someone's kids with me for money. At this point I was twelve years old and reading seven books a week. I could read very fast. I soaked up manners, customs, and life living skills. Manners and life living

---

2 Dorothy was later murdered in her apartment at age 25. See appendix.

skills were not taught at my house. I studied language in the books and spoke perfect English without a lot of slang and only an occasional curse word. This made most adults treat me better than the other children I was around. I was basically a miniature adult due to having had so much responsibility from an early age.

Words of Wisdom

You have to be able to see yourself with what you want, to hold an aspiration in your heart.

At twelve, I started cleaning houses for money for the old ladies in the neighborhood. I was a terrible negotiator when it came to pay, often saying "whatever you think". Well they never thought much of my cleaning, I guess, because I never felt the pay was worth the time I had in it. I switched to babysitting for 50 cents an hour. At least you knew what you were going to get paid. And I really liked the babies.

I hated being poor so much I spent every spare minute I could trying to find someone to hire me, so I could earn some money. Mark and I had a plan: if we could get $50.00 together, Pa would help him buy a car and we could get a paper route and earn money that way.

Cooking Steak Diane

My cooking had really improved. I started cooking "Steak Diane" a steak dish that I had in my mind and took years to perfect. I would buy a roast on sale and cut it into steaks. I would fry the steaks then add onion, tomatoes, and spices, then simmer the steaks in the sauce, which I would pour over mashed potatoes. I had a taste in my mind that I wanted the steaks to taste like. I could not get the dish to taste right to me. I cooked that dish six nights out of seven, trying to perfect my sweet

Words of Wisdom

Don't clean houses for pay in the poorest part of town. They pay poorly because poor people have poor ways.

and hot Creole sauce. It took me two years of cooking that dish over and over to get it seasoned to my satisfaction. Once perfected, I quit cooking Steak Diane.

No matter how often I cooked Steak Diane no one complained about the meal because even at twelve I was perfecting my ability to become an outstanding cook.

Diana's Steak Diane

1. Steaks floured and seasoned with Tony Chachere Seasoning and olive oil for browning the steaks.

2. After browning, remove steaks and set aside.

3. Add to the pan:

    Brown one diced onion

    2, 20oz. cans stewed tomatoes

    1 can Rotel

    1/4 cup brown sugar

    Garlic salt to taste

Cook tomato sauce down on low heat for 1-2 hours.

Serve over mashed potatoes, rice, or cheesy garlic grits.

1971

Eighth Grade: Doing Whatever Has to be Done to Earn Money

Eighth grade was a most difficult year. Mama was being laid off more often and called back less frequently. I just did not have the money to cover all the bills. Mrs. Fox was knocking on the door all the time asking for the rent. Mama was smoking up all the money. There was no money for food. Mark was eating all his meals at the Robinson's. I would not eat all day to go over to Buddy's after school to cook myself a hamburger. She would fix me a yellow cake with orange or peanut butter icing and always have it ready for me. Mark looked like a concentration camp victim, I was normal size, but Mama was getting fatter every day with no food in the house. I just couldn't figure that one out.

Mark and I finally scraped up $50.00. He bought a yellow 1956 Studebaker that barely ran and was a standard. Mark was eleven. He would get a chair and go out and open the hood of the car and work on it for hours. He was the only one that could drive it. I never learned to drive a standard until I was 15. But that old yellow car allowed us to get a paper route that summer. You might think a mother would be concerned that her 11-year-old son bought a car without her permission, had no registration, a stolen license plate, no insurance, and no driver's license. But not Mama. She was just glad we were working, and she wasn't.

To run the paper route, we had to get up at 3:00am to drive to the paper box where we waited with all the other unsavory characters that earned their living throwing papers. I was the only girl but there were other boys Mark's age and older. I actually learned how to drive two years later while waiting for the paper truck to deliver the papers. A man there told me I could sit in his lap and he would teach me to drive, so at 3:00 in the morning sitting in the lap of a strange man I learned to drive. This "nice man" let me sit in his lap and drive his car every night until I got the hang of it. God and my guardian angels truly protected because nothing bad ever happened to me.

Mark would drive our route. I would fold the papers, fasten them with a rubber band then toss one side of the street. Then Mark would reverse driving down the other side of the street. I would fold and toss so that we covered both sides of the street. There was one house I especially loved. The lady had poodles that yapped like crazy when we started throwing the papers on the street. They could hear us coming. The owner wanted her paper

Dian and Mark, 1971

slid into her mail slot in the front door. The poodles were already in a frenzy barking at me, but I decided to agitate them further for making me get out of the car, walk up to her door, and put the paper in her mail slot. Each morning, I shook the papers back and forth working the dogs into a frenzy. Then I would pitch the paper right onto the floor between them and watch with delight as the poodles tore her paper to shreds. One day she caught me shaking the papers. I dropped it and ran back to the car laughing all the way.

Throwing papers during the school year was not as easy as summer. We would get up, run the route, and get home at five. Mark and I would sleep until seven and then go to school. I was still walking to school every day with Trisha. Mama, however, had a good night's rest.

Babysitting

When I was 15, one of our neighbors got arrested while I was babysitting her two children, who were two and one. They were in my care at my house. I had care of the boys for the entire summer. When you live in the ghetto, you don't call the police or DHS; it is just not done. Mama had not let me go out with friends or do anything as long as I kept the babies; I just did not know what to do with them. I had an older boyfriend named Shane who drove a blue Mustang. He would come over to hang out on the front porch in the evening and drink beer. Shane and I never did go out on a date because I could never afford to hire someone else to keep the babies. I kept thinking of 50 cents an hour piling up all summer long, but I never saw any money from keeping the kids.

When school started back up, Mama said she wasn't keeping those brats any longer. She went down to the jail and got the phone number for their grandmother who didn't want them either. DHS came and got the boys. It broke my heart to see them go.

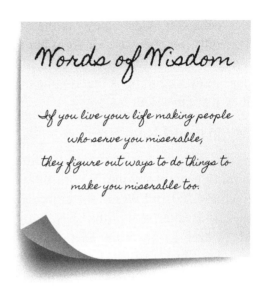

Later another neighbor had a baby girl who was just beautiful. She had black hair with blue eyes. She was nine months old. The neighbor said I could have Melissa, so I took her home. She was so pretty. I kept her two days when Mama said I had to give her back. Four years later that little girl shot and killed herself with a loaded gun she found in the house. If I had kept her she would still be alive.

Throwing Rocks

There was no ninth grade at Broadmoor Middle School, it was at the high school, so the love of my adolescent life, Luther, was no longer in school with me. He had moved on to Byrd High School.

Mama started collecting rocks. Anything that Mama did these days was cause for anxiety and concern, but what harm could there be with her picking up rocks? Mama would line her rock collection on the rail of the front porch. She took a lot of care in choosing just the right rocks and discussed them at length. Look how smooth this one is, this one is the perfect size, and this one is green, and so on it went filling the rails with the rocks. Then, one day, Mama started throwing the rocks. She threw rocks at anyone who walked down the street. People whose dogs pooped in the yard got the rocks. Children who came in her yard uninvited got the rocks. Bill collectors got the rocks. Young couples in love got the rocks - "how dare they rub their disgusting love in my face". Basically, no one was safe from her rock throwing. Anyone and everything that offended her got a rock thrown in their direction. The surprising thing is that no one ever called the police on her, they just ran.

My Friend Lisa

Mama also did not have a filter; she felt like she had every right to beat up anyone. No one ever called the police on her except one time. When I was in the eighth grade, Mama decided to beat up Lily Beaver, one of the girls in my class who lived on the next block over. Lisa was my friend. Damon was Lisa's little brother and was Mark's friend. Lisa had a mother and a father who were young and lived together, which was unusual in our neighborhood. They were married, also very unusual for our neighborhood. They also slept naked and spent a lot of time in their bedroom during the day taking naps. On occasion, Lisa's father would get up naked to scream at us kids to stop making so much noise.

I had worn a gold ring that my cousin had given me for Christmas, and it had gone missing. The ring was kept in the back of my panty drawer. At school that week I saw the missing ring on Lisa's finger and confronted her. She took the ring off and gave it back to me. She said that Damon had given it to her. I told Mama.

It wasn't long before Lisa came over to see if I could play. Mama started cursing calling her and her family thieves. Lisa started screaming back at Mama. Right then I thought Lisa was the bravest girl I had ever seen, until Mama grabbed her and started beating her up. Lisa fought back like a wildcat. I guess having five siblings a year apart helped her hone her battle skills. But Mama was bigger and stronger and had the home court advantage. She pushed Lisa off the porch, after giving her several punches. About 20 minutes later Mama was arrested. Later we all had to go to court. I got asked "what happened?" I had to lie under oath because if I told the judge the truth about what Mama did to Lisa, the beating I would have to take would make Lisa's look like a day at the spa. I was a lot more afraid of Mama than any judge, as I had to go home with her.

1971-72

Freshman Year

Just when I thought things couldn't get any worse, Mrs. Fox died. She left her house to her nephew who put it up for sale. He told us to get out as soon as possible. She left me an antique table. She didn't actually leave it to me in her will. She had asked if I could strip it for her, leaving it in my care. Mrs. Fox went home and died. I would have given it to the nephew if he had not been so nasty about us getting out of the place where we had lived for three years. People just don't get that they would be so much better off not being nasty to the little people...after all I was just a kid.

I had to go find another place for us to live with no money for a down payment, and no first or last month's rent. Sounds

Words of Wisdom

Children who are abused learn to lie. They are just trying to get out of the next beating. Every abused child knows that a lie is better than the truth because the truth will certainly get you beat. "Did you do this?" "No, the baby did it", or the dog, or anyone except you to take the beating.

Believe it or not, this was a great future lesson in dealing with employees. I learned that you never put someone in a position where they feel they must lie. The boss never asks a question that will encourage someone to lie.

impossible, not so if your standards are low enough. That's how I found 1116 College Street and Mr. Naser. Mr. Naser was an Arabic slumlord. I convinced him to let me move in with one month's rent of $50.00. I guess he just didn't have any other takers that day. It was a big, grand old home with white columns that was about one hundred years old. It had been divided into two apartments. We had the downstairs apartment, while the Barnes had the upstairs apartment. Behind us was what had been two separate servants' quarters located above the garage when the house was in its heyday. There were four families living in the old house. The house had peeling paint and worn out linoleum floors. But the rooms were large, with sun shining in through the many windows. No updates had ever been done. The house was in terrible disrepair.

Gary was long gone living in New Orleans, Sonny was living in Dallas. The moving was left to me and Mark. Everything we had was covered with roaches. Somehow, Mama didn't manage to do much of the moving. Mark and I did almost all of it in his Studebaker. Pa Robinson moved the refrigerator and the stove.

Even though we moved further away from Buddy and Pa and Nanny, we stayed overnight with them more. About this same time our paternal Grandfather, Papa, died. Louisiana law said if the father wouldn't pay child support, the paternal grandfather had to pay the child support. Our Grandfather had been forced to provide for us. Grandfather divided Fox's portion into three parts. The will stated if Fox could not pay the estate the entire amount of back child support in the sum of $30,000, his part would be divided between him, Mark and me.

Fox, of course, could not make restitution. Mark and I inherited part of our Grandfather's estate. I went to college on the money. Mark opened a business he has had for over 35 years.

When I started high school that year, several things were different. The girls' skirts were shorter, and the high school was integrated. They were busing black children to Byrd High School and white children to the black schools. The conflicts arose immediately when the black boys stood at the bottom of the stairs. They looked up the white girls mini-skirts. This threw the white boys into a frenzy and the fighting began.

The girl's gym was a battleground. We entered the locker rooms on the top floor then would take a small spiral staircase down to the gym. There were six black girls lead by a tiny 4'7", seventy-pound ringleader. She would pick out a white girl, start verbally haranguing the girl, then when the white girl started down the spiral staircase, the little girl would push the white girl causing her to fall into the other five black girls. They would gang up on the white girl and all beat her up. No one ever told on them. The gym teacher was terrified of this girl gang herself. She always seemed to be absent or claimed not to have seen anything when the beatings occurred. The white girls all just scattered and ran for their lives.

The ringleader wore a beautifully tailored yellow, orange, and brown plaid blazer that fit her tiny frame perfectly. It looked wonderful with her very dark, almost black skin. She was so proud of that blazer! She wore the blazer in any weather and even though we had to dress out in horrible one-piece shorts suits, she would put the blazer back on. The blazer was custom made. There was no telling how much it cost, but it was obviously very expensive. She had worn it every day for the whole school year.

I knew she didn't have anything else lovely to wear. I watched as the almost 40 white girls got beat up, one after the other. I knew my turn would be coming up soon because there weren't any white girls left to beat up except me.

My Aunt Carolyn was a young professional who had loved costume jewelry. When she died there was a large amount of it left at Buddy's house. There was a large metal bracelet that was about one and a half inches wide flaring out at the edges and sunk in towards the canter. The bracelet was ribbed and very heavy. I wore the bracelet every day. Many times, every day, I practiced sliding the bracelet up into my hand. Taking an imaginary punch with the bracelet, using it like brass knuckles. I got so good with the bracelet that I could basically flick my wrist out and find the bracelet perfectly in my hand to land a blow. Now keep in mind at that time I was not much bigger than the ringleader.

My day came in February, right around Valentine's Day. Why they left me until almost the last white last girl, I will never know. I was on my period, having a terrible time with very heavy bleeding, so I asked the gym teacher if I could skip dressing out. She said, "that would be fine but go downstairs and sit on the sidelines to watch the other girls." In my rehearsal for the upcoming beating I mentally prepared for the ringleader to start verbal assaults to signal that I had been chosen, but as I started down the spiral staircase there was silence.

I was surprised by a hard shove in the back. By the time I hit the bottom of the stairs, I came up with the bracelet in my hand swinging. I jumped back up the stairs to grab the ringleader. I had made up my mind when they finally chose to attack me, her jacket would not survive the fight. It didn't. I concentrated all my efforts on beating up the tiny bully ringleader. Any time one of the other girls came to help her I hit them as hard as I could with the bracelet. I had long hair and by the time the fight was finally broken up by the gym teacher I was missing most of my hair and black and blue. But I had had worse before.

The gym teacher must have thought I looked pretty bad because she sent me with another girl to the bathroom to clean up before I was to report to the principal's office. I bit my lip. I wanted to cry so bad, but I knew those kinds of people. If they sensed weakness of any sort they would beat me up every day for the rest of my life. I developed my lifetime motto right then, "Die Before Cry". I sucked it up, pulled myself up by my bootstraps, and marched into the principal's office fully expecting to be expelled that day. Fighting was against the rules. The six girls were sitting on the couch. When I walked in they pointed and exclaimed, "That's the girl that beat us up." It was ridiculous. I turned and looked at them and said, "That's right, you want some more?" To my shock and amazement all six of the black girls started crying and said, "no". They got suspended for lying about their part in the attack. I was rewarded for confronting them by not getting suspended.

Life in the new house was different; we were growing up. Mama was still mentally unbalanced, and throwing rocks, but we were not her main targets any longer. Moving had opened up a new group of neighbors for Mama to hate and think were plotting against her.

The upstairs apartment was occupied by the Barnes Family. Mark and I both made fast friends with the Barnes children. They were a family of three older boys who had their own band named Graveyard and two younger sisters who were named Wendy and Jane. Their parents were divorced. Their mother worked as a Certified Nurse Aide, CNA, every minute of every day to support the six of them. She literally was never at home. Life upstairs was a party every minute. There were music, drinking, drugs, and people, people, people. There was never a reason to be bored again, if I needed some entertainment I just went upstairs to the never-ending party.

Graveyard was a touring band. The boys traveled all over from Tulsa to New Orleans. Their band was very well known.

Words of Wisdom

I guess it just never occurred to the principal that I was just using one of the oldest tricks in the book. sometimes the best defense is a good offense.

Wendy (age 15) and Jane (age 12) and I (age 14) became best friends. This was not to be the best friendship for me but it sure was fun. Dirty fun, but still fun.

These girls never wanted to leave their home. They were content with each other like very few siblings I have ever seen. They were truly each other's best friend. When they weren't partying, they cooked wonderful teen age food like hamburgers, fish sandwiches, sloppy Joes, and basically anything else you could put on bread. They had every grocery stocked in their apartment. Every condiment, every chip, cookies, anything you needed to throw together a great sandwich party to keep the munchies away. And when their mother was off she cooked!

Everyone was having sex. Sex, sex, sex. For some reason, I still do not understand; I was not interested. I guess I was still in love with the middle school quarterback. Best yet, I like to think I had morals. I did have morals, I just don't know where or how I got them. Where they came from, I still do not know. I did not steal; I did not cuss (okay just a little); I didn't have sex. All in all, I guess I was boring. I didn't do drugs or smoke marijuana (that went against my strict anti-smoking stance). I would not do hard drugs because I wanted all my girl babies to turn out perfectly. I didn't want any chromosome damage. At school in the 1970's they talked about chromosome damage a lot. I guess they needed to because everyone I knew was taking LSD.

I invented my imaginary boyfriend that I had "sex" with, so everyone would leave me alone. I was always going and staying with my grandmother to get away from Mama, but I told the Barnes I was staying with "my boyfriend". I told them that I told Mama, I was going to Buddy's so not to blow my cover, it worked perfectly.

Life was good. I met another best friend, Carrie, my first day of ninth grade. Carrie was a sophomore as was my love interest, Luther. Carrie was from a family that the mom and dad were still married. Carrie's dad was really friendly and wanted to kiss me on the mouth whenever I came over or left.

Carrie's mom was 35 years old. My mother was 52. One day, Carrie's mother washed my blue jeans for me when I spent the night. She apologized that she had forgot to get them out of the dryer and the jeans had a few wrinkles! I was still washing all the clothes in the bathtub, ringing them out by hand and hanging them on the line. My clothes were WRINKLED! I loved being taken care of by Carrie's mom. Was that what a good Mom was like? I found out many years later that Carrie's Dad was a pedophile. Her dad had raped Carrie at the age of eight, then every day after that. Her mother claimed she never knew. Her Dad was a very bad man.

1972-73

Sophomore Year

Mama was a hock-a-holic. She was also a trash picker.

She was always on the lookout for anything she could hock. She rummaged through everyone's left over trash to make weekly to daily trips to the pawn shop to see what she could hock. Sometimes it was surprising what she could get money for. We had pawn tickets all over our house with no plan to ever redeem them to reclaim the merchandise. You had to be really careful with anything you brought home because if it was pawnable, Mama hocked it. I think it was almost a disease.

Luther was dating my best friend Tara. She was beautiful. They dated all through our ninth and tenth grade year. The summer after our tenth-grade year I started dating a friend of Luther's named Joey. Joey and I went out several times, but it did not work out well. Toward the end of the summer Luther and Jeannie broke up and he came directly over to my house. I was staying up all night with the Barnes, he stayed up with us. By morning he had forgotten all about Tara.

I did what I thought was the best thing to do for all concerned. I asked Tara, " if she was through with him, could I have him?" Of course, she said, "Yes!" I thought she really meant it. Boy was I wrong.

From then on Luther and I were together. He had blond hair and blue eyes, very big boned and thin. I was sixteen and he was a year older. Luther was selfish. He was negative, loved to abuse people smaller than himself, and smoke. He would cup the cigarette inside of his hand and never burn anyone or anything. I confused this with love because I had been burned so often by Mama. He had an unusual sense of humor. Luther had personality traits that were high strung. He had headaches frequently. Luther would make poor decisions fueled by his addictions and his unbridled temper. Luther was a bully and like all bullies he only attacked until someone fought him back. Then Luther would crumble and cry just like a baby. He cried a lot. He had so many character flaws, but it was what I was used to living with. I had fallen in love with him at twelve. Now I had him.

Luther was my boyfriend. I didn't have to continue to lie about the imaginary guy any longer. Luther was possessive. He hated the Barnes girls and forbid me to hang out with them any longer. This probably wasn't a bad idea. I let Luther boss me around. I was cowered down by Mama's abuse. I went along with a lot of things I probably should have put my foot down about. He hated all my friends, except Carrie and Trisha. Which, in hindsight, was probably a good thing.

Words of Wisdom

I learned a hard lesson; best friends don't date best friend's old boyfriends. She probably hates me to this day, but I promise she got the best side of things.

Luther worked a full-time job. I was very impressed with his industriousness. he owned his own car: a supped-up Pinto that he sometimes raced. He made all his own payments, insurance, and repairs. He was responsible. The first thing he did as a display of trust was come by my house on his way to work, have me take him to work, and leave the Pinto with me in case I needed to go somewhere. At 16, that was true love.

Luther was always looking to have a good time. He wanted to go, to do, and have fun. There was always a movie to see, a dinner to eat out, a picnic; the boy was just always on the lookout for a good time. I was a girl that had never had a good time. I never got to eat out. I never got to go to the movies. I was overloaded with responsibility and a crazy mother. What I got was an even crazier, but fun boyfriend.

Luther had every characteristic that Mama had. He would get manic and have paranoia; he would get violent; he would get migraine

Rule of Thumb

Be careful what you wish for. That one piece of advice would haunt me for years to come.

headaches; he would scream and curse. And he loved to fight. His senior year, Luther started wearing a black motorcycle jacket with studs and epaulets. He kept a chain swinging from the epaulets, around his shoulder, in case he got in a fight. He could quickly pull the chain off to beat someone with it. Luther had quite a reputation for fighting at school.

All in all, I guess I felt safe with Luther because he acted familiarly. He acted exactly like what the people were like that I knew. Besides, I could talk Luther down. Something I had never been able to do with Mama. I could never reason with her. But I could reason with Luther, or at least I thought I could.

I had no idea in my late teens that there were people in this world that were loving and kind. I had never been around anyone kind, except my grandmother and my aunt. To me, Luther's meanness was normal.

Mark hated Luther. He still does. Luther deserves it. For years this created a wedge between Mark and I as we were growing up. We were losing our close relationship. It seemed at the time I was always having to make hard choices. I loved Mark. I was in love with Luther.

Things were getting more serious with Luther. He asked me to marry him. We put our rings on lay-away. Twice that year we tried to get married. Once, we drove to Waskom because we heard you could get married there if you were 16, but that was not true, then, another time, we headed out for Tennessee. We didn't get very far on the Tennessee trip, just the edge of town, when we decided we would be in big trouble if we just ran off and got married.

Mama hated Luther. Luther hated Mama. They were so much alike in behavior and moods. I guess that no one likes to see their worst personality defects mirrored in someone else. One day she decided to throw a rock at him. Luther was a seasoned seventeen-year-old ball player. He caught the rock in the air. He threw it as hard as he could, hitting her in the fore head. It immediately swelled up, it was a goose egg. The blood ran under her eyes blacking both her eyes. She couldn't call the police because she had thrown the rock first. Like true bullies do, Mama never tried to physically challenge Luther again.

1973-74

Junior Year

Luther was becoming increasingly moody and unreasonable. He had so many issues that his parents decided to put him in a mental hospital. Charter Forrest was the name of the hospital. It was about one mile from our house. After a week of being shut up inside the hospital they let Luther go outside into an eight-foot fenced in yard. He jumped the eight-foot fence. He ran all the way to our house screaming, "hide me, hide me". I put him in my bedroom. I held him until he stopped shaking. In a little while his Father came to get him to take him back to the hospital. At sixteen, I couldn't see what all the fuss was about, Mama acted worse than Luther and she was three times his age.

Words of Wisdom

I am pretty sure if you are afraid you are going to get in trouble for getting married, its a sign you are too young to get married. You might reconsider getting married if you're worried about anybody not liking your spouse. Adults who are truly in love with the right person don't have concerns like these.

They put Luther on antidepressants. He hated them. He was too drugged up to eat. I was working full time at a pharmacy. They told me to give him some yeast and he would eat. It worked, but one day he threw the antidepressant medicine away and said he was fine. It was the classic syndrome: the medicine made him well, so he would quit taking it. He would get sick, have to go back on the medicine, then quit again. Luther repeated this cycle throughout his life.

Luther would play verbal mind games with me. He would also "test" me. I never knew his true motivation or his goal, or if something was a "test". He was predictably unpredictable. This was not a good place for a teenage girlfriend to be. He would declare that he loved the sluttiest shirt and beg me to buy it. When I refused he would say I passed the "test". He would accuse me of things, then after grilling me, he would say I passed the "test". It seemed like I was always having to "pass the test". When I would get fed up, trying to break up, he would cry and beg forgiveness. As I always felt a lack of love growing up, being held in his arms was very reassuring to me. I thought that physical touch was love.

That summer Luther escalated to physical violence. Once you cross that line, it becomes easier to cross each time after that. We broke up, but he begged and cried so much we got right back together.

I was always having to monitor Luther. He was a cheater and a beater. I now know that cheating and wife beating go hand in hand. In sixth grade, I had read a book on why Germany had very little wife abuse. In Germany, the wife is not ashamed of the abuse, so she goes door to door telling the neighbors what her husband has done to her, embarrassing her husband. In America, the women are too ashamed to tell anyone, so they keep the abuse secret. I had kept abuse a secret all my life.

With Luther there was always an incident with some girl. I would catch him giving me a gift with another one exactly like it to someone else. I would see him with another girl drive by in my car; it just went on and on. We would break up. He would beg forgiveness, crying. I would cave, taking him back.

Work

I was working every spare minute I had: first at a shoe store downtown, then later at a hamburger restaurant named Griff's. While working at Griff's, I met a fun younger boy. One evening, I was taking my scheduled break, watching the clock. I made sure my break was only 15 minutes, when the boss came in claiming I had been sitting there all night. This was a lie! When I said I wasn't, he said he'd been out in his car watching me. He was lying. Ten minutes earlier I had been dancing on the top of the restaurant counter with that dancing kid doing a dance called "The Bump". I was going to miss that dancing kid.

After Griff's I worked downtown at Selber Brother's, a big, fancy department store. I had been hired to work on the switchboard. It was a complex task to learn how to plug the lines in and out.

Mama had not worked in several years by this time. Money was scarce to non-existent. Things at home were getting uglier and uglier with more financially desperate times now that Papa was dead. Mama's brother, Howard, had gotten married. His new wife did not want him sending his money to his deadbeat sister. Mama had no income. We were fighting constantly over everything. I was staying furious with her.

My personality is very happy and kind but the pressure from two abusive people in my life was causing me to become a very angry young woman. "Anger is a much more useful emotion than despair", is a line from the movie Terminator 3, spoken by Arnold Schwarzenegger. I found this to be true. The more furious I became, the hotter the fire in my belly burned. The harder I worked, the more I accomplished. The more I accomplished my goals, the more recognition I received. Then the harder I worked, and the cycle continued.

Mama had begun to have chest pains. She had gone to LSU Medical Center where they told her she had had a heart attack. I don't doubt it. With a heart as mean as a snake it was just a matter of time before it turned around and bit her. She started a final chapter in her life where she would be sick for the next decade.

Words of Wisdom

I quit taking breaks after that. Breaks are not worth losing a job over. To get ahead, there has to be time on the time clock.

Buddy had a stroke and had to go to a nursing home. I was with her when she had the stroke. I had been staying with her almost full time while her health was deteriorating. I had to call the ambulance and report the situation to the family. At 16, it was very upsetting to see my grandmother begin to die.

1974-75

Senior Year

I bought an old car for $50.00 that didn't have a floor board in the front under the driver. Keeping your feet off the pavement was a bit tricky but it was all I could afford. After getting fired from the hamburger restaurant, I had to look for work, but because I did not have a phone, they could not call me. I decided that finding a job would be my job. I would get up early in the morning, walk or take the bus to a location, and apply at every place of business. I would make lists of where I had applied in a little spiral notebook. I averaged 15 applications a day. I would call them from a pay phone daily to follow up and see if they needed me. I literally looked for a job for eight to ten hours a day, every day for three weeks, before I found a job as a waitress.

I dropped out of school to go to work to support my family.

The Restaurant

A Hispanic restaurant manager finally ended my month-long job-search and hired me on the spot to work from 6:00 AM to 2:00 PM the next day. During the interview I was dressed in my best clothes. I had my hair fixed and make up on. He told me I had to wear a uniform and they would take the cost of the uniform out of my first two checks. He handed me a size twelve dress. I told him I was a size four and he replied, "when you work for me you are a size 12!" I was really frustrated about having to buy a uniform dress that would never fit, because I had no money to waste. To retaliate for the size twelve, I showed up the next day in flat shoes with the dress to my ankles. I could literally wrap the dress around me twice. I said nothing. My appearance was quite different from the day before. I had no makeup on, I had pulled my hair into a severe ponytail. I looked plain as a church mouse. After about a week of us both ignoring each other he ordered me to "hem up that dress".

I had two customers that stick in my mind to this day. One was a nice looking professional, black businessman who came in

121

and sat in the same chair at the same table every day. He wanted a

Words of Wisdom

Being unable to get a job was a life-altering experience for me, as I decided then that I did not want to ever be put in this position again where I did not have the education or the skills to get a job. I had always planned to go to college, but now I burned with the necessity of a degree. I resolved that I would get a career that had so much demand that I would never be out of a job!

Words of Wisdom

I think the inability to get a job that fall was a critical tribulation that I had to face in life to be the person I became. I had to face the despair of unemployment to understand the burning need to be employed. I had to face the shame of underemployment to want to provide good paying jobs for people that would not have the same opportunities that others enjoyed. Romans 5:3-5 says, "And not only this, but we also exult in our tribulations, knowing that tribulation brings about perseverance; and perseverance, proven character; and proven character, hope; and hope does not disappoint, because the love of God has been poured out within our hearts through the Holy Spirit who was given to us".

From this horrible experience of being unemployed I learned perseverance, character, and hope. And hope leads to faith through the Holy Spirit.

paper, coffee, cottage cheese, and fruit cocktail. One day, I asked him, "Are you going to eat the same thing every day?" and he said he was. From then on, I had his place reserved exactly like he wanted it. His coffee, cottage cheese, and paper cost $2.55, but every day he left me a $5.00 tip for having it ready and waiting on him when he came in at exactly 9 AM!

The other customer was less appealing. He was an old farmer, about 70 years old, whose wife had recently died. He decided that I, at seventeen, would be a good replacement wife. Every day he would sit there from 6:00 AM to 2:00 PM, my entire shift. He sat at the counter where we had to wash dishes and prepare the drinks and desserts. He would try to bribe me into marrying him with more and more material goods. He told me he had a really nice house. He would buy me a car, diamond ring, new clothes, every day; the list got longer with me saying, "No, No, NO!" He had me worried about my safety. I was scared he might try to abduct me. He was so crazy and wouldn't take, "No!" for an answer.

False Identity

Luther had altered my driver's license by taking the plastic cover off using a razor blade, he changed out a number for the birth date with one of the license numbers to make me eighteen. It was easier for me to work and we could legally go out drinking and dancing at bars. Luther refused to alter Mark's license because they didn't like each other.

Mark had dropped out of school. He and I drove to Haughton, Louisiana and there we paid the chief of police's son, Logan, to make Mark a driver's license that said he was eighteen. He could go get a job on the oil rigs if he was eighteen. Logan had the keys to the Driver's License Bureau. Mark would be making $8.00 per hour when minimum wage was $1.65. Mark was six feet tall at 14 years old, but only weighed about 130. In a couple of days, we got the license. Mark went to south Louisiana to work on the oil wells offshore.

I immediately decided that Mama should sign up for government assistance. Mama had always suffered from delusions of grandeur. She would prance around and act like she was somebody, and, frankly, it was just embarrassing. I told her that she had to go sign up for Food Stamps. She flat out refused, screaming at me, "DO YOU KNOW WHO I AM? I AM A JOHNSON!!! " From that minute on I wanted no part of the name "Johnson" if she was the representative of the name. I decided to get rid of that name as quick as I could, and never, ever use it as a middle name as so many women do with her maiden name.

Dian Johnson 1974

I ordered her to get in the car. Several months earlier she had tried to physically assault me again. All 108 pounds of me slammed her against a wall while telling her she better never lay another hand on me. She was still wary of launching an assault on me. Besides, she wasn't well. I drug her to the car. I drove to the Food Stamp office. She refused to get out of the car to sign up for assistance. I put my feet on her butt, using the steering wheel as leverage and pushed her out of my car screaming, "you go get Food Stamps and don't you come home without them". I was so furious as I drove off, leaving her stranded at the Food Stamp Office, that I decided right there and then to move out. I rented an apartment. I started moving out before she got back home from the food stamp office.

The Apartment on Wilkinson Street

I found a two-room apartment after looking for couple of hours, on Wilkerson Street, located in the back of a store. The rent was $65.00 per month for the apartment. Luther came over. He looked at it and decided to build a loft for the bed, allowing the living space beneath to be open and usable. After he built the loft He insisted we had to scrape the 100-year-old windows down to wood and repaint them white. Luther picked out the wall paint colors of mustard gold. When he got it fixed up it, it looked lovely. He was a hard worker who got manic on projects. He would finish the project quickly. Luther had learned his home repair skills from his parents who were always restoring an old property. I had never experienced the luxury of picking out paint colors combined with creatively shopping at yard sales to match the furniture to the interior decor. We bought the used furniture I needed and repainted it. We had a lot of fun fixing up that old apartment. When we were through it was beautiful. The nicest place I had ever lived. Luther went on to buy that house after he graduated from college. He lived there for several years.

The landlady was not fair. She did not allow me to take the supplies off the rent. She felt like I was a free fill-in clerk anytime she needed help in her shop in front of my apartment. She never paid me. I do not know why I didn't tell her no when she came back and ordered me to come and help her. I guess I was just too afraid she would kick me out of the apartment. I felt that she was unfairly taking advantage of me by not paying me for my work. I struggled every time I was left in the shop alone to rearrange the beautiful clothes and jewelry, not to compensate myself by stealing something. She owed me compensation for the work I was doing, after all I had to pay her rent to live in the apartment. She should not have expected me to work for free. I realized right there at seventeen that most people would have stolen her money or some of her clothes because she wasn't being fair. But I did not steal from this woman.

Later, I was able to realize the shop owner didn't have any money herself because everything she had was tied up in the merchandise. She did not have that many customers as she had just opened the store.

The instant I left Mama's house, my standard of living went up straight up. I could not believe that making minimum wage, living on my own, I had so much more money than when I had lived with Mama and Mark. It seemed that no matter how hard I tried to work, budget, and manage the household finances, Mama had a way of destroying us financially. Without Mama, I had so much money left over each week that I could buy Mama sacks of groceries or sundries and take them to her. I refused to give her money because I knew she would just spend it on cigarettes, material, and novels. Sometimes I even paid her bills. All my life, I was used to never having anything, not even toilet paper, so it was sheer delight to have my own money.

The Fire

On a Friday night, Luther had to work 3 PM to 11 PM as an offset plate maker. I spent the night with my Aunt Tirr. Luther came by my apartment on his way home. The house across the street was engulfed in flames. He was able to get the old woman who lived there out, but her son died in the fire. He had been smoking in bed. There were articles in the Shreveport Times newspaper about how he had risked his own life. He was interviewed by the news to tell his story. Luther was a hero. The old woman died of her injuries about three weeks later.

Words of Wisdom

Always be fair to your employees and the people who work for you. Do not expect to get something for "free", especially labor, because most people do not work for free and will compensate themselves in some way you will not like.

Youree Drive Drug

It wasn't too long before I got a better job working at a pharmacy from 2:00 PM to 8:00 PM. I received several job offers from when I had applied everywhere. I had tried for about a month to work both jobs. I just could not make it work as I had only 30 minutes between jobs and the travel distance was 30 minutes. I had to change out of the terrible uniform into cute clothes in the pharmacy rest room.

I loved the atmosphere of the pharmacy and quit the restaurant. The young pharmacist who had recently graduated from pharmacy school reminded me of Sonny, so I had a fondness for him. He would let me help him out in the back of the pharmacy, packaging the medications and watching him mix up the tinctures. In the 1970's, the pharmacist mixed up more of the medicines than they do now because there were less packaged products available. I loved it; it was exactly like cooking, my favorite hobby. The young pharmacist encouraged me to go back to school and be a pharmacist. He will never know how much I needed that encouragement or how much it meant to a young seventeen-year-old girl to have a much older man (I think he was 23) believe I could do something useful with my life. I was no longer the only one who thought I could be successful. He believed in me because his wife was a foster child that had gone to college. She was also a pharmacist.

When I was hired at the pharmacy, I was told about two ladies that came into the store and shoplifted. We were to follow behind them, writing down what they stole, and then bill their husbands, without confronting the women. Imagine my surprise when one of the women was none other than Luther's mother, Mary. She had a real problem with stealing. She took anything and everything. She lied constantly about stealing. She lied about her recipes. For some reason if she cooked something you liked, and you asked how she cooked it, she would start telling a recipe that had none of the ingredients you were eating. I had been cooking since I was little. It incensed me that she would think I would be so stupid to believe that the recipe she gave me was even remotely close to the dish we were eating. While my future mother-in-law didn't curse, she was an alcoholic

Words of Wisdom

The law of averages is one out of 10. If you apply to 100 jobs you will get, on average, about one job for every 10 applications. 10 people will call you back for a job. If you are marketing a product, one out of 10 people will buy your product. When I started The Right Solutions, I would propose nurse staffing to 10 hospitals and only one would sign up with my company. Try this in your life it works every time. The more you market, the more you get.

and smoked almost as much as mother. She was a real jewel.

Eighteen! April 10, 1975

My birthday was on a Thursday. I was turning 18! I spent the day taking the GED exam, that I passed with flying colors. I was now legal to drink. I don't know why that was important. I had possessed a fake license since I was sixteen. The next morning, I was scheduled to take the ACT, so I could attend college in the fall. In all of my 18-year-old wisdom, I decided the best plan of action

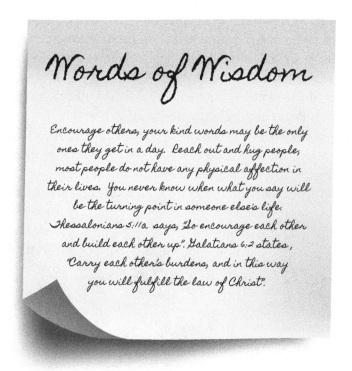

Words of Wisdom

Encourage others, your kind words may be the only ones they get in a day. Reach out and hug people, most people do not have any physical affection in their lives. You never know when what you say will be the turning point in someone else's life. Thessalonians 5:11a says, "So encourage each other and build each other up". Galatians 6:2 states, "Carry each other's burdens, and in this way you will fulfill the law of Christ".

would be to stay out drinking all night because it was my birthday. That way I wouldn't have to get up early for the test. I would just go straight to the test the next morning without sleeping.

Luther and I went out partying and dancing but didn't make it all night. We got very drunk. I had no phone. The next thing I knew, Luther was in my apartment waking me up to go take the ACT test. If you were one minute late they would lock the doors.

Then they would not let anyone late take the test. I don't remember driving to the test or taking the first half of the test. I "woke up" from the booze about noon. I still scored a 22 on my ACT. I had passed the GED and the ACT in two days; I was on my way to college! Taking the GED in April, I "graduated" from high school before the rest of my class did in May. This was amusing.

Aunt Tirr was thrilled about my decision to go to college. She said, "The only thing no one can ever take away from you is your education." She said this often, which I found unusual as she did not have a college degree. She encouraged me to be a nurse because "nurses could always get a job". I was forever scarred from the month-long job hunt. I didn't want to be a nurse, I wanted to be a pharmacist. There was only one pharmacy school in Louisiana and it was in Monroe. I decided that I needed to go to Northeast Louisiana University in Monroe, Louisiana. Aunt Tirr drove me over during the summer. We went to orientation then visited dormitory rooms. The campus was located on Bayou DeSiard, complete with big old trees hanging with Spanish Moss. I loved it.

Northeast Louisiana State University 1975

About a month after summer orientation, I went off to college. I was using my grandfather's trust fund to pay for school. I moved into a tiny, dark, brick-walled dormitory room, with a roommate that I had never met. I felt like it was a prison cell. My roommate, a sophomore, and our two suitemates had lived together the previous year. All three had matching bedding and accessories. Having never met any of them before, I was the odd one out. My first day of class I arose early for an 8:00 AM class to get in the shower. Within minutes, both of the suitemates jumped naked into the tiny little shower with me. I jumped out with my hair still soapy with shampoo. This was traumatic. I was just about hysterical by the time I got to class with soap covered hair and soapy skin. My personal space had been invaded. By girls!

To add more discontent, my roommate was terribly sick. She suffered from a serious liver illness that started during the summer. She could barely get out of bed. She wouldn't go to the cafeteria to get herself anything to eat so every day; she was losing weight. I didn't know this girl. We did not talk at all, she was too sick. But I started caring for her, bringing her some food while encouraging her to eat. She was too sick to be at school. Sometimes, she could barely walk to the bathroom. I would have to help her.

The bathroom continued to be a big problem for me. Having been raised with brothers, I was not used to having anyone in the bathroom with me. I could not go into the bathroom for even a minute without being immediately joined by one of the other three girls. If they had designed a plan to get me to move out, it was working!

That's when I found Emma. After a week at college, I had made no friends. I had been taught not to speak until spoken to. That just doesn't work well for making friends at college. Standing behind me in line, at lunch that day, was a beautiful girl named Emma. I turned around saying, "I haven't met anyone this week, my name is Dian." Emma replied, "You are the first person that has spoken to me this whole week! Do you want to eat lunch together?"

Emma and I were both having roommate problems. We decided right then to move in together in her dormitory room on the third floor of Casper, the oldest dormitory house on campus, complete with a nosy housemother who locked the outside doors at 11:00 PM. She gave demerits if the room was not clean or curfew was violated. Other rules were that no boys could visit except Saturday and Sunday, when you had to sign them in. The door had to be kept open with the trash can stuck in the space. Our big bedroom was sunny with lots of windows, but very run down. It looked just like my bedroom on College Street. I felt very comfortable. I loved it! The community bathroom was down the hall with multiple showers, bathroom stalls, and sinks. I never had to worry about any of the girls seeing me naked or on the potty. Also, my roommate was not deathly ill. I was liberated from caring for anyone. Life immediately improved 100% again. Emma and I were having fun!

It was to be very short lived.

Out of the Frying Pan into the Fire

Luther and I were still fighting and breaking up and getting back together and breaking up again. I never even knew if we were on or off again. In those days we didn't have cell phones or dorm phones, so Luther would drive the 100 miles. He would show up at the worst possible times to see me. It was always awkward because Luther was so much like Mama. There was never any pleasing him or satisfying him. If I had to go to class or to work when he showed up (with no notice), he would throw a fit and make me choose between him and my responsibilities. Nothing I ever did was good enough for him. But I still loved him because he was what I knew: predictably unpredictable.

For some reason I had recreated the same unhealthy relationship that I had with Mama. He and Mama were both alike: they were unhappy unless they were making me miserable. Both were experts at it.

Because of my previous switchboard experience at Selber Brother's Department Store, I was able to land a job working the campus switchboard. The job was great, with good hours and good pay. Luther would frequently accuse me of having another man when he would show up unannounced. I was scheduled to go to work. I was determined not to get fired from this job. I loved it. I would have to make him stay outside until the previous workers left. Then when I was working by myself, I let him in. I hated him being there because he

Words of Wisdom

If you're not happy, make changes in your life. Life is too short to be unhappy. By staying in unhappiness, you are missing out on beautiful opportunities. Take chances; they pay off.

snooped in everything, opened every drawer, and read everything.

I wanted to completely focus on my job as the switchboard operator for a college campus that was very busy at night. But I couldn't say anything to him because I knew it would send him spiraling into a fight. Everything sent him into a fight, so we were off again real soon.

Luther had decided not to go to college until I went to college. Then he enrolled late in Shreveport at LSU-S. He decided to be a photographer like his father.

Pregnant at 18

College was wonderful! Everywhere I turned I met new people that were exciting and wonderful. I joined the Union Board, a college committee that planned all the fun activities that a college hosts, like speakers, bands, dances, movie nights and other fun events. The president of the Union Board took a special liking to me and asked me out on several dates, that sparked the interest of another Union Board young man. Now everyone in Louisiana knows about the feud between the Fontenot's and the Thibodeauex families. One of the boys was a Fontenot and the other a Thibodeauex. There was no way this triangle was going to turn out well. I didn't have to worry about them for long. Both the Fontenot and Thibodeauex boys each invited me to Homecoming. I had declined both invitations because I was politically trying to salvage both relationships and my position on the Union Board. Once again, Luther showed up unexpectedly, driving the 100 miles without notice.

We went to the homecoming football game and had a wonderful time. Luther had rented a hotel room, so he would have somewhere to stay. I got pregnant with Dana that night, October 28th. I knew as soon as I woke up that next morning I was pregnant. I told Luther I was pretty sure I was pregnant. A month and a half later I passed out in the cafeteria hitting my head sending me to the doctor who confirmed what I already knew. I was definitely pregnant. Luther and I had been back in our relationship, so we decided to get married. At this point, we had been together for two and a half years. This is a lifetime when you are 18 years old.

About the same time I found out I was pregnant with Dana, I met a lovely black woman with light-skin the color of coffee with cream, Marilyn. She worked in the college financial office and we became fast friends. We both loved Popeye's Chicken, so we would meet there and have lunch. One day Marilyn told me about financial aid and how to get a BEOG grant. I had already applied back in the summer. I had the BEOG paperwork in my room, but I thought I had been rejected because I could not understand how to read the document. Marilyn took one look at the paperwork and wrote me a check for $1464.00! It was more money than I had ever had or seen in my life! I called Luther and told him to please help me find an orange Volkswagen. Within a week, he drove a beautiful orange Volkswagen to NLU. Life was just getting better and better, especially when Marilyn explained that I did not have to repay the money.

We planned a simple, quick wedding at his grandmother Meme's house. Meme and Papa had a built a new house. They had just moved in. It was beautiful with everything done in green. Meme's favorite color. Meme loved me. Mary, Luther's mother did not. What Meme and I had most in common was a mutual hatred for Mary. Mary was always devising some evil scheme, stealing something, and causing chaos in general. We would try to catch her to thwart her evil plans. It kept things interesting. Meme and I bonded over always trying to outsmart Mary.

The Wedding, December 22, 1975

I got married in my baby blue and cream lace Gunny Sack dress I had worn to my junior prom. I had found it on sale for $27.00. It was still a fortune for me at the time when I was earning $1.65 an hour! I had to work 16.25 hours to earn that dress! For me this was worth it: the dress was so beautiful!

In typical Mama fashion, she had plenty to say about why I couldn't wear my beautiful dress (wrong color, too cocktail like, used, etc.), but there was no other dress option and no money for another dress. She knew there was no other option. I had to wear it because it was all I had. (I still love that dress.)

Mama surprised me with a blue and cream lace veil that matched the dress perfectly. She had sewed it with little seed pearls. I thought it was beautiful. I knew she had to go buy the material to make the veil because all the boxes, tubs, and closets of material she owned were brown. This was one of the few things that Mama ever did for me that was nice.

Mama was a terrible seamstress, so the veil was not perfect. But, it was for me. Everything she sewed was lopsided, uneven, and brown. For once, Mama had considered my feelings, by making me a bridal veil that was something I would like. It was very unusual for Mama to consider someone else's feelings besides her own. This was a very big step for Mama.

Luther and I had a simple wedding on December 20, 1975. Our honeymoon was a one-night hotel stay, then we moved into Luther's parent's house until after the holidays. We moved into the one-bedroom apartment I had found for us in Monroe, Louisiana, where we would both be going to school.

I continued working at the college switchboard while going to college.

Spousal Abuse

Life with Luther was bad. Because of his abuse, every time I came home I had a stomachache in anticipation of the abuse. I left for the weekend two months after we got married and went back to visit Mama. I had not stayed overnight in her home for a year and a half at that time. She told me I couldn't stay with her. I had to go back

Words of Wisdom

Every purchase I have ever made has been a calculation of how many hours I would have to work to pay for the item. I look at the price and divide it by the number of hours it is going to take me working to pay for it. I decide if that material item is worth the number of hours of work. This puts things in perspective.

to my husband even if he was physically abusive.

I left him for the weekend again at four months. This time I went and stayed with Trisha in her dorm room in Ruston, Louisiana, where she was going to college at Louisiana Tech University.

When I was six months pregnant, I came home from work unexpectedly to find Luther in our living room with another young man and they were bagging marijuana into baggies. I stood at the door and said, "I'm not losing my baby for you. Get that out of my living room before I come home from work or the police will do it for me."

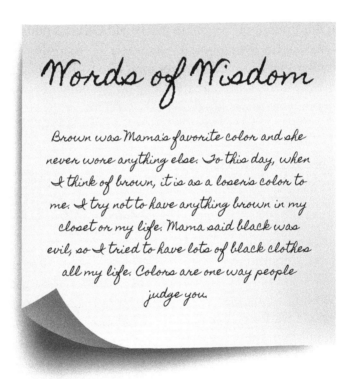

Words of Wisdom

Brown was Mama's favorite color and she never wore anything else. To this day, when I think of brown, it is as a loser's color to me. I try not to have anything brown in my closet or my life. Mama said black was evil, so I tried to have lots of black clothes all my life. Colors are one way people judge you.

We moved into a two-bedroom apartment, so we had room for the baby. When I was eight months pregnant, I came home from work at the switchboard and my husband had his old friend Liam visiting with his new girlfriend. I had no idea they were coming so I was surprised to find them in my home. I loathed

Liam with the passions of hell. I always had. I pretty much hated everything about Liam. After a few hours, Liam and the girlfriend asked to spend the night. They wanted to go to bed. Luther and I were downstairs, when the girlfriend appeared naked to ask us to join them upstairs. Luther grabbed his camera. He couldn't get up the stairs quick enough. I reluctantly followed because I did not want my husband sleeping with another woman. When I got upstairs, the three of them had cooked up the idea of a swap before I got home because Liam (who I hated even more after this!) wanted to have sex with a pregnant woman. My husband had" traded me" to his friend.

I said I had to go to the bathroom, grabbed my purse, and went out the front door! I went to my friend Olivia's house. Olivia and I worked at the switchboard. She was a 32-year-old divorced, single mother that Luther had never met. I knew he would not know where I went. Olivia let me sleep on her couch because she was someone who understood marital problems.

The Aftermath

The next day when I went back to the house, Liam and the girlfriend were gone. Luther slapped me as hard as he could. I fainted and fell hitting my head. When I roused, Luther had left. I took his undeveloped film from the night before of the naked pictures of Liam and his girlfriend, put it in an envelope and sent it to myself at my mother's address. It was inevitable I was going to have to get a divorce. I figured I might as well start collecting evidence.

Words of Wisdom

Home should be SAFE. The world is so mean that home should be a safe place to be. You should never worry about coming home. If your stomach is hurting, take this as a warning.

When Luther came home he started after me, having much

Words of Wisdom

Blood is thicker than water. Choose family first. Realize who family is; it is not a spouse who is not related to you, your children are dependent on you.

more experience that he did with abuse, I tore up the stairs with my eight months pregnant belly shaking. I flattened out on the wall at the top of the stairs. He charged past me. I hit him as hard as I could in the back of the head with my wooden high heel shoe, using the toe strap as the hand grip. He dropped on the floor face down. I beat him black and blue with the high heel until he was screaming and not trying to hit back any more.

I grabbed my purse and got out of there. I stayed away for hours until it was well after dark. When I got back home, I cowboyed up, walking into the house with an attitude. I marched in the door with the wooden high heel dangling in my hand demanding, "Do you want some more?" He just looked at me and started crying, "No, please don't hit me". "You are going to get a job and you are never going to hit me again!" I screamed at him.

Luther went to work at the state hospital where I planned to deliver the baby for free. He got a job as an Emergency Room Clerk signing in patients that needed to be seen. That incident bought me some time from his abuse. The abuse stopped long enough for me to have my daughter.

<u>1976</u>

Dana's Birthday! My luck changes!

Luther and I had always had a name for a son: Adrian Shawn Smith (the initials ASS was starting to bother me). We both loved it. We had agreed three years earlier on that name. But the night before Dana was born, he decided he wanted to name our son Thurman Clarence Smith II, after his dad, who I could not stand. He said he had decided to call the baby Top Cat since his dad was using the initials T.C. I was horrified! My son would not be Thurman Clarence Smith II! And never Top Cat after a cartoon character! I felt 100% confident that the baby would be a boy because I wanted a girl so badly. Nothing had ever worked out the way I wanted in my life. I knew if I argued he would not budge, so I used my calmest voice and said, "yes, but the baby is most certainly a girl, and if we are to change our name for the boy what about changing the name for the girl?" Since high school, we had decided our name for a girl was Melanie Elaine. He said that he had been thinking about that. He liked the named Dana Erin, because it was similar to Dian Karen which was my name combined with his sister's name. Elaine was Karen's middle name. I replied, "You can name the girl and I will name the boy Britton Thurman." The night before Dana was born I traded away her name of Melanie Elaine so a boy would not be named TC.

The birth was long and difficult. The baby was three weeks premature with respiratory problems but weighed eight pounds two ounces. I did not realize I was in labor on July 6. I had a caesarean section scheduled for August 3, Trisha's birthday. I had been having stomach cramps during the night with diarrhea. I thought I had a stomach virus or food poisoning. It never crossed my mind

Words of Wisdom

Always fight back. Get smart. Don't play fair. If someone is abusing you, do whatever you can. Take whatever steps necessary to stop the abuse. If that means waiting until they go to sleep and beating him with a baseball bat, that's okay. All is fair in love and war. Make no mistake, abuse is war. Abusers and bullies tend to stop abusing when the person they are abusing finally fights back. They want an easy target that does not fight back. Tell everyone about the abuse, do not keep an abuser's secrets.

I was in labor because in my 19-year-old wisdom, surgery was already scheduled.

Luther was taking final exams for the end of the first summer session. He was not at home the morning Dana was born. Late in the morning, one of my neighbors James, stopped by. He realized I was in labor. James physically carried me to the car. He drove me to the hospital. James carried me into the ER. Dana was stuck in the birth canal with no gynecologist on duty for the July Fourth weekend. She was delivered by two twin ER interns who managed to cut me down both legs and completely through my rectum then pull Dana out with forceps. The entire birth was a mangled mess. I was injured. Dana was injured with a forceps mark on her forehead that did not go away until she was two. Both of us were so sick I could not delight in having a daughter. But that night I remember realizing, with the birth of my beautiful daughter, that my luck had finally changed!

Dana

The hospital had a new policy of "rooming in" where they let the baby stay with the mother but no "germy" dad could come in and contaminate the mom and baby. I was in a ward with seven other mothers. The one next to me was 27 years old and having her seventh baby. I already had made up my mind when I was 13, I was having three girls. I had asked God every day since for the girls. That first night after she was born, Dana quit breathing several times. I did not know what to do! Each time, I grabbed her little blue body up by the arms, holding her out at arm's length and ran screaming out in the hall for a nurse. The hospital did not have the nursing staff to open the nursery. The third time Dana quit breathing they decided to have a nurse sit at my bedside where she could watch the baby and resuscitate her if need be. For the remaining stay, I had my own nurse in a packed ward of seven other mothers and seven babies. I couldn't sleep with the baby so sick, I was frightened that she was going to die in the night.

The hospital had ridiculously cruel rules. At 4:00 AM in the morning, all seven mothers had to get out of bed to stand at the foot of the bed while the two nurses on duty changed the seven beds. The RNs gave us seven basins of water to wash up with in front of everyone else. I fainted from blood loss causing "them" a fuss. But the next two nights they managed to find me a chair to sit in. I did not have to bath in front of six other women. There was a shower right down the hall.

I finally went home on the third day. To my surprise, my husband had found me a babysitting job, taking care of a seven-year-old girl and a four-year boy, who were waiting on me when I got home. He had not discussed this with me. Dana was having respiratory problems, while I was very sick, and the children were extremely active! In no time I was hanging on by a thread, getting sicker by the minute, when Meme, Luther's grandmother, showed up.

I had not prepared for a baby because we had no money to buy anything. I literally had only two outfits, five summer blankets my Grandmother Fearn had made me, and no diapers when the baby was born (in those days, no one had disposable diapers). The day I came home from the hospital, I was given a baby bathtub that I put a pillow in for Dana to sleep in. Then all my neighbors started bringing over their used baby clothes and diapers. I am still grateful to one neighbor who brought me three dozen cloth diapers.

Meme brought a baby bed, some little pink clothes and blankets, and homemade tuna salad. The longer Meme stayed, the sicker I got. When the baby was a week old, I could not get out of bed. I was running a high fever with an infection. Meme was frantic and made Luther take me back to the Emergency Room. They called in a very good gynecologist who took one look at what used to be my lady parts but was now the mangled mess that the twin brother interns had created. He announced that everything had to be surgically opened up and re-sewn right there in the Emergency Room with no anesthesia. After two rounds of antibiotics I recovered somewhat but really did not get back on my feet for six months, which was to be my usual child birth recovery period.

When we got home, the children Luther had gotten me to babysit were nowhere to be seen. Meme had called their mother who sent them to the grandmother's permanently.

Mama Got Saved

Diane holding Dana

After Meme left, Mama showed up. In true Mama fashion, she did exactly nothing except tell me what to do, give orders, and hold my baby. I was rapidly becoming one really pissed off nineteen-year-old woman.

Mama didn't smoke anymore, or curse, or do much of anything else except read her Bible. Mama had been possessed by a smoking, cursing, rage demon. All that was completely gone the instant she had become saved. It really was a miracle. I was so angry at her for the years of abuse I could not fully appreciate the transformation. I had spent a lifetime anticipating her actions. Now she was truly unpredictable. I would tell her what to do and she would...listen. She was still eaten up with laziness. She did nothing to help me the few days she was at my house except hold my sleeping newborn. I finally sent her packing. Besides she and Luther still did not get along.

Ruston

In August, Luther decided we needed to move 30 miles from Monroe to Ruston, Louisiana so he could go to school there. Ruston was the only place that he could get his photography degree. I planned to stay home for one semester with the baby and then go back to school, driving the 30 miles to Monroe.

We settled into a subsidized housing apartment with Luther making us redo every surface until the apartment looked beautiful. But it was ridiculously hard, worthless work. I was so sick that we really should not have done it.

Luther became threatening to Dana. "Get your "thing" out of my living room!" He would snarl, whenever the tiny baby was laying on a pallet on the floor. I was scared of his behavior towards her, but I did not know how father's acted and thought maybe this was normal or would change. I had never been around a father before. I thought maybe they had to grow to be attached to the child.

I took Dana to get her first immunizations at the health unit when she was two months old. Her leg swelled up, turned bright red, she developed a fever, and screamed for hours. The only thing that would shut her up was to dangle her leg over the air conditioner and let the cold air blow on the tiny little leg. Luther screamed at me to turn off the air conditioner, but it was late August in Louisiana, the hottest part of the summer. I ran it anyway to soothe the baby. Luther got belligerent, I locked him out of the bedroom and continued to hold her leg over the A/C. Luther went outside and turned off the electricity to the house. In no time, my baby was screaming again. I could forgive Luther for being cruel to me, I had been treated cruelly all my life, but I was not going to have my child treated cruelly.

Shortly after this experience, Meme and Papa showed up at our apartment unexpectedly. After I cooked dinner for them we were holding the baby in the living room. Luther said, "Tell her what we decided." So gently, Meme said, "We think it would be in everyone's best interest if we took the baby home and kept her until you get out of college." I flat out refused. This was my baby. I was keeping my baby. That issue was not to be discussed again. After they left, Scot tried to talk me into giving Dana up for adoption. I made up my mind right then that I was giving someone up all right, but it wasn't going to be my baby! I just had to find the right time to get out because I still was very sick. I needed a plan.

James

A couple of weeks later, Luther brought James, our old neighbor from Monroe, to our home. Luther said that James was going to live with us from now on. We had two bedrooms, one with a twin bed and baby bed, so space was not a problem. I loved having James around as he diffused everything that Luther did. He would always come home happy and delightedly pick up Dana. James would swing her around in the air. When she needed to be fed, he would beg to feed her, change her, get up with her in the middle of the night, and do all the baby care that Luther refused to do. Whatever I cooked, James gushed over the meal and said it was delicious. Luther was going through a liver and onions phase where all he wanted to eat was liver and onions with brown gravy and rice. I could not eat this. I was living on cottage cheese. James even gushed over that. Every evil thing Luther did was in stark contrast to the kindness that James showed me and the baby.

Each day, when Luther got home from school, he would go from room to room in the small little apartment to look for

Dana Smith, 1977

something out of place, so he could pick a fight. Just like with Mama, I would try in vain to have everything perfect to try to appease him. One day everything was so clean he couldn't find anything that was out of order, so he pulled the toilet tank away from the wall in the bathroom to have something to complain about. He was spoiling for a fight, but right then James came in gushing over how great the house looked, how wonderful supper smelled, and how terrific the baby and I were to do all this for him and Luther. Luther looked at me, still wanting to fight. I stared at him with hatred. James wanted him to go out drinking, so off they went. I had absolutely no love for Luther and felt very trapped.

Because James was setting a good example, Luther could not stand it. He started to participate in holding the baby a little. One day Luther decided to change her diaper. Dana was screaming and crying, which was not like her. I tried to take her out of his arms to see what was wrong with my three-month-old daughter. He physically threw her very hard into the crib and blocked the door to her room. Luther was screaming, "You have spoiled her rotten and she can just cry it out." I physically struggled with him while the baby screamed until she finally went silent. When I finally got past him, to my sleeping baby, she was lying in a pool of blood because he had stabbed the safety pin through her side and pinned it into her diaper. I had to get her out of there. This environment was dangerous.

The next day I had an out of body experience. I was so depressed and upset over the diaper incident and his mean spiritedness to both of us that I literally felt like my spirit moved out of my body. It was hovering above me near the ceiling while I was washing dishes. I was looking down on my body; I got so scared that I decided I had to leave.

I went to visit Mama. I told her I was getting a divorce. It was close to Thanksgiving. In true Mama logic she said you can't leave before the holidays; it'll mess up everyone's holiday's. You have to wait until after New Year's. I guess that has stuck with me because no matter what employees have done over the years, I try to never fire anyone between Thanksgiving and New Year's; you just don't want to mess up anyone's holidays.

1977

Life without Luther

1977 was a year that life got better. I waited like Mama said to move out January 2, 1977. By this time, I was convinced that I might be in love with James. He truly was the first nice man I had ever been around in my life. It wasn't love, just high contrast with evil. As soon as we were no longer roommates, I never thought about him. Other than the time James had carried me into the hospital, we had never had any physical contact at all.

Dana and I moved back in with Mama, who was now saved, and Mark. Mark thought that Dana was the most adorable baby he had ever seen. This caused me much anxiety when he would just pick her up and take her off somewhere for hours without telling me. Once, when she was 10 months old, he took her fishing all day with no bottle, no sunscreen (they didn't have that back then), and no diapers. He fed her Kentucky Fried Chicken and coke. I was just so relieved she returned alive but a little burnt I didn't say anything to him because I felt like a child had to have more than her Mother to love her. Mark loved Dana very much.

Luther and James were still rooming together (without me and the baby), living a calm life in Ruston. Mama was a different person, but unfortunately, I was not. I was an angry young woman. I decided my child would not be abused. I decided I would stay

144

single and never be abused again. It simply would not happen. I still had it in my mind to be a pharmacist. I was going to college at LSU-S still, working on my pre-pharmacy degree, which was a lot of chemistry, math, and science. I was going to get a degree. I planned be able to provide a good life for us both, without a man.

Being a "Nurse" for the Wealthy

Here I was, back in my old life, living in the ghetto with a baby of my own. Not much had changed since I was 15, except Mama was acting more like a normal person. She adored Dana. I was still going to school, only this time it was college and I was working. We didn't hear much from Luther for a couple of years as he was busy with college and dating.

Since Mama got saved she decided she needed to go to work. Mama got a job sitting with an old lady, Miss Anne Elizabeth, who was hit by an ambulance driving her maid home when she was 95. That car wreck broke her hip. She was housebound to her bedroom on the second floor of a big house. When Mama started sitting with her she was 100 years old. She still lived in the mansion complete with a chair elevator. Everything in the house had been state of the art when it was new about 50 years earlier. It had not been updated since that time.

Miss Anne had an only daughter, Miss Evelyn Avery, and only one grandchild, Charlotte Avery Evelyn. Miss Anne's maid had been with her since the maid was 18 years old. Now 80 years old. She had helped raise Miss Evelyn and Miss Charlotte. The maid could barely hobble so her daughter hired sitters to come and take care of Miss Anne. Mama had the evening shift. I had the night shift. I would have the baby in my car at 11:00 when I came to work. Mama would take her home to put her back to bed. She would come get me when I got off at seven the next morning, then I would go to class. Mama still didn't have a car.

This job was great! All I had to do was go to bed when I got there. I would lie down on the guest bed in the room next to Miss Anne. I had to lay on top of the bed because I had my nurses' uniform on, but at twenty, sleep is sleep. When Miss Anne needed to go to the bathroom during the night I would get up and take her, put her back to bed, and go back to sleep myself. It really wasn't a lot different than taking care of a baby. At 6:00 AM Miss Anne would wake up ready for breakfast and I would go cook it for her. She ate the exact same breakfast and supper every day.

Breakfast was two eggs, two strips of bacon, chicory coffee, and butterflied toast (the bread was toasted in the oven then you cut the crust off, ran the knife down the center of the bread making two thin slices and then re-toast them again). Supper was a bacon sandwich, apricots, avocado and tomato salad, with homemade mayonnaise, and a Manhattan. Miss Anne ate lots of homemade mayonnaise, butter, and bacon. She said all the news about not eating fat were lies, besides, the reason she drank her Manhattan every night was that the alcohol cleaned out her veins.

One of Miss Anne's great grandsons had just graduated from law school. He was a lovely young man. When I worked evening or day shifts, he would come in and hang out with me. Miss Anne did not like the household help to fraternize with the family so whenever Will was home she made me come sit in her room, so she could keep an eye on me. She was so quiet and silent all of the time, barely speaking. I was surprised she could figure out he had a crush on me. Will and I became friends for several years and kept in touch. When you go out with one lawyer, all the other lawyers think they should go out with you too, soon all of Will's "friends" called me for dates. I had many lawyers calling to go out on a date. I didn't like the aggressiveness of the attorney personality. I could not get close to any of them. It didn't matter how many I went out with and rejected, another one would call. I never allowed any of the attorneys to physically or emotionally get close to me. Will's interest in me was a positive influence, as it made me realize I could remarry a professional man.

Miss Anne outlived her only daughter, Miss Evelyn, who died at 73, then outlived her only grandchild, Charlotte, who died at 54, and wound up in the custody of her great grandchildren at 105, Evelyn Avery and Will. These young people immediately put Miss Anne in a nursing home where she died at 105 years of age.

Garage Apartment Neighbors - The Murderer – Jimmy Wingo

Living with Mama during this time was better than it had been at any time during my life. Gone was the cursing, raging, and cigarette smoking. The rocks no longer lined the porch rails. She had conversations with the neighbors. She loved our garage apartment neighbor named Jimmy Wingo. Jimmy told Mama he was in law school. Mama would invite Jimmy in for a glass of tea. Jimmy was the single most scary man I have ever been around. We had a phone that I paid for. Jimmy would knock on the back door and ask to use the phone. I was so scared of enraging him I would take my baby and go sit on the front porch to "give him some privacy". My body would scream with fear as tingling would start at the back of my neck. My anxiety would be so intense I could hardly breathe. I felt we were safer sitting outside on the porch than in the house with Jimmy. I absolutely knew that Jimmy wanted to kill me. Mama wanted me to marry Jimmy. She said I should go on a date with him.[3]

Mama loved the baby too much. I did not want her to influence my child and still did not trust her behavior was a permanent change. It wasn't. One night she fell "off the wagon". I was in my closet trying to reorganize some clothes, when she flew in my room in a rage over some imagined wrong. She grabbed hold of me to draw back her hand to hit me. Mama was about 225 pounds and I was about 110. She towered over me. But enough was enough. When she grabbed hold of me, I retaliated fast and hard,

Words of Wisdom

Men like a challenge. The more aloof a girl acts, the better they like the chase and the more likely they are to call.

---

3   A couple of years later, Jimmy wound up in jail. He broke out with another inmate, walked 3 miles to Dixie Inn, LA where the two inmates murdered a nice couple named Newt and Earlene Brown on Christmas Eve in a robbery. On June 21, 1987 Jimmy Wingo was electrocuted. See appendix.

shoving her massive bulk into a doorframe while grabbing her by the neck. I screamed two inches from her face, "You will never touch me again." Mama was a bully and like all bullies when they think they might be the one to get hurt they are terrified. This was the last time she ever tried to abuse me. I was twenty years old.

I think she was shocked by the force of my reaction. I realized by the spirit of Jesus that she was wrong to assault a grown woman. She never thought anything was ever her fault. While she acted like a raging banshee, she thought she was the victim all her life. She never once associated her behavior with how people reacted to her. She never admitted her fault because she couldn't see her responsibility. A lack of responsibility sums up her life.

I doubt she ever asked forgiveness for her sins of child abuse and neglect because she felt she was only using discipline. I hope I am wrong. I feared for years that she had gone to her death thinking she was the perfect person, because the devil had blinded her so badly. I do wonder how she felt when she got to heaven and they reran the video of her life, how it must have felt for her to see herself as the monster she truly was. I do truly pray that she asked forgiveness. It has taken me years since her death to finally believe she went to heaven and Jesus forgave her. I forgave her.

1978

I went back to Monroe, Louisiana and college working on my pharmacy degree. Dana was a difficult toddler. The college daycare complained about her often. She was just 18 months old and there wasn't a whole lot I could do to change an 18-month-old baby's behavior. I moved into the same apartment complex Luther and I had previously lived in, because that is where my friends lived. I got a job at Saint Francis Hospital in the Laboratory. The old pathologist I worked for loved red haired women, so he was extra kind to me. He allowed me the extra opportunity to learn to read microscopic slides and watch the morgue after I completed my clerical duties. I spent many hours working alongside him, staining slides and writing up what he saw. I loved that job.

Life in the low rent apartment complex was interesting. There were lots of single women with low class boyfriends, a few trashy husbands, and lots of snotty little kids. The men started calling me "tight ass" which I thought was because my behind was so firm. One day one of the wives enlightened me and told me it was because I would not sleep with any of them. Talk about double offended, they were ALL married! I found out my fanny was not in as good a shape as I thought they thought it was.

My cousin started to visit me almost every weekend. Bryan was four years younger than I was and at seventeen he was 6'4" and husky. Bryan drove a big white pickup truck and wore a cowboy hat; we had a great time together. We never did a lot, just cooked, hung out, and played with Dana. We didn't have any money, so outings were limited. One day one of the ladies asked

Words of Wisdom

Sometimes just acting brave is enough to stop a parental bully. All bullies are terrified to get hurt themselves and they love getting a reaction. They are trying to control or hurt another person in a harmful way. In bullying there is a difference in power, and the bullying behavior is intentional and repeated. Parental bullying is evidenced by threats, physical and verbal abuse, and mental and emotional manipulation. Report this behavior to everyone. Never, ever, keep their secrets.

about the man I was living with. I was offended because I was NOT living with a man. "Yes, you are," she insisted, "I see him here every weekend in his pickup truck and cowboy hat". Oh, my cousin.

A Very Bad Baby

Dana was becoming more and more of a challenge. She could escape from any enclosure, get out of baby beds, and open any door. Dana could open any bottle cap. She had a natural tendency to push down and turn so every cap came off easily for her. I put screen door slide hooks on all my inside doors. I took to locking everything down to keep her out of things. She would eat or drink anything she got into her mouth. One night, when she was 21 months old, at 3:00 AM, she climbed out of her bed while I was asleep. Dana went downstairs to the kitchen where she dragged a chair over to the refrigerator. Dana then carried about 50 little golden books downstairs which she stacked up on the counter to climb up onto. She got into the cabinet over the refrigerator where I kept the household cleaners. She drank bleach.

I was soon on a first name basis with the poison control center personnel. It seemed I was calling them daily. She would eat whole lipsticks, drink face makeup, or anything she could get in her mouth like rocks, toys, plants, etc. She didn't seem to differentiate between food and sundries. She ate everything. Keeping her safe was a challenge. I took to locking her in her room for her naps. The neighbors thought I was crazy. But try as I might, I could not keep everything out of her mouth. One day I had her strapped in her car seat while I stopped for less than five minutes at the ATM to get $20.00. I was planning on driving back to Shreveport for a visit. Strapped in her car seat, she hooked my purse with her foot, pulled it up, got into a prescription bottle, and ate the entire bottle of pills with no water in less than a minute. I was just getting $20, less than three feet from the car! I turned my car from the bank parking lot into the West Monroe Hospital Parking lot. Instead of visiting my friends and family in Shreveport, I got to spend my Saturday afternoon in the ER with a young doctor who later asked me out on a date. I had long since stopped taking her to the hospital where I worked, it was just too embarrassing.

A Very Sick Baby with Encephalitis

The semester ended with beautiful Louisiana summer

weather. All the ladies in the apartment complex sat outside in the evenings after supper, supervising the babies playing on their little riding toys. One night, I put Dana to bed in my bed because she would not stay in her bed. I learned to sleep holding her foot, so I could keep her in my bed. I used her for my alarm clock because she was up every morning at 6:30 AM on the dot. I had to get up with her every morning because I had to protect her from trying to kill herself.

That morning I woke up at 10:00AM: Dana sat up, unconscious, threw up all over my bed without opening her eyes, then laid back down, unconscious. I jumped up, grabbed my jeans, a T-shirt, flip flops, my baby covered in throw up, and ran to the ER. My child had encephalitis caused by mosquito bites. Our apartment complex was right on the Bayou Desard and there were several cases in the ER already.

Dana was in the hospital for almost 60 days. When she got out, my pediatrician, Dr. Hall, had his wife keep her at no charge to me, so she wouldn't have to go back to daycare at the university. He never charged me anything for the medical care he gave her. I had sat at her bedside, never leaving for a minute, even though I was taking a summer class. I finally figured out how to study that summer sitting in the hospital room with nothing to do but read my microbiology book. Even though I never attended class, I passed the final exam with an A. I had several friends that visited me daily to stay with Dana, while I went and took my tests, so I could finish the summer session. One girl, who had not been that good of a friend until Dana went in the hospital, climbed into the metal hospital crib to entertain Dana for an hour almost every day. She gave me time to take a shower, get cleaned up, wash some clothes, and get something to eat. God is good to give us angels on Earth when we need them.

Dana's immune system was compromised. I could not put her back in daycare, so the only reasonable thing for me to do was to move back to Shreveport. Trisha was going to Northwestern University Nursing School. This was a block from my Mama's house. She talked me into changing from pharmacy school to nursing school with her. I had completed the first two years of classes and my hours transferred. All my electives also transferred. I was able to be accepted into the Baccalaureate Program to go directly into clinicals.

Roomies

Trisha and I rented a house in Broadmoor on Ockley Street while we went to school and work. Mama and Meme worked out a schedule where they alternated Dana every day. When Dana got sick at 22 months, she was potty-trained and speaking clearly. She was way above her age level. She was counting to 50, knew all her colors, and had known all the animal sounds since she was 15 months. She was my party trick. I would have her perform. Everyone was always amazed by her. The encephalitis knocked all of that out of her. She had to learn everything over again. After the illness, she was much more irritable and fussier. She was sick with a virus or bacteria all the time; skin rashes were common, and she seemed to be allergic to everything. Her immune system was a mess.

While she regained her basic life skills quickly, she stayed sick. The allergies kept her down and me frantic. The year I left her rotating between the grandmothers was a year that little sick child became the most spoiled little brat you have ever seen. She minded no one. She didn't have to because the grandmothers would put up with anything for one day knowing she would be somewhere else the next day. Besides, she was sick. After a year, she was better, however, the allergies seemed to be permanent. For my mental health I had to put her into a day care program. She was so spoiled she was impossible.

The Dreaded Guest

Trisha was a party girl. She liked a good time and while I was working, going to school, and taking care of a baby she was in a different position. She was smarter than I was. She didn't have to study. At all. She had always studied trivia and loved to compete in bars and radio contests. Trivia contests used to be a 1970's thing. Trisha always won. She would read whole encyclopedias and trivia books. It must have prepared her for nursing school.

I was always cutting my time extremely close. If I had to be at work and the drive was fifteen minutes, I would give myself five whole minutes extra to put on my uniform and get to the hospital floor where I worked as a Certified Nurse's Aide. One night, with 20 minutes to get across town, to my unit, by 10:45 PM, I came running into my bedroom at 10:25. I didn't turn the light on in my bedroom as I had a walk-in closet with a light. I was planning on stripping down, putting on my uniform in the closet, and dashing out. As I stripped down, I heard a man's voice from my bedroom say, "Hello there". I freaked out. Always one to have a gun and a knife in the closet, I exited the closet armed and ready for blood. Trisha, in her loving consideration, had met a man at a bar and brought him home because she thought I would like him. He had taken off his clothes and climbed in my bed to wait for me. A total stranger! I screamed him out of my house. Somehow, I still made it to work on time.

1979

Trisha and Mason

After the man incident, Trisha's judgment was worrying me. I felt that the situation was too risky for myself and my child. I decided to move out to Greenwood, to Meme and Papa's, where they had a double wide trailer.

Living in the double wide was like living in a new house. It was nice. We were living in the country away from everyone, with Luther's grandparents right across the street.

That winter Trisha met Mason, her future husband. They married June 9, 1979 in Waskom, Texas. A couple of weeks later, Mason fixed me up with one of his co-workers, David Wright. Trisha and I giggled and laughed like young girls do, while David didn't say a word. The date didn't go that well. David didn't ask me out again. David was the only man I ever went out on a date with that did not ask me for a second date.

Luther had been relatively out of sight and out of mine and Dana's life, enjoying college life in Ruston. We had seen each other infrequently since I took Dana and left. I guess the move across the street from his grandparents and his upcoming graduation caused his grandmother to want us back together. Meme had always loved me and Dana. I suspect she started putting pressure on him to get back as a family with us. Anyway, as summer approached, he asked me to re-affirm our vows in September and move in together to be a family.

That is right after he went to Italy again for the summer. With Amelia. He had spent the summer in Italy the previous summer with Amelia. It was so spectacular that he had to do it again. His plan was for me to drop out of my last year of nursing school and work full time to pay for his summer in Italy...with Amelia. Then after one last spectacular summer in Italy, he would settle down to family life. How can any girl refuse that offer? I told him if he left (with Amelia) I would be engaged to someone else by the time he got back. He went to Italy. I got engaged.

I had a neighbor that had the only other child in the neighborhood. Our houses were five acres apart. His name was Jake and lived with his parents and four-year-old Isabella. Jake would come borrow things. I never let Jake in the house but would let Isabella come over and play. Dana was NEVER allowed to go to his house and play. One evening, Jake came over and asked for a screwdriver like he had done many times before. I left him standing on the porch. I turned to get the screwdriver out of the kitchen drawer, when, suddenly, Jake was standing right behind me. Having had lots of experience with abuse, I calmly asked Jake, "Don't you want a drink?" I showed no fear. This disconcerted him. I know if I had screamed he probably would have killed both me and Dana.

He said, "Sure". I made him the strongest drink I had in the house. He drank all the bourbon, then started on the Amaretto, drinking it straight; it had been a Christmas present from a friend. I had a frozen casserole in the freezer I was saving for a future party. I popped it in the oven telling him I'd just make us something to eat. Every time I stood up, he beat his fist on the table. I would just calmly keep him talking. When he had finished the last of the liquor and eaten the entire casserole, he told me that he was too drunk to get it up to rape me that night, but he would be back. He said he was going home to rape his four-year-old daughter. As I dead bolted the door behind him I was terrified. I called my best friend, Alex, and had him bring some guns and come spend the night. I called the police. When the police got to my house, they said that Jake had driven his car into a tree and wrecked his car. Jake had been taken to the hospital.

Alex and I packed up my house. I moved out the next day. Jake would come back to haunt me years later.

The Custody Battle

I had to find a place to live. I had moved so frequently since I was seventeen, I could scarcely keep count. I needed security and stability. I only saw that as a possibility if I owned a home of my own. I started looking at homes and decided they were too expensive, so I bought a brand-new trailer. I found a lot. I had the trailer moved and set up in less than a week. I finally had a home of my own. Even if it was a formaldehyde (cancer-causing chemical) filled trailer that could not have been healthy. Later, several reports came out on the dangers of living in formaldehyde-filled trailers.

My new trailer came with a next-door neighbor who became a new best friend, Mia, and her little girl, who was a year younger than Dana. I was happier than I had been in years. Then Luther came back from Italy. When I refused to be with him, he abducted Dana. I knew that to find her all I had to do was call every babysitter in the paper because he would have left her at one of these. My new finance was horrified. He insisted that I hire a lawyer instead and we go to court and settle this. He was sure that Luther was reasonable. He didn't know Luther. Luther had no intention of being reasonable. We went to court. I went through hell. I was finally awarded custody of my child. I had decided that if I lost custody of my child I would wait until my first visitation when I would take her to live in Mexico, never to return to the US. The fiancée only lasted as long as the custody battle he insisted on was over.

Value Questions

I had to change my life and the men in it. I desperately wanted another child. I decided that I would make a list of value questions detailing what I had to have in a man to get married again. If I couldn't find it, I would stay single. I always had total confidence in my plans. I knew my plans worked. The problem was perseverance. Working the plans long enough for them to come to fruition was always the challenge, as different goals took different lengths of time to achieve. I started interviewing potential husbands with the following value questions:

Value Questions

1. He had to love me more than anyone else in the world, even his family.
2. He had to be faithful to me and only me.
3. He had to have a college education. I didn't want to be poor.
4. He had to own something of value that he had paid off to show he could make payments: a house, car, motorcycle, boat.
5. He had to like my child and want more.
6. He had to like his family and they had to be nicer than mine.
7. He had to like animals, especially dogs, and be kind to them.
8. He had to have blonde hair and blue eyes.
9. He had to be six feet tall.
10. He could not be a liar or a thief.
11. He could not have ever gone to prison.
12. He had to be smart.
13. He had to go to work every day.
14. I needed stability. I wanted to set my watch by the time he came home every day - doctors were out.
15. He could not be lazy; he had to be a hard worker.
16. He could not smoke; Dana had asthma.
17. He could not cuss.
18. He could not be abusive.
19. He could not have children. I felt like my one child was enough and I didn't want him liking any other child more than mine.
20. He had to be clean and bathe every day. He had to wash his hands after he went to the bathroom.
21. He could not be a sissy crybaby. He had to be stoic.
22. He had to be handy with his hands and fix things. I had lived in houses all my life where many things would be broken. I decided I would not live that way any longer.

I started going through the men. One after another. There always seemed to be someone else to go on a date with. First dates only, I never accepted a second date with anyone who was not a potential husband candidate. Sometimes I would be asked out and when I replied, "I have to get a babysitter", the man would retract his invitation and tell me he didn't want to date people with kids. Good riddance! My children have always been my greatest assets.

As soon as the date started, I would start the conversation by casually asking the questions in a friendly, conversational manner. Most of the men loved to answer the questions about themselves. It really made them feel like I was interested in them. Most people really want to talk about themselves. I was regarded as a great conversationalist without saying much. When I would dislike the answer to a question, I would complain of a headache or something similar, and make them take me home. There was no reason to tie up anymore of my time with a candidate that failed the test and not husband material. I used this technique in interviewing potential husbands. I have always used this exact technique in my business also, when someone I interview is not a candidate, there is no reason to waste any more of my time or their time. When I would get to an answer I just could not accept, while interviewing candidates, I would just stand up and thank them for coming, wish them luck, and escort them out.

This semester was so rough that I had to drop down to only five hours. To me, that was the equivalent of dropping out of school, so I felt very down about my life. Luther had succeeded in making me truly miserable. But I still had my job and the baby was in Genevieve Daycare, the same day care Trisha had gone to herself. The best part was because I was low income, it was free.

I could not stay in this negative spiral of depression. I signed up for a Catholic program called Beginning Experience where people who have experienced the loss of a loved one through divorce or death came to begin the grieving process. I was the youngest person at the conference by about 15 years, but everyone there accepted me and made feel a part of their group. I met a dear friend, named Don, who had also just been through a custody battle for his three-year-old daughter, that he won, obtaining custody of Donna. From then on, Don and I shared the children, clothes, and babysitting. To this day Dana and Donna are best, lifelong friends and visit each other often.

That Christmas was one of the worst Christmas' of my life. While I was used to not having good holidays, my two grandmothers had made up where Mama fell short: they always had a present for me and my brothers.

This year was different, I had absolutely no money. I was depressed to boot after the strife of the semester. The custody battle had really done a number on me and Luther had never paid a dime in child support from the day she was born. I was dead broke. For Christmas, I bought Dana a couple of very cheap dollar store toys, two, terrible, sugar cookies, and a quart of eggnog. That was our Christmas. Later that day, Trisha brought me two African Violets. As I took the plants in my hand all I could think was that now I have something else to take care of that I would probably kill. It didn't take long for me to kill them.

Trisha was worried because I had been so depressed throughout the holidays, that she decided the perfect thing to cheer me up was for me to go out on a date. Because my first date with David had not been stellar (he had never called me back), I refused to go out with him again. Trisha said she had the perfect man named Rodney. Imagine my surprise when we drove up to "Rodney's" house in Broadmoor and David answered the door. As I was standing on the porch, with Trisha and Mason behind me, she was whispering furiously, "Be nice, be nice". David looked lovely that night wearing a blue shirt to bring out his blue eyes.

That night we played games. We had a fun evening at David's house. David was a nervous wreck. No man could answer my value questions accurately. They could get one or two, then everything would start to fall apart. I probably had 15-20 first dates before Trisha fixed me up with David for the second time.

I asked David the value questions and to my surprise he answered everyone exactly as I wanted my husband to answer my questions. It was freaky, because he didn't look like what I had imagined my husband to look. He totally missed number nine. He was not six feet tall. The man I wanted mentally and emotionally wasn't wrapped in the external package I had imagined. I thought I wanted a man who wore suits, David wore work boots and jeans. David was a typical Arkansas man: a hunter and fisherman, windblown, physically fit, loved the outdoors, OCD, and rustically handsome. I loved his blonde hair and blue gray eyes. And that man can fix anything. Literally anything. I also really love his OCD (Obsessive Compulsive Disorder). That man loves order and cleanliness. Best of all, he thinks he is the only one that can-do cleaning right, so he doesn't want my help! My favorite people always have OCD. I love cleanliness and order and timeliness as long as they don't expect me to return those same qualities.

I didn't have a phone, partly to keep Luther from bothering me, but I decided to get one so David and I might have a chance. I knew it would be impossible to cultivate a relationship with him with no way for him to call me for a date.

Mason kept setting us up on dates. David would not take the initiative. I refused to pursue a man. If he wasn't interested in me enough to call me, I wasn't going to call him. After about four fix ups, David finally took the initiative and asked Dana and me to dinner. David never just asked me to dinner. He always asked "us" to dinner.

PART FOUR

Becoming a Nurse

First Day of Nursing School

On my first day of nursing school the instructor said, "Look to your right and to your left, those people will not be here when you graduate. I mean, if you graduate." There were 129 young men and women in that nursing class; when I graduated there were only 40 of us left. I was not thrilled about being a nurse. It seemed to be ran as a second rate, low-class, blue-collar profession when it was so much more.

I thought it was laughable that the instructor would fail us all out of school, but that is exactly what she and her fellow instructors proceeded to do. They assigned us Interdisciplinary Care Plans, which included the care delivered by the other care team members, like the respiratory therapist, the social worker, and the doctor. We didn't yet know what nurses did and now we had to identify and know what every other member of the team should do for every disease because, according to the instructors, we were the "supervisors" and the patient "belonged" to the Registered Nurse. Every care plan had to list every disease or ailment a patient had and also include patient education.

There were no resources for this that any of us students found. We didn't have the Internet. We had to spend hours pulling outdated books from the library and sorting through the information trying to determine what information was correct. Because the Interdisciplinary Care Plans were so new, there were no resources for them at all. Actually, in 1979, there were very few care plan books available at all. We were all struggling and failing miserably to write the nursing care plans that made up the majority of our grade.

About that time a most interesting thing happened that would change my life. I unexpectedly got a package in the mail containing the *McGraw Hill Handbook of Clinical Nursing*. This was a $75.00 book of interdisciplinary care plans that I could never have afforded to purchase. How I got it or where it came from, I never knew; I think my guardian angel must have sent it to me. If it was a gift from God, I was going to use it. That book saved my life in nursing school. Immediately, it eliminated 75% of my work.

I pledged to tell no one as I rapidly copied my care plans

from the book. At first, I took care to rewrite them in language you would expect from a junior nursing student: however, late in my senior year, I just copied them and changed the words to keep from being accused of plagiarism if any of the instructors ever located the book. Until this writing, I have never told a soul about the book that allowed me to be a single mother of a young child, work full time, and take a full load of classroom and clinical hours in nursing school. Time and money were so short that I just could never afford a babysitter to spend the hours I needed in the library to make "A's". With the *McGraw Hill Handbook of Clinical Nursing* I didn't need any other resources; I had straight "A's" on every care plan from then on. I like to think that I learned a lot from my copying days. Studying the clear, concise way the book was written gave me a better understanding of nursing concepts than many of my fellow students. And best of all, my grades were great!

Metpath Laboratories

I was working for Metpath Laboratories, which was headquartered in New Jersey. Metpath had an interesting work flow process in the late 1970s and early 1980s. Drivers were sent to all area doctors' offices in three states to pick up lab samples, which were brought back to the office to be boxed in a large cardboard box. The samples were then raced to the airport, where they would board the 6:00 PM flight to New Jersey, and where they would be tested. My job was to buy a ticket to let the samples sit on a seat, because they could not survive the freezing temperatures in the cargo hold. The results were electronically transmitted to the Shreveport office the next morning, where they were run off on a large printer. In those days, no one electronically transmitted anything, so this was state of the art processing which appealed to me.

I was hired as the office manager. I loved every aspect of my job. I got to practice my blood drawing skills, which were critical to becoming a successful nurse. I got to operate the printer, the size of a large chest freezer. The best part was I got to drive a company car. Because I lived the closest to the airport, it was my job each night to drive one of the company cars to the airport to make sure the box of samples got a seat on the 6:00 PM plane to New Jersey.

The company car was specially supped up with flashers and a siren just like a police car. On the sides of the station wagon were magnetic signs that said laboratory specimens were on board. At 21 and 22, I thoroughly enjoyed turning on the flashers while speeding 100 miles per hour to the airport. I also felt blessed to have a company car to drive because affording a car was always a challenge in my life. I kept two "beaters" or very low-cost cars so that I could keep one running and the other one in the shop. It was cheaper than car payments.

In July, my paycheck bounced. My boss in New Jersey said that everything was okay, just hang in there; they would cover the check in a few days. Week after week my check bounced. Week after week my boss talked me into staying on the job. I had saved every cent I had earned and lived frugally so I had enough emergency money for about six weeks. On week seven, my personal checks started bouncing. I could not figure this out because I should have had $75.00 in my account. It was at zero.

I never balanced my checkbook. I keep a running tally in my head. I add and subtract mentally to keep a correct balance. When my checks began to bounce I pulled out the still sealed banking statements, and I found the error almost immediately. I was supposed to be on a student checking account that charged no fees. At some point several months back, the bank had started charging me a finance charge every month. Now, on top of that, I was accumulating added bounced check fees. I started crying hysterically. I couldn't quit.

David had a habit of calling me every afternoon at 1:00 PM from work, after he'd finished lunch. So when I heard the phone ringing, I knew it was him and that I had to answer, but I just couldn't talk to him right then. I had to figure out what I was going to do. I answered the phone, still crying, to tell him I couldn't talk right now I was too upset. I told him I'd call that night and then hung up the phone. Then I unplugged it because I knew he would just keep calling.

I got all my bills out. I figured out that if the bank refunded the account fees and the bounced check fees that would take care of the immediate problem. I still could not pay the rent, utilities, or groceries because seven weeks of my paychecks had not been covered by the company. I cried some more. I really loved my job, but that was a low point in my career. Now that I am the one issuing the checks, I have always made it a priority that the nurses I staff get paid well and on time.

I went to the bank, who reversed all the fees and notified all the holders of the bounced checks that there had been a bank error. The hardest thing that day was that David told me I had to quit my job. In Louisiana, an employer has three days to make complete restitution after an employee quits. I quit my job that afternoon. Three days later I received the seven weeks of pay. I never did pay David back. He never asked me too.

Becoming a Registered Nurse

I was finally in my senior year of nursing school! The last fall semester, we worked at the large Catholic Hospital, Schumpert Hospital. Catholic ownership and religious doctrines meant that Schumpert held to special rules that the other local hospitals did not. In particular, Schumpert did not allow any type of sterilization procedures to be performed. The only birth control method allowed to be taught was the Rhythm Method. According to WebMD:

> *"A woman practices the rhythm method of birth control by learning to recognize the days she is fertile and not having sex before and during those days. The rhythm method does not work for all couples. Another term for this is "natural family planning."*[1]

The instructor who taught the Rhythm Method was the same instructor that informed us on our first day that our class would be cut to less than one third. She had been a military nurse. I can still see her marching back and forth, back and forth, while she drilled us on this "very excellent method of birth control." I had never taken birth control pills. This sounded perfect for David and me! So we used the Rhythm Method for one month and on the 27th day of my cycle I conceived my beautiful daughter Melanie.

David and I were getting married anyway, so we just moved our wedding date up two months. On November 22, 1980 we were married.

When we married, I owned the new trailer that I had lived in one year, while David owned a two-bedroom house in Broadmoor. The first time I went to David's house alone I was intimidated because every surface in David's house was covered in plastic. Someone had made lamp shade covers and covers on the chairs; the bed was covered in a plastic mattress cover and pillow covers. All I could think was that I was in the home of a serial killer that was going to kill me. Life had taught me that the best defense is a good offense, so I immediately confronted him demanding, "What is the meaning of all this plastic? I don't like it." He replied, "My ex-wife wanted to protect everything, so she put the plastic on it."

'It has to go", I replied, and proceeded to tear all the plastic off his furniture and throw it away. He didn't know it, but I was looking for bloodstains or anything else that would signal that this kind, loving man was a nut case. I had just never encountered anyone as calm and stable as David.

David and I got married the Saturday before Thanksgiving in the trailer park clubhouse where I lived. We were married by a Baptist minister, who made us promise that we would never separate unless we got marital counseling. We readily agreed.

That day was like so many had been in my life up to that point. Everything went wrong. I woke up with bronchitis. I got up early to go to the beauty college to get my hair done in an updo. The young man that was doing my hair insisted on doing my makeup, for free, which caused me to get behind on time. He put so much makeup on me I looked like a streetwalker. Sonny was waiting for me at my trailer when

Mr. and Mrs. David Wright
November 22, 1980

Words of Wisdom

My sister-in-law Sue once told me as a wedding present: Never learn how to do something you don't want to do. For example, if you don't want to mow the yard for the rest of your life, don't learn how to start the lawn mower when someone tries to teach you. If you don't want to be known as the typist, don't learn how to type fast. It's as simple as that.

I got home and said in disgust, "GO wash your face, you look ridiculous!" I always minded Sonny. Mama was there causing as much conflict as possible by upsetting Dana. My sister-in-law needed me to hem and iron her skirt. The entire family kept asking if I could get them something to drink, eat, this, that, or another. Here it was my wedding day. I felt like Cinderella. As usual, I was taking care of everyone else with no one taking care of me. I was really sick with bronchitis, and pregnant. Finally, Grandma Fearn and Mama's sister, Aunt Maxine showed up with their family and helped get Dana dressed. This was the first nice thing my family had done for me all day. Worst of all, it was raining cats and dogs.

Because four-year-old Dana was a real challenge to take care of, Mama had told me she would only keep her the one night of the wedding and I would have to be back by 8:00 AM to pick her up. Unbeknownst to me, until after the wedding, Mama announced to her entire family that she had "cooked" Thanksgiving supper at her house for after the wedding. Since David and I only had about 14 hours for our honeymoon, I had made reservations at Shorty Leonard's Restaurant for our first meal as husband and wife.

Since I had cooked for many years, Mama's previously bad cooking had deteriorated. Mama had taken to pouring vinegar into everything she cooked. According to her "recipe" green beans needed half a cup of vinegar while creamed corn only took one fourth cup. Mama didn't have a good oven, so the Turkey would be burned on the outside and raw, possibly still frozen on the inside. The house was covered with roaches. It was unsanitary because I had not lived there in several years, which was the last time it was cleaned. All in all, the meal would be disgusting, the surroundings would be depressing, and the company miserable. I would NOT be spending my valuable 14 hours of my only honeymoon with Mama. I flat refused to go. I said, "Absolutely NOT, I would not go. It was not in my plans and that was final." David was clueless to what was going on. He was horrified that I was adamantly refusing to go to Mother's house to eat with my relatives. David had never been to Mother's house. As I think back about it I really should have never let Dana go to Mama's that night. It was just not safe or clean.

David and I went to Shorty Leonard's Restaurant for our first meal as husband and wife. I still remember that I had Scallops Au Gratin, which was delicious. We spent the night in a hotel. Then we picked up Dana early the next morning.

We married just five days before Thanksgiving, with final exams starting the second week of December. David and I decided not to move into his house in Broadmoor until the week of Christmas. I was achieving one of my goals! I was moving to Broadmoor.

While David was working, I moved everything into his house that I could by myself, finishing on Christmas Eve. When David came home from work Christmas Eve, I had set up a small tree and cooked a lovely meal of roasted Cornish Hens in a happy atmosphere. The Christmas of 1980 was very different from the previous one just one year ago.

Christmas morning would start a "tradition" where Luther would come get Dana. He would keep her until early afternoon, so she could have Christmas with his family. We would anxiously wait for her return so that we could immediately get into the car for the drive to Little Rock to David's parents' home.

David had five sisters. When we got married, he had four little nieces older than Dana. The Wrights would not get a grandson until their eighth grandchild was born. Dana was the youngest of the stair steps at four, then Stacy at five, Angie at six, Kerry at seven, and Amy at seven. Rosemary bought all of the girls matching nightgowns and they looked adorable.

That first Christmas with the Wright's I learned that Pauline, David's mother, was a prolific gift giver. She loved to give many, many gifts at Christmas. I would learn that it was not unusual for Pauline to give 25-30 gifts to someone, especially if she favored you. The more she liked you, the more gifts she gave because gifts were her love language.

Gifts had always been scarce in my lifetime. I had learned to ask for nothing and expect less. I still remember David asking me what I wanted for Christmas that first year. I asked for two pairs of knee socks and a pair of gloves. I thought he would get me a little something else as a surprise, but my practical husband got me exactly what I asked for. Nothing more, nothing less.

But that Christmas evening at Arlis and Pauline's house David, Dana, and I opened presents alone because the rest of the family had opened their presents for Christmas morning. Sitting on the floor with Dana, the stack of presents in front of me grew higher and higher. I had never seen anything like it. I had over 40 presents. Dana had about 20. I didn't know what to say. I kept saying, "Are you sure all these are for me?" My cheeks flushed redder and redder as I was finally the only one in this room of 30 relatives opening presents. Pauline had bought each of her girls a matching wardrobe. Everyone got exactly the same 15 outfits. I got tops, slacks, dresses, pajamas, robes, jewelry, and candy. You would think with all the deprivation I had suffered it would thrill me to no end to have all these clothes, but none of them fit. The few pieces that did fit didn't look right on me. It didn't dawn on me at the time, but Pauline had less than a month notice to buy Christmas for me. She divided out what she had bought all year for her other girls. That is why I received clothes in all different sizes that Christmas. After that, Pauline always did a great job of gift-giving.

Pauline was a wonderful mother-in-law and a good friend. She was everything Mama and Mary were not. Pauline was the smartest person I have ever known. She read everything: two newspapers a day, 20-30 magazines a month, a book almost every day. She remembered everything. There was nothing Pauline did not know about. She specialized in financial concerns. She knew how to make money from investing money.

One day, many years after we had first met each other, we were sitting at my dining table reading. We often enjoyed sitting together looking through a sales brochure while critiquing the home decor. On this day I was reading the newspaper someone had been arrested for "crank". I spoke up inquiring of Pauline, "I wonder what crank is?" For about fifteen minutes I got an oral dissertation on the chemical differences between crack, meth, and crank with the pros and cons of each drug. I mean there was nothing Pauline didn't know. She was a walking encyclopedia. This woman was amazingly brilliant.

Pauline was also quiet, retiring, self-depreciating, almost timid, and extremely introverted. Sometimes she would talk to me nonstop and other times I would say, "Hello" and she would not acknowledge me. I finally figured out she would not talk to me in a crowd, only if we were one on one. Early on, I had mistaken her lack of communication as moodiness. It took me awhile to figure it out.

Pauline did not have many friends. I really do not know if she had ever had a best girlfriend until me. But that is what she and I became over the years. She could tell dirty jokes, drink wine, and let her hair down with me, things she could not feel comfortable doing with her daughters. We would go to the movies and out to eat. Pauline loved going out to eat. Pauline was always entertained by the things I was doing. David and Pauline had the same personality and they both loved hearing about my day. My outgoing cheeriness always entertained them. They were truly happy.

Arlis was a different person altogether. Arlis was outgoing with a top-level position at a power company. He was a pilot. He had done quite well for himself and his family over the years. I always liked Arlis because he was nice to me. David struggled with the years of scars from his father's drunkenness. At the time I came into the Wright Family, Arlis was no longer drinking.

But as I know so well, when a parent has bad behavior that has lasted for years, the child's bad feelings don't immediately go away when the parent suddenly stops committing the bad behavior. Interestingly, this is exactly what people with a history of abuse expect. They want total forgiveness for changing and stopping the atrocities that normal people would never dream of doing to anyone, much less their own child. Unfortunately, most of us do not have perfect forgiveness, which only comes from Christ, of anyone's behavior.

It is such a personal attack when the parent, who is supposed to protect the child the most, mistreats the child. The child has no recourse for escape and over time the scars of parental abuse are exhibited differently in each different adult. Two children can experience the exact same event, yet the outcome and scars can be exhibited differently as adults. Dr. Joshua Garren once told me, "Child abuse leaves the least scars when the child does not buy into the abuse".[2] If the child feels the parent is wrong and the abuse is undeserved, the child is less affected than if the child feels ashamed or feels that he deserved the abuse in some way, such as by being bad or unlovable. David felt his father's drunken stunts so strongly they were physical pains just as sharply as I had felt Mama's wire coat

Words of Wisdom

Forgiveness is a walk in faith every day. We need to say every day, "I forgive everyone, everything, I can, I will, and I do." Then the Father will forgive us.

hanger.

Arlis favored David: his good, quiet, well-behaved son, to the exclusion of all other people. When David was a child, Arlis took David with him everywhere he went. Arlis never stayed home with his family. He worked constantly; when he was off on the weekends he went hunting or fishing (A.K.A. drinking) with his buddies. Some of Arlis's friends were well known. He went fishing with actor Robert Mitchum. Pauline would save Robert's cigarette butts to hand them out to the neighbors.

Diana and Dana, 1981

Unfortunately, my introverted husband hated the drunken parties that Arlis brought David to every weekend. David was often left to clean up the mess the men had made. One late Sunday night, when David was fourteen, his father was too drunk to drive. He charged David with driving them home while he slept it off in the back seat. My sweet husband came upon a wreck. He had to wake Arlis up to help the dead passengers. A fourteen-year-old child should have never been expected to drive his father home late on a school night.

The beginning of the final semester of nursing school filled us nursing students with joy. We had one two-hour class and one eleven-hour class left until we graduated. Each class required two exams and an optional final exam. As graduating seniors' final exams were optional, we could take them in hopes of raising our grade, or skip them, our choice.

The first test for the two-hour class was so easy that everyone in the class made close to 100%. The content was exactly what was taught in class. By studying our notes, the test content was straightforward. Evidently, that upset the instructor because the second test contained no class or textbook content whatsoever. Where the questions came from no one knew, with only the smartest girl making a "D," while everyone else made a "F."

172

My grades of an "A" and a "F" averaged a "D" for the semester. I decided to "stick," meaning I would not risk taking the final exam. If I failed the final I'd fail the class and not graduate. To me, this was a no brainer. Why would anyone risk not graduating? Well, that is exactly what 25% of my class decided to do. 75% took the final in hopes of raising their grade and failed! They did not graduate in May. I was graduating, no matter what!

Diana Wright,
College Graduation 1981

By the final semester of nursing school, the class of 120 had shrunk down to 40, exactly as our instructor had predicted. The Rhythm Method of birth control had produced six pregnant girls, all due to deliver in July, exactly nine months after our enlightened rhythm method education.

Loving Together and Building a Family

As my belly swelled with new life, our RN State Boards were scheduled for July 7 and 8, 1981. Melanie was to be induced July 1, which also happened to be my mother's birthday. There was no way I was going to be physically able to sit for my state boards until the following February 1982, when the boards were offered next. That meant I could not become a Registered Nurse in 1981. As I would not be qualified to work until I could get my license, I stayed home for the first nine months after graduation to care for my new baby, and my eldest daughter, Dana (my first husband was her father) who was then four years old.

If I had any doubts about what David would be like as a father they were quelled the first night we slept in his new house that was perfect for young couples. The first night that David and I moved into his adorable two-bedroom house in Shreveport, at four in the morning, Dana came down the hall screaming in pain; vomit streaming out one end of her body and diarrhea out the other. David didn't think twice about running a bath and taking care of little Dana. The house had new carpeting. I was happy that David cared more about the baby than any damage she had done to the carpet.

When we had been married about half a year, I was seven months pregnant. I started leaking blood, David did everything right. He picked me up, elevated my hips, listened to the baby's heart tones then called the doctor with his findings. He took care of me, too. The next day I went in for an ultrasound and Melanie was fine.

I received my Bachelor of Nursing May 15, 1981.

Nursing 101

Ever since I began nursing school, I had wanted to work at Schumpert Hospital ICU. It was the biggest hospital in Shreveport, with the latest technology. In 1982, there was a severe nursing shortage. I was immediately hired to work in Schumpert's Intensive Care Unit, which was the largest in Shreveport. There were multiple intensive care units that specialized in different areas: Regular Intensive Care Unit, Medical Intensive Care Unit, the Pediatric Intensive Care Unit, the Surgical Intensive Care Unit, the Cardiac Intensive Care Unit, the Cardiovascular Intensive Care Unit, Neonatal Intensive Care Unit, and the Neuro-Trauma Intensive Care Unit. I wanted to be trained in both the Cardiac Intensive Care Unit and the Medical Intensive Care Unit.

As a Registered Nurse you have to obtain your "flare". Each Registered Nurse is required to obtain certifications applicable to their specialization. I had to obtain CPR, ACLS, NALS, PALS, and Arrhythmia Strips, before they would even allow me to step into the Intensive Care Unit to train. All of the classes bestowed initials to write behind "RN." I used to say I had twice as many letters behind my name, as I had in my name. Many

Melanie and Dian Wright
July 1st, 1981

Dana, Diana, and Melanie
July 4th, 1981

of these certifications come with pins that the nurses wear on their chest, similar to how Jennifer Anniston did in the movie Office Space. In nursing, you can never have too much flare, or too many initials. This signals to other nurses that you know what you are doing. Nurses spend their entire careers proving every day to all the other nurses they know what they are doing. It never ends.

Newly graduated nurses have no flare. They have no initials, usually not even RN. They have no applicable job skills because reading about a medical procedure is not the same as actually doing the medical procedure. All in all, they are one scared, pitiful group of brand new employees in their first job. They usually get the worst hours, nastiest patients, and generally the short end of every stick, at least in the beginning. They are the brunt of hazing, practical jokes, and sabotage. Being a graduate nurse is risky business. Some nurses get so distraught at how they are mistreated that they never make it through the first year on the job, dropping out of nursing to pursue a different career path due to the sheer abusiveness of the professional nursing staff.

For some reason, these "professional nurses" cannot remember the time when they did not have the level of knowledge that comes with years of experience. I cannot understand how a woman who is the most loving mother at home can turn into a monster in the workplace who expects new graduates to instantly attain the knowledge and skills needed to function alone in a clinical setting. These same loving mothers refuse assistance and refuse to answer questions of new nurses. There are multiple articles about this—called, "Nurses - Eating our Young."

I am proud to say that I have never, ever treated anyone with this abuse. My philosophy is what I like to call maternal management. As I came up in the healthcare ranks, I projected authority, but I was not afraid to also project tenderness and care. Today, as the CEO of a nurse staffing agency I do not hesitate to put my arms around one of my nurses if I think she or he is in need of reassurance.

I feel so strongly about the need to mentor younger less experienced nurses because of how I was treated. After six weeks of classroom training and multiple certifications, I will never forget how I was mistreated. My boss was a Catholic nun who was a Registered Nurse and the Assistant Director of all of the Intensive Care Units. Nothing I did was right. I was used too many linens. I was accused of being wasteful, although, to this day, I cannot think of how I could have used less linens to make the beds. I was forbidden to wear gloves because she said that was a waste of good supplies, when I could just wash my hands. And so on and on it went.

My first patient was a beautiful, 27-year-old wife and mother of a three-year-old daughter. She had run a 107 degree temperature for two months with nothing to bring it down. Sometimes her fever would go higher than 108, which, at the time, was the highest any thermometer would register. She was so sick that the nun assigned her two RN's: Megan, a nurse that had graduated the year before me, and me. I was following Megan's lead because this was my first patient. But Megan and the doctors had no lead to follow, because no one had ever seen any disease like this. The diagnosis was disseminated tuberculosis. She had tuberculosis everywhere. This didn't make any sense because usually tuberculosis appears only in the lungs.

This beautiful girl needed to be on a ventilator to breathe. Although much of the time she was cooperative and appreciative of the care we gave, her hands had to be restrained. If given a chance, she might rip out the tubes and IVs. She became extremely agitated whenever her husband visited. She wrote on a chalk board that she wanted him to leave and that he had killed her. She constantly asked for her brother, a police officer, and

Diana working as a nurse

then begged him in writing to save her daughter from her husband.

One day it came to a head. Her brother was visiting when her husband showed up. This beautiful girl ripped the ventilator out of her throat and started screaming at her husband: "You killed me, you killed me. You gave me this terrible disease." We didn't lose her that day, but her husband never came back to see her. Her brother stayed at her bedside for another week until she died.

In the chaos, that afternoon, Megan was stuck by a contaminated needle. Six months later Megan and I each received a letter from the Louisiana Health Department warning us to go and get tested for a strange and unusual disease. My first patient was the first AIDS patient in Louisiana. It turned out that her husband had been working in Haiti. He had brought this disease back to his lovely wife. And the nun had not let me wear gloves.

My next patients would turn out to be my last at Schumpert. I had a hard day of two patients load in this very busy ICU. In those days, medications were given from "Med Cards," which were tiny little cardboard cards about one half the size of a business card that were handwritten for each medication. They were placed in a slot on the wall. The RN would then go to her 8:00 AM time slot, remove the cards, with the idea that they would never miss any of their 8:00 AM medications. Each nurse had her own wall board for her own medication cards.

I was sitting at the nursing station desk with its two-foot high pony counter. I was taking off orders. This was a task I was never very good at, as I worried incessantly that I would miss something important for a patient. I would pour over and over the orders, taking way too much time. The nun was leaning on the counter overlooking my work, scrutinizing my every move. I had limited work space for the multitude of paperwork I had to finish before I could leave for the day. I was writing my medication cards. As I wrote them, I placed them on the counter above my head out of my work area and right where the nun was standing. One patient had seventeen new medications, another patient had only three. I finished the 20 medication cards and moved on to completing my nurses notes for the day so that I could be ready for report. When I looked up all of my medication cards were gone.

I couldn't confront my boss because I knew I would be fired. I ran into the medication room and the cards were not in the slot. She had not placed them there. I knew she had the cards in her pocket but what could I do? I gave report, clocked out and rewrote the 20 medication cards, placing them in the medication slots in the med room before I left.

The next day when I arrived for work, I was allowed to receive report to take a full load of patients. Then I was pulled off the floor, into the ICU Director's office where the nun was sitting with a smirk on her face. I was handed a "write-up" for writing two sets of medication cards! I was told to bring the write-up to the basement and report myself by logging in the incident report with medical records. I was not allowed to say one word to defend myself. All the way down to medical records I debated with myself about quitting. I imagined walking out the door with the slanderous write-up and never coming back so no one would ever have that lie in writing. Instead, I decided to do as I was told. I was furious that I had been set up by my boss; I had only been on the job two months.

When I arrived at medical records, as far as the eye could see, there were "write ups" stacked in about three-foot-high piles. "What do you do with all these?" I asked the clerk.

"We file them as soon as we can," she said.

The stacks of "write-ups" frightened me. I did not want to have my first job end in a firing. I saw no way for me, a new RN, to win with my boss setting me up, and she was married to Jesus! I have wondered to this day what he thought about her behavior when she went to chapel and told him about her day.

I promptly turned in my resignation.

1982

Taking the Nursing Boards

Louisiana Registered Nurse State Boards were held in the New Orleans Gold Dome in February and July each year. I had delayed taking the state boards due to giving birth to Melanie, but as it turned out all of my closest nursing school girlfriends were taking state boards at the same time I was in February 1982.

As we girls loaded up in one car together to head down to New Orleans, our group was a mess. Carol Kaye had always been a year behind me. Ella, Madison, and Scarlet had failed the two-hour class. I had left a breast-fed baby at home and immediately my breasts became so engorged that by the end of the trip I had mastitis.

Madison had just learned that her husband had been cheating on her. Madison had three children: eleven, five, and a three-year-old she still breast fed. (She also got mastitis on the trip.) The day before we left for state boards, the three-year-old had told her about Daddy's girlfriend. When Madison drove the children down a road close to the girlfriend's house, the baby had said, "Daddy's girlfriend lives down there."

Madison had a 11P to 7A job in Newborn Nursery as a graduate nurse. As soon as she left for work at 10:30 PM, her husband would wake the sleeping children, load the children in the car, and they would all spend the night at Daddy's girlfriend's house. He was a Surgery RN and would get the kids dressed at the girlfriend's then drop them off at daycare, so he could be at work by 6:30 AM. He had threatened the children with their lives if they told their mother. The girlfriend and Madison looked like identical twins except that Madison was 4'11" and the girlfriend was 5'8".

During the trip, Madison was an absolute mess. She was taking Ativan and Valium and drinking large amounts of alcohol that had me frantic with worry because that was how all the movie stars died. Ella's husband also had a girlfriend and wanted a divorce, but Ella was trying to work things out with him. In my experience, that never works because for a relationship to work both people have to want it to work. Scarlet was also a mess because she had severe test anxiety and was not likely to pass the boards. Carol Kaye was smart; she dumped us and decided to stay with her friend Nancy.

I slept by Madison's side and she sobbed all night, so no one got any sleep. Madison was so hung over the next morning that I had to physically dress her. She insisted on wearing ridiculous outfits, such as a skirt with knee socks. She could not walk into the testing area by herself. I had to pull and guide her as she staggered. She didn't remember taking the tests, but she was so smart that she was on autopilot and scored really high on her State Boards.

Despite the three days of testing dissolving into one of the worst trips of my life, in incredible breast pain while running a fever, I too scored high on my State Boards. When I got to the pediatrics section, I somehow didn't turn the last couple of pages and neglected to finish that portion of the exam, but I still passed with a very high score.

When you travel with someone you really find out who they are. Frequently who they are is not someone you like. Or want to travel with. My take away from this trip was to always take your own car and get your own hotel room. I was so glad to be back home, away from my crazy miserable friends and back to my stable husband.

One day I left Melanie with a babysitter to attend a funeral for a close family friend. When I returned home from the funeral, my baby, that I had never left with anyone, (except her father) was not acting right. I stripped her down and noticed a water vesicle skin lesion that was consistent with a cigarette burn. I was livid. No one was going to burn my child. These were not the days of cell phones. I attempted to call the sitter to read her the riot act when I noticed another lesion had popped out, then another. By the time five-year-old Dana got home from school, she was covered with chicken pox. I realized that Melanie was in the early stages of breaking out with chicken pox. That night I found out what kind of father David was. Dana was miserable and could not sleep. I had to wrap her hands with gauze and put socks on them to keep her from scratching the sores and making scars. She cried incessantly. I tried rocking her to no avail. As a 45-pound kindergartener, I could no longer walk around and carry her.

David stripped her down to her underwear. In the cool, February night air, he carried her up and down the street until she finally fell asleep on his shoulder, so we could put her into bed.

Riverside ICU

I was now a Registered Nurse. After the nightmare at Schumpert was over, I was faced with the decision of either trying another job or giving up nursing. David insisted I try working as a RN again. I decided to go to a brand-new hospital, Riverside, that had recently opened in Bossier City, just over the bridge from our house.

Betty Grace was a beautiful, South African head nurse of the Intensive Care Unit, who worked 7A to 3P. She promised me I could work five days on and nine days off every two weeks from 11P to 7A! This job was perfect for my family. The ICU was small and rural with only eleven beds; however, in the early days, we would often go for days, weeks, and months without a patient. I was making $8.35 per hour. Unlike my previous boss, Betty was kind. She was the most competent nurse I have ever met, but a terrible schedule creator. She would patiently explain to me how to do a procedure then send me out with total confidence that I could do it. She believed in her staff which made her staff believe in themselves.

After two weeks of orientation, with hardly a patient to practice with, my first night was approaching. I had made Betty and the DON (Director of Nursing) both promise that I would work with an experienced nurse. Having the only BSN degree made me the likely nurse to be in charge if there were ever more than two ICU nurses working. The charge nurse had to make the schedule and know what to do in every situation. I didn't feel qualified yet. That first night I was relieved to know that an experienced nurse was going to be working with me on my first night shift. Imagine my surprise when Victoria exclaimed, "I am so glad you showed up, I have never worked ICU before!"

I flipped out for a second and then realized my error. I had made Betty and the DON promise I would have "an experienced nurse" not an "experienced ICU Nurse." Big, big difference. I was the "staff" assigned to the ICU Unit. That night, my first night ever working in the ICU unit as an RN, I was the official Charge Nurse. I sucked it up and decided that I would do the best I could because the patient needed me. Victoria said, " We will be OK, because the doctor is sleeping right down the hall." We were fine.

The hospital was so new, there were hardly any patients in the ICU the first year. I was always the Charge nurse because of my four-year degree. I was required to be present in the unit in case any patients showed up. The other nurse, an LPN, always had to float. That four-year degree finally came in useful for something. I would usually show up for work, have no patients, set my alarm, crawl into a patient bed, sleep all night and get up in time to make coffee for the day shift, then go home. One night, after months of not having a patient, I showed up to three patients. It had been almost a year of having one patient or less a month and we had never had three at one time. From that night forward, the ICU Unit was packed with patients. Sleeping was a thing of the past. I had to hire a babysitter because I could not go home refreshed after a full night's sleep anymore. I couldn't take care of my children all day. I had to work hard at night. Life got real. But with all that experience, I learned how to be an excellent ICU nurse.

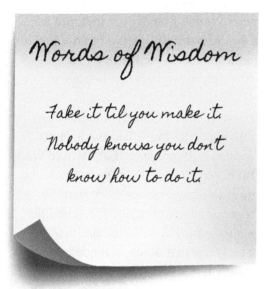

That Christmas, Riverside planned a wonderful Christmas Party for the entire staff. It was to be at the La Bossier, a new hotel in Bossier City. There was a meal, band, dancing, and glory! All the free alcohol the staff could drink! At 25, I was the average age of the rest of the staff. We were all young and looked forward to a rowdy party. Most of the nurses had been pregnant or breastfeeding the previous Christmas, in the early stages of motherhood that limits drinking. So, there was great anticipation for this party. Grace, one of the 3-11 nurses, even weaned her baby so she could drink that night. She frequently proclaimed, "I am going to get snot slinging drunk." Everyone thought this was very funny!

The night of the party arrived, and I wore a beautiful, new, red dress. We had a wonderful time dancing, eating, and drinking. Towards the end of the night, Grace could barely wobble out onto the dance floor when she passed a table, she grabbed the edge of a tablecloth and blew her nose on the tablecloth that covered the table at which the CEO and DON were sitting! Everyone, including David and I, roared with laughter. Grace had accomplished her goal to get snot slinging drunk.

Julia

Well, so did the rest of us, as David and I passionately arrived home, we had a wardrobe malfunction with a prophylactic. That night Julia was conceived. I knew that I was pregnant immediately. David and I were expecting again. We were both really happy and life was wonderful.

The pregnancy was unlike either of the other girls. I had never had so much as a stomach queeze with the previous pregnancies and now I vomited constantly. I spent my days throwing up, feeling famished and dehydrated, eating and throwing up. I was doing everything I was told. I ate dry toast, crackers before I got out of bed, limited water, sipped ginger ale, always kept potatoes baking. Absolutely nothing stopped the nausea.

I was working 3-11 PM in the ICU Unit, still in charge at Riverside. I worked with Aiden, a young, gay LPN. Aiden and I spent 24 to 40 hours a week together. We sat at the desk, shared secrets, and I felt like we were good friends. By then I was pregnant again. I had to have a trashcan in front of me at all times. I would be doing a procedure on a patient, lean over to vomit, and go back to what I was doing. Aiden started throwing things at the wall near where I was standing when I threw up, jokingly screaming at me, "I hate pregnant women!" When I would finish my patient care to come back to the desk to sit next to him, he would make up with me by saying, "But you are a damn good nurse."

This is the highest compliment for a nurse. You see, the world of nursing is made up of "good nurses" and "bad nurses," period. It is that black and white. Once a nurse gets a reputation as a "bad nurse," there is nothing she can ever do to fix it. Her only recourse is to leave the position to go work somewhere else. The sad thing is that this is so subjective that a nurse's reputation can change quickly with a change of staff or boss. The one thing that usually didn't change a "good nurse" into a "bad nurse" was the doctor's opinion, but of course that was pretty subjective as well.

Lucky for me, I looked the part of the "good nurse." I was trim, fit, neat, and looked good in my scrubs, which were always clean and fresh. I wore a lab coat over my scrubs primarily because the coat was warm and the scrub pockets over my breasts were not at the right angles to hold supplies, while the lab coat pockets were roomy. I owned the lab coats from having worked at Metpath Laboratories. Wearing them made me look more professional than my co-workers and because of the deep pockets I was more organized.

I learned several "tricks" to get along with the other staff members. Before I gave report, I made sure that my patients' rooms were completely clean. After I gave report, I would walk back through my patient rooms again to make sure that there was nothing out of place that could cause me to be negatively judged. I cannot tell you how many times a patient had thrown up, pooped, knocked over water, tried to climb out of bed, or otherwise made a mess that the oncoming nurse would have judged me by. But that never happened to me, because I made double sure that when I left the hospital, everything I touched was in better shape than when I found it.

There was a second thing I did to prevent staff judgment. I sat down one Saturday while in nursing school to figure out how to achieve an "A" on my nursing notes. I developed, memorized, and wrote the perfect narrative note that emphasized any patient exception. I needed a way to chart every day on multiple patients, while never missing anything. I needed my nurse notes to be reviewed, scrutinized, and stand up in court. From that day forward, I would use this style of charting throughout my nursing career. No one taught me how to chart like this in nursing school. My detailed nursing note, which was always the exact same nursing note on every patient, was exceptional. My nurse notes started at the top of the patient's head to the bottom of their feet, charting any IV or oxygen line and what was running through the line, detailing all injury, sore, bandage, drainage, bleeding or pain. My assessment notes left nothing out. The other nurses were all over the place with their notes and left things out all the time. I never left anything out, of that you can be certain.

After having been falsely accused at my first job at Schumpert, I never had another reprimand in over 40 years of working in the nursing field. I was always the boss and in charge from my first shift.

God blessed me with the ability to rapidly create a schedule and the inability to understand why no one else could do one. For me schedules were just so simple. You write in the staff's requested days off, the weekends they need off, and then fill in the rest of the days. Period. I could have the schedules done in a flash and staff were happy because they always had their requested time off.

As the pregnancy progressed, so did the nausea, until, one day, I just could not function any longer. I took a leave of absence at 33 weeks. I was at my wit's end with the throwing up. It was causing a serious depression, as I felt so bad. David and the children were affected. I decided I had to go to the library to try to figure out if there was anything that I could do to help myself for the last two months. After about five hours of reading articles on nausea and pregnancy, I finally found what I had been looking for. The article said that the fatigue, nausea, and vomiting of pregnancy can be blamed on hormones. When the vomiting is severe, a negative nitrogen balance occurs because of the starvation. The cure for the nausea was to eat pure protein and NO carbohydrates at all. I had been living on a carbohydrate nausea diet for 33 weeks while getting sicker and sicker. I went home and ate slices of cheese, hamburger patties, eggs, and protein shakes in a can I had frozen. I cut out the bottom of the can and ate the frozen protein shake like ice cream. It was June, July, and August in Louisiana; it was hot! Within hours the nausea subsided and went away. For the rest for the pregnancy, as long as I ate pure protein, I felt fine. When I added carbohydrates, I got nauseated. This was my first

Dana's ballet recital and Diana holding Melanie

experience where what was generally accepted medical practice didn't work, wasn't accurate, and made me worse.

This pregnancy was hard on me, and, as a result, it was hard on David. I was sick for seven months. Our relationship suffered. I complained about never being pregnant again, so, at the end of May, David scheduled a vasectomy.

David never listens to my medical advice. He usually dismisses it immediately while frequently doing just the opposite of what I advise. This approach never seems to work out for him. But this is our modus operandi. I advise, and he devises.

I had experience with vasectomies. My good friend Matthew had a vasectomy; I had gone with him. Matthew is an unmarried pharmacist that I had known for years before I met David. You never knew when Matthew was going to show up at our house. He would just appear in the evening to stay for hours. Frequently, David and I would get up, go to bed, leaving Matthew watching TV, drinking beer alone in our living room. Matthew didn't really have much of a life; he never wanted kids. Matthew wanted me, a nurse, to go with him to make sure that the doctor did everything right. I held his hand during the procedure, then took him home, got his prescription, and made him something to eat. Matthew wanted the strangest thing to eat. He wanted me to take a can of black eye peas and boil a cup of instant rice with the peas. It was Hoppin' John[3] made with no nutritious ingredients. I was horrified he ate this way.

Matthew had received IV Valium and pain medication. He had local anesthesia at the incision site. All in all, the procedure did not appear to be terrible. Matthew was not in pain. When I left he had taken a pain pill and was laying on the couch. Later that afternoon, Matthew felt so good he decided to pull the engine out of his car. He suffered a testicular hemorrhage.

David and I met with the doctor. He explained the procedure then asked David if he wanted the IV Valium and pain medication. David asked, "Does it hurt?" "No", replied the doctor, so against my medical advice, my husband declined all meds, except the local for the incision. Unlike Matthew's straight forward procedure, the doctor could not find David's second vas deferens, so he had to probe, dig, look, and cut. All without anesthesia. By the time we left the doctor's office David was so worn out that he laid on the couch the whole weekend to recover. Unfortunately, David had to go back for rechecks for 10 months after the vasectomy before we finally got an "all's clear". We never got pregnant again.

I unofficially went into labor with Julia on Sunday night, four days before she was scheduled to be induced at 37 weeks. I had been in and out of Braxton Hicks contractions for months. That Sunday morning, I awoke with terrible respiratory congestion, so I called my friends at the ICU unit, went up to work, and got several nebulizer treatments so I could deliver. I had been preventing contractions by drinking four ounces of wine, taking two Tylenol, and taking a hot bath. In the four days before Julia was born, I was doing this protocol about every four hours.

On Thursday, August 18, 1983, I was to be at the hospital about 5:30 for the induction. As David and I got into the car, I told him, "I think I am in labor, as the contractions were regular and hard". The hospital Labor and Delivery Unit was completely full, with no beds available. The night staff placed me on a gurney and put me in the supply room, then failed to check on me. My doctor was a friend of mine. He had delivered Melanie, so he and I had developed a rapport over the years. At 6:45AM, shift change, a nurse came running in the supply room to get something for another patient and I called to her, "I think I am in labor." She snapped at me, "You'll be in labor when I start the drip!' And rushed out of the supply room leaving me and David alone. About 7:30 AM, Dr. Jenkins came in to check on me. The nasty nurse came in with him to start the IV and the Pitocin drip, while Dr. Jenkins did an exam. He looked up and said, "Turn off the drip! Didn't you check her when she told you she thought she was in labor? She's at an 8! We need to get her out of this supply room and down to the delivery room right now, this is her third baby! Call Anesthesia for an epidural!" With Jenkins firing off orders the staff jumped into action, performing like a Labor and Delivery Unit should.

The Labor and Delivery Unit was in chaos because the

Unit Director, Layla, who I went to church with, was also in labor that morning with her third child. Layla had two boys at home that were about two and four years old. Our children were in the

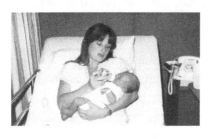

Diana and Julia, August 18, 1983

same classes at church. The nurses were all excited about her delivery and were fixated on Layla. They ignored the rest of the delivering and post-partum mothers. They were having a party in Layla's room, betting on what time she would deliver. I delivered Julia at 9:30

AM, my third girl, several hours before any of the other mothers delivered. I recovered quickly from the birth and did not feel sick. Layla delivered her third boy at 12:00 noon.

Late that afternoon I was relaxing, peacefully marveling over the beauty of my new daughter, when Layla came in to see my beautiful baby girl. I always thought my babies were more beautiful than anyone else's children (but doesn't every mother). Layla started talking about how pretty my girls were. She talked about how we were both nurses, our husbands were both engineers, how we had three girls and she had three boys. Our families had so much in common. Then she dropped the bombshell: "You know, no one would know if we exchanged babies. Then you could have a boy and we could have a girl. It would be perfect, we would both get what we wanted." Except I had already gotten exactly what I wanted! I wanted this beautiful, gorgeous, perfect, little, baby girl. I wanted our baby, not Layla's son. I was terrified! Here I was in her Unit and she wanted my baby! She had the ability to change the names on the birth certificates and the sex in the birth records, so no one would ever know. All I could think was, "Of course she wants one of my kids, hers are all so loud!" But I was really scared. I thanked her but said I could not part with Julia. Layla sadly said she understood and quietly left the room. I wanted to leave with Julia.

I had requested a single room a month in advance but because of the number of patients delivering that afternoon I soon had a roommate named Nora. Nora had a baby die the year before at birth. When she arrived in my room, she was running a fever and throwing up all over the floor. There were so many patients the nurses fell terribly behind. They were not cleaning the vomit up, so the room reeked with the smell of vomit on this hot August evening.

Nora was distraught because she had not been allowed to see her baby, because of her fever and vomiting. The baby had been kept in the nursery; the staff were refusing to bring the baby to the room because they did not want Nora to contaminate her own baby with an illness. (And it was perfectly all right for Nora to contaminate me and my baby). I buzzed and buzzed and buzzed for help to no avail. After waiting for almost an hour, I finally walked down to the nurses' station for help and there was no one there! This was unheard of. I waited for 30 minutes and never saw a staff member. I was forced to return to the sobbing Nora. I was growing furious. It was ridiculous that this mother was being denied the mental security of knowing if her child was all right.

Nora was convinced her baby was dead. The staff had the knowledge that her baby was well and it was being withheld from her. Her husband was useless. Nora's biggest problem was her husband was not sympathetic to her emotional distress. He was intent on seeing me naked. I would close my curtains to try to feed Julia who was not eating, and he would open my curtains. I would go to the bathroom; he would open the door. It was harassment: embarrassing and uncomfortable. My husband was at home caring for our other children. So here I was, alone, in the hospital, feeling very vulnerable the day I delivered my baby, having to deal with a potential kidnapper, a pervert, and his sobbing wife.

With my nerves pushed to the limit, I finally pitched a fit with the Newborn Nursery RN telling her how cruel she was being not letting Nora see that the baby was alive by just bringing her to the door. That worked. After two hours the RN finally walked the baby down for Nora to see so she would stop crying. I asked her to get our nurse to come to the room to help Nora (and clean up vomit). I had not seen a nurse since 10:00 that morning and now it was 5:30 pm. When the nurse showed up, Nora said, "I need some apple juice, that always stops me from throwing up. I need some medicine for nausea." The RN looked at me to order me, "Go get her some apple juice, stop by the desk, and I will give you her meds!" By this point I was beyond done with this staff, but because Nora needed help, I worked as an unpaid nurse on the day I delivered my last baby!

Just when I thought the day couldn't get any worse, Julia would not feed. The baby cried and fussed and struggled. She suffered from torticollis where her neck muscles on one side were longer than the muscles on the other side, causing her cheek to lay on her left shoulder. This was caused by her head being wedged in an odd position in the uterus that limited her movement in utero. What I didn't know at that time, was that the reason Julia would not feed was because her collarbone had broken, as her head could not turn properly during the birthing process. It hurt her to put her into a position to nurse. So, as I struggled to feed this crying baby, Nora's pervert husband peeped through the curtains.

Words of Wisdom

A crucial lesson that David and I learned from this experience is that no one should ever be left in the hospital alone. I should have had someone with me the entire time I was in the hospital to protect me from the abuse I suffered.

By 5:00 AM, twelve hours after Nora became my roommate, I had had all I could take. I was going home. I called

David and told him, " Come get me I am leaving without medical consent." He refused to come get me. I was furious and entertained myself by showering, putting on my makeup, and packing all of my things. When Dr. Jenkins arrived about 7:30, he discharged me home with medical consent; David showed up about 30 minutes later. I was so relieved when we finally arrived home with our daughter; we were safe from a pervert and potential kidnapper. Just when I thought things couldn't get worse, my neighbor showed up.

Paula, David's sister, and her new husband Robert came to pick up Dana and Melanie to keep them for several days so that I could recover from the birth. David was exhausted from the birth and the fact I had called him every fifteen minutes starting at 5:30 AM that morning, begging him to come and bring us home from the terrible hospital. *Julia Wright, August 28, 1983*

I was napping in our bedroom; David was asleep on the couch. I was awakened by the back door opening and someone walking into our kitchen. By the time I got up and walked barefoot to the kitchen, my neighbor, with her Double EE boobs, had sat on the side of the couch, pushed her boobs in David's face and was crooning softly, "David, David, wake up, I need some help. Can you come down to my house and help me out with my bicycle right now?" I was furious. It is a low blow to hit on your neighbor's husband the day after a birth!

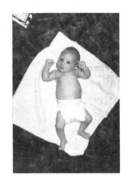

I decided to give David enough rope to hang himself. I stood very still and said nothing, watching his every move from the kitchen doorway. David jerked, stiffened, and tried to pull away from the giant boobs with nowhere to go except deeper into the couch. His reaction told me everything I needed to know. My husband was not interested in her. David then firmly and possibly too loudly shouted, "NO!" I stepped out of the kitchen and she ran from the house. She had never been my friend.

My week was just getting better. The next day was raining and hot, when the electricity went out. Back then when the electricity went out, we did not have phone service. Or air conditioning. So, Paula did not have a way to call me to let me know she was bringing the children home early. I was sitting in the living room rocking Julia when Paula and Robert drove up, depositing Dana and Melanie. They said they had to get back to Hot Springs immediately. Dana and Melanie had been with Paula for less than 24 hours. It was a good thing I felt fine and was able to care for my children.

Halloween

Halloween rolled around that year and I dressed the children to go trick or treating with my friend Don and his daughter Donna. We took the children trick or treating up and down Patton Street then to A.C. Steer Elementary School for a carnival. I was always very particular about my children being in bed at 8:00 PM, but that night we stayed out later. When we arrived home, David told me that Mama had called, she could not breathe, and I needed to go get her. As usual, these days whenever she called with some last-minute emergency, I did a slow burn. It was just like her to call on Halloween and get the holiday focused on her. She was intensely jealous of the children. She threw a fit if I took care of one of the babies before getting her whatever she wanted.

David and I had enjoyed three years of marital honeymoon pretty much without Mama or Luther's interference. Mama had a job she liked working nights and sleeping days. It did not leave enough time for her to create chaos in our lives. She was busy for the first time in her life. Luther was busy starting his own photography studio and chasing women who he felt he had to introduce to me for my stamp of approval. All of that was fixing to change, and not for the better.

I drove over to her house on College Street, not knowing if she was just wanting attention or was really

Diana, Dana, and friend Destiny, Halloween

sick. She was really sick. I loaded her in the car and took her to Riverside Hospital where she was admitted to the Intensive Care Unit. Mama had been sick since August with a sore throat but because she was working at night in a state-run facility for the mentally challenged, she felt that she could not take off work to go to the doctor. It was interesting she developed a work ethic in the last years of her life.

Mama had received no medical care for strep throat that simple antibiotics would have cured. She had full blown scarlet fever when she was admitted to the ICU. Dr. Hannah Evans, a cardiologist, began the work up on her. Hannah and I had worked together for several years. She was the best cardiologist available. I was still on maternity leave. Because I was the best cardiac nurse present in the ICU unit that night, I worked unpaid beside Dr. Evans to stabilize Mama to save her life that night.

The Intensive Care Unit is a closed unit, meaning visitors are not allowed to stay with the family members, with strict visiting times enforced. I knew I couldn't leave when the new nurse on duty did not know the equipment cart well enough to gather the supplies that Dr. Evans wanted. Together, we put in a Swanz-Ganz catheter, multiple lines, and gave cardiac medications. We basically performed what is known as a slow code, on Mama. Dr. Evans and I worked together until well past midnight that Halloween night to save Mama's life. Finally, she was stabilized.

Dr. Hannah was a young, female, homosexual doctor, just a few years older than me. We occasionally hung out at her house where she lived with an older nurse practitioner. Because she was always struggling with peer recognition as the only woman physician, surrounded by male doctors, she was very strict with her title. I could call her Hannah out of the hospital, but only Dr. Evans in the hospital.

One day, Hannah went to the ICU bathroom. She was dressed in the fashion of the 1980's with a full, floor length skirt, a large collared shirt, and a sweater vest pulled over the shirt. As she exited the bathroom her skirt was tucked neatly into her underwear with her entire behind showing. "Hannah, Hannah!" I furiously whispered, desperate to get her attention just feet away from the male doctors sitting at the desk, who had not yet had time to notice. They loved to harass Dr. Evans. She whirled on me, "I have told you repeatedly NOT to call me Hannah at work! I am Dr. Evans to you!" This was possibly the worst thing she could have done because when she turned to upbraid me, this exposed her fanny to the male team of doctors, who looked at each other and smiled maliciously. I was furious, here I was, trying to protect her and keep her exposed behind a secret. She was quite literally, "showing her butt" to the very men I was trying to protect her from. I said, "Yes, Ma'am!" and hurried away quite wounded that she would talk to me so forcefully. A short while later she came over to me and asked, "Were you trying to tell me about my skirt?" I replied, "Yes, Ma'am" and walked away.

I would like to say that Dr. Evans learned I was on her side, but we had several more incidents where she thought I was not respectful enough to her, when I was trying to save her butt. Literally.

One night, I arrived at 11 PM to find Dr. Evans admitting a patient to the ICU Unit. I got coffee, took report, everyone left, and I went in to see the patient. I was working alone in the ICU Unit when my patient cardiac arrested. I pulled the CODE Blue cord, ran for the crash cart, and no one came. The Code Blue button alarmed in the Emergency Room. They did not have any patients and it was a beautiful night; the staff were smoking and sitting outside. I started CPR alone, desperately waiting for help, but no one came. I screamed for help every time I did heart compressions. No one came. I finally ran to the door that joined the Medical Surgical Unit and screamed down the empty hall for help. That got an LPN to help me. I got her started on CPR and ran to page overhead the Code Blue. The Emergency Room Doctor was there in a flash and started running the code, I had started pushing the drugs to hopefully save the man's life when I realized I had not called Hannah! OMG! You did not work on one of her patients without her. I raced to the phone and placed a call to the sleepy doctor. I explained that 103 was a Code Blue and she flat out called me liar! Really??! I have never ceased to be amazed that people who are not present when something is happening can decide to call you a liar. "Okay, Dr. Simmons (the ER doctor) and I are coding him; I can't talk" and hung up the phone. I knew that would get her because she didn't like anyone else working on her patients, especially an Emergency Room fill-in like Dr. Simmons.

In a few minutes, way too few for the drive she had to get from her house to the hospital, she was there. As she walked into the room she had left less than an hour before, she didn't recognize the man in the bed. People in the throes of death look very different than they do when they are alive. "That is not my patient", she glared accusingly at me. I never said a thing; I never looked up; I did not challenge her; I just kept pushing the drugs ordered by the ER doctor. A few minutes went by with Dr. Evans staring at the unrecognizable patient, until the ER Doctor finally asked her if she wanted to assume control of the code. Recognition began to slowly resolve her doubts that the man in the bed was the patient she had known. Dr. Evans snapped back in full control. Now that was the Hannah I knew. Hannah really was the best physician ever.

Hannah diagnosed Mama with a strep throat that had not been treated. Her heart valves and pancreas had been destroyed by the strep. She was on the verge of death. Mama would be a diabetic from this day forward. She would have open heart surgery with a pig valve to replace her ruined valve. Mama could have prevented all of this damage by a prescription of antibiotics.

Just before Thanksgiving, within two weeks of initial diagnosis, Mama had open heart surgery. Julia was not even three months old and breast fed. My neighbor said she would keep her, so I could be with Mama the day of open-heart surgery. That day, I ran to the hospital, then back home to fed Julia, then to the hospital, and back to Julia again. Mama had prayed that she would have no pain with her surgery and, miraculously, she did not have any pain after open heart surgery. She never took a pain pill at any time, but her energy was limited. She died in inches over the next four years.

Mark told me he would stay in the hospital that night since I had been at the hospital all day so that I could go home and breast feed three-month old Julia. I waited all day for him to finally get to the hospital, running back every four hours to feed a new baby that wanted to eat every two hours. I left, thinking everything would be all right with Mark there. I was not home 30 minutes when the nursing staff called me, wanting to know where the family was, as Mark had left Mama alone the minute I was out of sight. He just couldn't emotionally take being in the hospital with her. I soon found out that David and I were the only people that would physically and financially care for her until her death.

Mama never had a pain after her open-heart surgery. God had answered her prayers. I was completely allopathic at that time and could not integrate God or any naturopathic medical concepts into healthcare (Thank God that all changed later). So, I really did not understand her painless recovery. She was released from the hospital almost immediately to came home to David's and my house.

Our home had a guest room with a bathroom that Mama could use. She was on oxygen full time. This limited her movement in the house to where the 25-foot extension tubing would reach. The tubing reached almost the entire length of the house.

I soon found out how much David loved me. David, like everyone else, did not like wisdom from Mama because Mama spent all of her time saying things that made her as unloving and unlovable as a person could possibly be. Mama had a talent for discerning the soft spots of a person's heart and exploiting them. My husband was anti-racist and a pacifist. Mama would make racial comments and talk about beating people up in his presence, which hardened his heart against her. But she was sick, and she could not get up to go to the bathroom alone, so my sweet husband assisted Mama to the bathroom, waiting on her when I was not at home. Now that is love and sacrifice.

Before Mama moved in with us, she thought the girls were cute. After she moved in, she saw them as a direct interference in my attention to her. Mama was always eaten up with jealousy. She was jealous of everyone and anything. Mama became so jealous of the children, that life became more and more difficult. They were the enemy. The children: ages seven, two, and three months were obstacles in her self-centered universe; she wanted them gone. She started causing as much conflict as you could possibly cause with very small children, two that didn't even talk. I think in her demented mind she thought I might give up my children and just take care of her, if she caused enough conflict. She was doing everything possible so that I was not able to care of her and the children both.

If I was preparing lunch and started putting the plates on the table, woe unto me if I put a child's plate on the table before Mama's, because in her mind she came before everyone and everything. She would get hysterical screaming, "Me, not them!" If a child was crying and needed something, she would immediately pitch a fit superseding the child's need and making herself a priority. There was no peaceful recourse except to mollify her, then take care of the child because one thing for sure, none of my children could ever escalate to the fireworks of Mama. Nobody could, except Luther.

Luther had behavioral problems with everyone. He fought with, stalked, and verbally, emotionally, and physically abused his girlfriends. He fought with his parents and his friends. When he was getting out of control he would call me. The problem was, he called me three or four times a day, so I would talk him down from whatever crazy behavior he was considering. I was very good at talking crazy people down, I had a lifetime of practice with Mama. Luther started the crazy calls about 7:30 AM under the guise of talking to his daughter, "What is my child doing?" He would ask. "She is eating breakfast", I would reply. "What is she eating", and here is where it always got sticky. No matter what I replied, his response was exactly the same. No matter if I said, "Oatmeal", "Eggs and Toast", or "Donuts", his response was, "I do not want her eating that, I am on my way over there right now!" I then would start the talk down therapy, where I would attempt to reason with him, without ever challenging him. I knew that if I challenged him it would be World War III and I had better be prepared to take it all the way. So the hill I would die on had better be a good one. Until that day arose, and I made the decision to enter into a full-fledged war, I would try patiently to appeal to him, as one of his only friends in the world. I pretty much was.

197

He picked up the calls again as soon as Dana was home from school. "What is my daughter doing", again the response did not matter, "Homework", "A snack", "Playing with a friend", it was all an excuse for him to escalate into, "I am coming over". Interestingly enough, he did not want to talk to his child in the morning or afternoon but would want to talk to Dana before bedtime. He called to talk to me. Years of experience with Mama taught me how to deal with this very angry, sick man. The basic reason he called several times a day is that after he spoke to me, he was calmed down enough to not do the crazy thing he was considering.

Mama continued to have bad behavior, which escalated. She acted out continuously. Mama never acted out as badly with Mark or David as she did with me. She felt like she had immunity with me. My female opinion didn't count, so she could do whatever she wanted. She always had. One evening we sat down for supper, and Mama started slapping at Melanie, our two-year-old. David firmly in a very hard voice said, "You are to NEVER slap one of my children again". She stopped and never tried again.

All I knew was that Mama had to get out of my house. Between Mama and Luther, I was squeezed and torn up every day. I could not live life like this and stay married. Which was exactly what Mama wanted. She would say, "If you would get rid of David we all would be happy". No, I wouldn't!

Get rid of David??!!! He supported us: he worked every day, he cleaned the cars, the yard, and probably worked harder in the house picking up as much or more than I did. But the real reason I could never let him go was that he was the love of my life. In my heart, he came before the children, Mama, or anything or anyone else. We had a healthy, mutually exclusive relationship. We were deeply in love.

Mama had to go. It was apparent that Mama would never be able to work again. She had to have health insurance. I went out to the state-run facility, where she had worked, and found out about Cobra. I got Mama's insurance extended 18 months. Each month for the next 18 months, I drove her health insurance payment 22 miles to the state home for mental retardation, where I would get a receipt that I kept. I also signed her up for Social Security, Disability, and Medicare.

Mama could not go back to the shack that she had before. It was drafty, overrun with roaches, and packed with belongings she had rummaged from other peoples' trash. 1116 College was cold in the winter and hot in the summer. She had to move to an apartment where the temperature was constant.

David and I paid for her to move into an apartment not far from our home. With a two-year-old and a three-month-old in tow, I singlehandedly moved Mama into her new apartment, hauling a double bed, triple dressers, recliners, a TV set, table, chairs, and too many other filthy items in truck load after truck load to furnish the apartment. I asked David and Mark, but neither of them had time to help me. I did it myself.

As I cleaned up Mama's house and packed up her belongings, I found outdated checks tucked everywhere. When I would bring one to her she would laugh and say, "I forgot where I hid it." They were everywhere and dated from 1959. The relatives had literally sent her thousands of dollars over the years that she had squirreled away and never cashed. The checks represented money that could have prevented us children from going hungry or cold. What was surprising was that the checks came from so many different people who had tried to help this crazy woman and her children. Mental illness is a hideous affliction.

As bad as this sounds, I could not bring myself to clean up the disgusting mess that was 1116 College. There was roach poop two inches high in the pantry. The holes in the floor let in rats and dead rat carcasses were stuck to the floor under the furniture I moved out. I had no idea how to get rid of the mounds of pillaged trash she had drug home for years. I decided to leave it in the apartment when we moved out.

For some reason I will never understand, Mark came over to see what was left in the filth covered apartment and decided that he would move his wife, Michelle, and baby, Kevin, in that mess. So, he did. I have always felt guilty about leaving Michelle in that mess that day and walking away. But I had all I could say Grace over. I was overburdened.

Mama's furniture that she had received in the divorce 25 years ago was beyond use and infested with vermin, so David and I allowed her to pick out a brand-new set of living room furniture. In true Mama fashion, she picked out the ugliest, most uncomfortable, most expensive, brown, flower print couch and loveseat. It was so dreadful I knew I had just thrown $1000.00 away. It truly was the worst couch and loveseat imaginable.

1984

In February 1984, David had to go to Gentry, Arkansas to work at Flint Creek Power Plant. He specialized in taking the huge turbine engines apart that made the electricity. The turbines were the size of a 3000 square foot house. As a mechanical engineer, he was responsible for knowing how every bolt and screw came out and, more importantly, how they went back together. If any part was not in the correct position when it was reassembled, it would cause tremors, shaking in the engine, and tear up these multi-million-dollar engines. It was a huge project that took weeks to disassemble, clean the parts, then reassemble the engine.

The minute David left, my life started to fall apart. Mama had to go back into the hospital. I struggled balancing her and the children alone. I decided to wean Julia because I was having so many problems trying to be at the hospital with Mama and at home breast feeding Julia. This caused Julia to immediately start having one ear infection after another. So now I had a sick Mama and a sick baby.

But it didn't stop there. We had a hail storm that ruined the roof of our home. The ruined roof leaked water into the kitchen and living room. About this same time my dishwasher got stopped up, overflowed, and the water ran up under the cabinets and the floorboards. The linoleum buckled. It was like walking in a fun house when I walked in the kitchen. As we had home owner's insurance to cover water damage, I called my insurance agent who sent a man out to inspect the damage. This man cut a three-foot by three-foot hole in the center of my kitchen floor, taped a plastic bag over the hole and promised he would be back the next day to fix it. I had a crawling baby, a two-year-old, and an out of control seven-year-old, with a large hole that dropped four feet under my house in the center of my kitchen floor for over a month. Of course, he did not come back. I called the insurance agent to accuse him of sending his brother-in-law. The insurance agent had a crew out fixing the hole and replacing the linoleum the next day.

David did not send any money or pay the bills. He was working 12-hour days, seven days a week, living in hotels, and not completing his expense reports. To get ahold of him I had to have him paged over the loudspeaker at the power plant. Then, I had to wait for him to come to the office to take the phone call. In those days, everyone was terrified of long-distance phone bills. I don't think I was afraid of them because I had not grown up with a phone or the admonitions and fear of the long-distance phone call. David, however, was just not going to run up a phone bill with long distance charges. He did not call me during this time period. I became increasingly distraught with the obstacles I was dealing with at home. He became less and less inclined to call a woman on the verge of a nervous breakdown, when he was exhausted. We were both at an impasse. I needed physical, emotional, and financial support, while he needed rest. I asked him many times why he didn't call me during that time and he replied, "You yelled at me".

Unfortunately for David, his short-term decision to avoid conflict by choosing not to call me caused me to make long term decisions that were not in his favor for many years to come. This was a dividing point in our marriage, that his picking up the phone could have prevented. By the time he got home, my heart for him was hardened. David never considered coming home to see his family and he would never agree to allow me to visit. His refusal to see his children and me was unhealthy for our relationship.

David's Grandfather died during this time. He told me I was not allowed to go to the funeral, so I called Paula, his sister. Melanie, Julia, and I drove to Illinois to his Grandmother's house. To my surprise, and delight, David met me there. We had a wonderful reunion under the bleakest of circumstances.

Since David was no longer paying the bills, I had to go back to work full time in the ICU. There was not a full-time position at Riverside, so I took a 11P-7A position at P&S Hospital in the ICU Unit. It was a miserable experience. Not at all exciting and fun like Riverside. The staff were mostly fifty and sixty-year-old black women who were LPN's, Nurse Aides, and a Ward Clerk. They were not thrilled about the arrival of a young, white, BSN RN. Instead of my salvageable cardiac and trauma patients from Riverside, P&S had a surplice of terminal stroke and cancer patients that were old and dying. The only other young, white nurse was the girlfriend of a doctor with narcolepsy I had worked with at Riverside, who frequently fell asleep with his head in unusual spots on the patient's bed. I had actually called

Julia Wright, 5 months old

the DON and had her come down to experience it for herself when he could not be awakened, with his nose stuck to a patient's rectum. While the girlfriend did not know me, I had heard too many unflattering stories about her from him. I felt very awkward working with her. Work was a disaster. Home was a disaster. I was a total mess.

My best friend Trisha decided to help me by babysitting for an entire weekend 7A-11P (working doubles), both Saturday and Sunday, so I could get caught up on the bills. It usually took both David and I working to pay the current bills. It was becoming increasingly apparent if David did not show back up, I was not going to be able to continue the current Broadmoor lifestyle. I was facing a divorce, a move, the care of three small children, Mama, and worried about a crazy ex-husband. It was overwhelming just to think about.

That weekend, while Trisha babysat, the TV blew up. I have no idea what happened; I was at work. I came home to a very large black spot on the living room wall and a TV that did not work. Trisha had dead bolted the screen door hook into the dead bolt. I had to call a locksmith to come out to take the door apart to fix it. Another $50.00. But whatever it cost that weekend was worth it to me mentally.

Trisha will never know how much that weekend helped me

emotionally. The ability to go to work in the Intensive Care Unit to get myself together was invaluable. I got caught up financially and emotionally. I don't know how taking care of the sickest of the sick patients could reground me, but it did. I was rested. I had moved from despair to anger. I was furious with David for abandoning me and the children. Anger had me full of energy with the ability to take action. I decided to go to counseling to help me decide what to do about David.

I had never been to counseling in my life. I always disagreed with the advice. I decided to go to counseling anyway. The counselor told me that there was nothing left of the relationship, that David had abandoned me, and I needed to move on with a divorce. I was not there mentally or emotionally, but I was growing increasingly furious with David every day for not calling me, when he knew all that I was going through.

Julia was increasingly sick; the pediatrician said she had to have tubes surgically inserted. I had kept a sinus infection since I was nineteen, when Luther had hit me in the eye, fracturing my orbit and causing a continuous infection that could not heal. The doctor said I could no longer put off having a repair as the bone was "soft" from the infection. Mama had returned several times to the hospital with congestive heart failure. Dana was having asthma with terrible allergies. I had to figure out how to continue to go to work to support us and take care of everyone at home. Life was increasingly difficult.

Julia had surgery. I had surgery. My surgery was more than I thought it would be. Pauline, David's mother, offered to keep the children while I had surgery. My surgery did not go as well as anticipated: I spent eleven days in the hospital. In retrospect, I should have waited until David returned, but I did not think he would. I had his insurance, so I agreed to have the surgery. Mama had my car while I was in the hospital. One Saturday, she locked the keys in the car. That cost me $50.00 to call a locksmith out to unlock it in the hospital parking lot. The next Wednesday, she wrecked it. So now I was out a car. That was life with Mama.

Mama drove like a bat out of hell. She only knew one speed: the accelerator pushed completely to the floor and the other foot on the brake. David says Mama never learned from her mistakes. This was certainly true of any car she ever touched. She wrecked, stripped, dented, ripped headliners out, and tore up anything she could with brute force, in a car. Now she had (almost) totaled my car. The car had been a disaster when David bought it for me. Now, after the repairs, it rattled and made such funny noises that people would get out of their cars at red lights to come see what was going on with my car. This was embarrassing. I drove the disaster car for twelve years.

That early warm April day I got out of the hospital weighing 105 pounds. I had lost fourteen pounds in eleven days. That afternoon, so weak I could hardly walk, I attempted to get my health back by walking the sidewalk. My neighbors came out to check on me and advised me to "Go eat!". But despite my lack of health, I was still responsible for the children. God is good! In a few days I felt well.

I woke up on my birthday, April 10, 1984, when I turned 27 years old. I had not heard from David in weeks. He had not sent flowers when I was in the hospital. I called him at the power plant. While I waited the 20 minutes for him to walk to the phone, I thought about my day. Finally, David was on the line. I said, "Hello, it's my birthday. I am letting you know what I am doing today. I am moving you out. I am starting with your stereo, speakers, clothes, and finishing with all your tools in the garage. I am putting everything out on the street. I should be through about 5:00 PM, so if you want any of it, maybe you should come get it." I hung up without his reply and unplugged the phone. I would not be taking any phone calls that day.

Somehow this promise resonated with David. By 4:00 PM, he had driven the six hours that had been "too far to come home". His job was over (the turbine was repaired) and he did not return. David had always been very gentle. He had never been physically aggressive, but that day, when he charged into the house, he took me down to the floor with his kisses. The man who had not seen me in two months was overcome with passion, but we had three little children so that had to wait.

I wish I could say that I got over my anger with him that

year, but the difficulty of this time changed me. I no longer trusted that David wanted the best for me or the children. I think the financial withdrawal had just been the final blow for me. I knew "if it was to be, it was up to me". I started slowly, first by changing the way I shopped for groceries: I started by clipping coupons and shopping on Tuesday for Double Coupon Day. I would only purchase items that I had a coupon for. I would then write a check for the amount of the groceries and pocket the money from the coupons. I was not stealing any money from the household, I only pocketed the exact amount of money I was given, to secure my children's future. I would not be stuck again like I had been when David had forgotten to help me pay the bills. I hoarded money any time I could get it. I hid my coupon money in a chest of drawers of sewing supplies up in the attic. My goal was to get six months of survival money in the event the children and I had to experience another "departure". I would have enough money to pay for deposits, rent, and buying groceries.

Words of Wisdom

You cannot get ahead with a car note. Cars are a depreciable asset. Money should never be invested in depreciable assets such as clothing, cars, CD's, or eating out. I have always tried to invest my money in non-depreciable assets that make money over time such as guns, gold, and houses.

I decided to stay with David because he was a very good father and roommate with many good qualities. He was so clean, paid the bills, and was good to the children. David and I had never combined our money by his choice. This probably would have helped at this point to improve solidarity in our marriage. David wanted to keep his money separate from mine. David did not share his money. The problem was David had money, but I didn't have

THE UNBELIEVABLE PLIGHT OF MRS. WRIGHT

any. We had only been married for three years. I was to pay for the childrens' education, medical care, my gas, the groceries, any lessons the children took, and Mama. David paid the mortgage, utilities, insurance, car repairs (we never had a note), and credit card bills (which we did not use). I never had a dime. I literally bought my and the children's clothes at Goodwill and Salvation Army. One summer, when Melanie was two, Mama found a box of size four little girl clothes that had been thrown out on the side of the road. It was a Godsend. Melanie, Julia, and Trisha's girls, Amy and Tracy, all wore that box of used clothes. Rosemary, David's sister, was still sending boxes of used clothing for Dana. I do not know what I would have done without these clothes. I had absolutely no money. Whenever I complained to David, "I have no money for groceries", he replied, "McDonald's is hiring, maybe you ought to take a second job". He thought this was funny. I thought this was mean. I was working as hard as I could.

I was fed up with not having money. I decided that I had to make a plan and develop some goals. I would divide my goals into tasks, the tasks into steps, and do the steps, thus accomplishing my goals and my plan for financial success. I was done with being poor.

So, I started working my steps. Just like my Aunt Tirr said, I needed to be prepared in life, because it became increasingly apparent that no Prince Charming was going to swoop in and make everything perfect. I decided that I needed to get a master's degree. I wanted to go to Law School, but there wasn't one in Shreveport. I started working on getting accepted at LSUS for my MBA.

I was not able to manage any additional problems. I just had too many problems of my own. My nursing school friends had continued to deteriorate into divorces, self-destructive behavior, all of them losing custody of their children. Our relationships had dissolved into me trying to talk them out of one bad decision after another. I was spending all my time talking crazy people down until one day I just got fed up. The girls I knew in nursing school were not my friends; they were draining me emotionally. I could not continue friendships with these negative women and their bad decisions.

David and I had let Ella and her new husband move in with us for a month. He threatened to rape me. The only thing that stopped him was my couch breaking. He broke the leg off my brand-new couch with me bent backward over the couch, with a baby in my arms, and Ella's little boy on the couch beside me. I started screaming, "You broke my new couch!!!" and went hysterical on him about it. He got so distracted that I was able to get outside of the house into the front yard with my baby. Of course, when I told Ella about it, she didn't believe me. They moved out that night.

I was done with the emotional abuse of supporting these crazy women. I could not continue to have a life that was emotionally unhealthy with these women. I called them up one call after another and said, "I can't be friends with you any longer. Please never call me again." None of them ever did. My life was immediately better.

Diana with Julia

1985

Mama was draining David and I financially. Miraculously, I found her an apartment across town for low income elderly people. It was lovely: two bedrooms, a large living room, and a kitchen. It was on the second floor with a view looking out over the courtyard. Best of all, there was a nurse on duty 24 hours a day. The apartment came equipped with call bells if the resident needed the nurse AND best of all, the government was paying for it all. The only problems were that it was thirty minutes away and Mama didn't have a car. I would have to take her to all her doctor appointments and shopping. It was eating up all my time running her around, but at least it wasn't costing as much as our mortgage, so that was an improvement.

After 18 months, Mama took a turn for the worse. She wound back up in the hospital with congestive heart failure. I had no choice but to bring her home to our house again. It was the June of 1985. I was just 28 years old, but the stress of Mama's illness turned my hair gray overnight. I was sure that she was going to die. I decided to throw her a birthday party and invited all the relatives and friends. To my surprise we had a big turnout.

You may wonder why I was kind to Mama financially, physically, and emotionally supporting her after the way she treated me growing up. It is about responsibility. I always felt responsible for Mama. That overwhelming sense of responsibility for her and many others over my lifetime has driven my actions. That was why, as a child, I was always trying to pay the bills and balance the household. I took on the responsibility when Mama neglected it; our roles reversed. I felt responsible for her as a mother would for a child, but she felt no such responsibility in return for me.

Dealing with Luther was also about responsibility but different. If I did not deal with Luther, my daughter would have to, and it was NOT her responsibility as a child to deal with a crazy man. It was mine. I had brought this man into our life. I would deal with the consequences, to do the best I could to protect my child from her own father. That was what love was all about. Protecting your child.

Words of Wisdom

If you want to be successful, you must associate with successful people. That is one of the laws of life. The Bible says in Proverbs 2:20, "Thus you will walk in the ways of the good and keep to the paths of the righteous."

The month before Mama's turn for the worse, an interesting invitation was extended to me and all of the nurses I worked with. Dr. Bryant, a young plastics doctor, told us that if we wanted a breast augmentation procedure, he would do it for free, but we would have to pay the hospital for the anesthesia and surgical suite. For some of the girls he got the manufacturer to provide the implants for free. I had my breast implants done one morning, after I got off working all night.

This procedure proved to be both a blessing and a curse. The blessing was that my husband had a much-renewed interest in me, as did every other man. It seems that I jumped way up the attractiveness scale. Everywhere I went, the men turned around and stared. My confidence started to rise. As my confidence went up, my attitude went up. I had long known what was attractive to a woman is not the same things that men found attractive. I also discovered that men could be deceived into thinking a woman was highly attractive by her attitude. If a woman thought she was attractive, a man would also. I improved my dress and grooming. I developed the habit of never leaving the house unless every hair, makeup, jewelry, and piece of clothing was the best it could be. I had worn high heels since my early teens, so the heels just got higher and the skirts shorter.

The curse was that within one month I was back in the hospital with a ruptured axillary artery. I almost hemorrhaged to death. David and I got so frightened, we ran out of the house in the middle of the night, to the hospital, leaving our two, four, and nine-year-old children asleep in their beds. David rushed me to Riverside where my friends would care for me, while he returned home to the children. This foreshadowed the future surgeries this decision created. In total, I would have five breast surgeries before I would finally have the implants permanently removed in 2011.

After Mama's birthday party, she came to me and told me she needed to go to a nursing home; it was the one and only totally selfless acts I ever saw her do in my whole life. I think God was working on her. She said," I have to go to a nursing home because as hard as you are working taking care of me and the children, you are going to die before I am." I cannot imagine what inspired this woman to make her request to go to a nursing home.

But I jumped at the idea. I began interviewing facilities. I did not want her to be in a pee-smelling, run-down, poor-care nursing home that I was used to as a nurse. I knew from my nursing experience if a facility smelled like urine, it was because of patient neglect. Any good DON would NOT allow a urine smell in her facility.

I interviewed facilities at lunch time. Any facility that had patients still in their pajamas was out, as was the smell of urine, or lack of staff. I found what I was looking for at the Health Center at Live Oak Nursing. It was a retirement facility with apartments, then, as health deteriorated, the resident could move down to assisted living, then, finally, full nursing home care. They had an opening for Mama in the assisted living unit, with a roommate. In true Mama fashion, she hated her roommate on sight. Chaos reigned, until I finally gave in and paid the remaining balance of $1000.00 a month for her to have a private room. If I hadn't, she would have been right back in my home for me to take care of.

Mama loved her new facility; she became the "belle of the ball". She participated in everything. The staff loved her. She took over decorating all the facility bulletin boards for every holiday.

Words of Wisdom

I picture the slow human decline as a staircase the person walks down toward death. Each step taken down is a point of no return from the level of wellness they had previously enjoyed. As they land on each new lower step and gain homeostasis there, they adjust to the new normal, then await the next downward decline until they finally reach the bottom landing, which is death. Mama had started to walk down the stairs fast. 2 Corinthians 4:16 says, "Therefore we do not lose heart, but though our outer man is decaying, yet our inner man is being renewed day by day."

They gave her free design to do whatever she wanted. She went to ceramics classes and painted many items I still have: my nativity set, Santa Clause, Easter eggs, and more. There was a beauty shop where she charged a daily hairdo every single day to me until I got the bill and had a fit. She charged what she wanted from the convenience store to me. I was working full time to cover her expenses. She piled the bills up.

Live Oak was built around a fish-filled pond. The residents could go out and fish if they wanted. Sonny, Mark, and I brought the children to see her several times. We had a picnic while the children fished. This was one of the few normal memories I have of my children with their Grandmother.

Unfortunately, Mama's health was failing fast, so she was moved to the nursing home side within a few months. This would begin a yearlong descent unto death.

Doctor's Hospital

In part, because I wanted to climb the ladder and move up in hospital management, I started a new job at Doctor's Hospital as the Hospital Supervisor, working nights. I loved that hospital. I loved Dr. Evans, who had leased the hospital to a management company just before I was hired. My first assigned task was to terminate all nurse aides that worked at the hospital, except for Dorothy, who was the hardest working woman you could ever meet. Mrs. Dorothy was to stay employed. That first day I called person after person terminating their employment. I got the job because I didn't know any of them. It was a test to see if I had the intestinal fortitude to terminate employees.

Dr. Evans had owned the hospital for over 50 years. He fired anyone he didn't like. It was a very black and white thing. He took a quick look at a new employee and fired them on the spot if he didn't like them. Fortunately, he liked me.

Dr. Evans was then 85 years old and kept an unlit cigar in the corner of his mouth that he chewed 24/7/365. Even when he operated. You could not question him. He was old school and did not tolerate any criticism. The surgical nurses were accustomed to putting his surgical mask on to the side, so the cigar could hang out. But the new management company had decided that Dr. Evans couldn't operate like that anymore. Furthermore, he shouldn't operate at all at his age.

One day I was working the day shift, which I was frequently called in to do, as there were some problems with the Assistant Director of Nursing. Dr. Evans called for me. "Mrs. Wright, I need some help, come with me." I came running. Dr. Evans led me out to the parking lot, to the trunk of his car, where he had chains and padlocks. "Those big city boys didn't read their contract too close."

Melanie, Dana, and Julia, 1985

He kept laughing to himself as he piled the chains and locks from his car into in my arms. I was loaded down like a pack mule when he finished. He guided me to each entrance of the hospital and chained each door closed, then secured them with padlocks. At the last entrance, he showed me in, secured the door with me inside (and him outside), and stood watch. He instructed me to wait for the phone call from the "big city boys" I was sure to get real soon.

We didn't have to wait long. Chaos soon ensued. People wanted out. People wanted in. Complaints started to flow into my office. Someone called the police; they couldn't get in and someone called the new management company. The fire department was called because you cannot padlock people in a hospital.

Dr. Evans's son, Henry, was the Hospital Administrator; I think he was the one who probably called the new management company. It quickly became apparent that the contract recognized that Dr. Evans owned the hospital facility completely. He could close it any time with or

Dana, Julia, and Melanie, 1986

without warning; it was in the contract. From that day forward, the new management company "let" Dr. Evans operate with the cigar hanging out of the corner of his mouth.

After I had helped Dr. Evan with his little stunt, he liked me better than the other nurses. I never bucked him. I jumped when he told me to do something. He decided to invest in me. He sent me to a seminar that would change my life.

However, life was still very difficult. David and I had

Words of Wisdom

I always ignored everything that I did not want to fight about. I had found in school if you ignored the mean girls and just smiled and spoke to them, even though they were being mean, even if your stomach was in knots, it made the mean girls a nervous wreck. It was always fun to watch, and everyone thought I was being really polite and nice. Try ignoring behavior you don't like and see what happens.

never returned to the relationship we had before illness, neglect, and raising a family got in the way. We were drifting further and further apart. I started working on a plan to rehab David, so our relationship would improve. David was saying things that were piercing my heart: "We don't have enough money for anything." "We are on the verge of bankruptcy." "We will never go out to eat again and you can forget about ever going on a vacation." David was not interested in me as a wife, much preferring to stay up drinking by himself than coming to bed with me. He was completely focused on saving up $40,000.00. For him that was some kind of magic number after which everything would be alright.

I decided things had to change. I picked the smallest thing I wanted to change. I worked on that as the first trial to see if my plan actually worked. I did not tell him what I was doing. David had not taken me out to eat in over a year. I waited until Friday night when I told him, "The children and I are going out to eat at El Chico's, your favorite restaurant, would you like to go with us?" David had taken up a charming little habit of screaming, "NO!" while slamming his fist authoritatively on the table. Which he did, and I ignored. I was a master of ignoring things, I had years of training.

I smiled sweetly and replied, "I am so sorry you can't make it, can I bring you something back? Like crispy tacos?" (his favorite)

Again, he forcefully said, "No!" So, I took my children and loaded them in the car, while ignoring his orders telling me we couldn't go. He actually followed my car out of the driveway telling me we were not going. I smiled and waved like I didn't hear him. At El Chico I had a miserable time. The children were not used to restaurants, so they were impossible. The food was the usual disgusting, expensive mess. But we had plenty to take home, just not crispy tacos.

The next Friday night at the exact same time, I launched the exact same scenario, this time he agreed to come along. We had a lovely evening out (even if I had to eat El Chico). My husband is a man of process. Everything has a time, a place, and a process. Now the process included going out to eat at El Chico on Friday night.

It took me ten months to work though the list of issues I wanted to change: each time devising a way of not really changing David's behaviors, but changing the way I had previously approached and responded to David, causing him to take a different approach to me. By the time we had worked through all the issues, David and I were more focused on being friends, but we were still not a couple. David pretty much refused to go with me 100% of the time when we received an invitation. It took me years to realize his first answer would always be, "No" and that I should ignore that and let him think about things. For me, his refusals would be a lifetime of disappointment, but I soon learned to go and have a good time without him, even though I would always prefer to have him beside me. David's refusal to accompany me to afterhours work functions created problems for me that would have never occurred if he would have just gone with me. It forced me to be paired with the single men, which caused uncomfortable workplace interest that could have been avoided if my husband had just gone. He never understood this and sent me single to too many things in life. He is a homebody who prefers his home to any other place. He placed his comfort before mine.

When the Assistant Director at Doctors Hospital stepped down, I was asked to move from night supervisor to Assistant Director of Nursing, which was a day position. Part of my job was to prepare for a new inspection by the JCAHO by creating a Standards of Nursing book. To prepare me to write the book, I was sent to the JCAHO seminar where I saw the graph that foretold my future. Or should I say that seeing that graph solidified the plan I already had been turning over in my mind: to move up in hospital administration, not only for my own ambitions, but also because I could see the difference between good and bad management. I wanted to be in charge of a well-run healthcare system that would professionalize nurses and improve patient care. That has always been my goal.

It took me a year to write the Standards of Nursing book. Back then there were no computers, so everyone had a secretary that did the typing. My goal every day was to work enough on the nursing standards book that I kept our precious secretary busy. When the JCAHO surveyor arrived, she asked for the book, took a glance, and moved on. Horrified that she was not even going to open my book, I said, "No, you have to really look at this book, I have spent every day of my life for a year writing this four-inch-thick book and you have to look at it."

She replied absently, "Yes, it is very nice."

A year's work for that!

Mama's Death (January 29th)

Mama's health continued to decline. She was on a no salt diet and she refused to eat the institutional food, so she was losing weight. I now had to scour the grocery stores for no salt cheese and bread because all she would eat were grilled cheese sandwiches. The nursing home would cook those for her if I brought it in. I would also cook her low salt meals then bring them to her every night. I would work all day as a DON, come home and cook, get my small children to bed, then take Mama her salt free meal. She always liked oyster stew for Christmas Eve, so I often took to cooking this for her with no salt. She thought it was delicious.

Mama decided to die the last week of January. It was a bad week because the children were all sick with the flu. Julia was the sickest with the flu. Mama also came down with the flu, as did most of the nursing home. Illnesses like the flu and diarrhea are known to spread through institutional residences, killing off the patients. I needed to be with Mama while she died but I couldn't leave Julia. I did the only thing I could do: I pulled eleven-year-old Dana out of school to stay with four-year-old Julia and begged Michelle to come sit with my children. She got someone else to keep her own children, so they wouldn't get sick while she came to my house.

During the night, Mama had tried to get out of bed and had fallen. The nurse at the nursing home thought she had broken her hip. She had lost her ability to talk the day before. Her cardiac function had decreased to the point of no return. I told them not to move her, not to take her to the hospital, and to heavily medicate her so that she had no pain whatsoever. By the time I arrived, her room was flooded with the people from her church all praying over her and telling her she was so lucky she got to go to Jesus. By this point, I had sat at the bedside of many people who had died. No one had as unconventional and eclectic group of people with them when they died as Mama did, all telling her to "go toward the light". She died on January 29, 1988.

Mama's Funeral

Mama had burial insurance. I went to schedule her burial. The funeral home showed me a plastic box with a snap-on lid that looked exactly like a very big sandwich keeper. I was beside myself. This was exactly the plan. The funeral home then showed me an expensive, giant casket that looked exactly like our entertainment center. I really don't know which one horrified me more. This funeral home definitely took advantage of the emotional loss of a family member.

David said, "We took care of her in life and we will take care of her in death. Go somewhere else." I called Luther's Grandmother, Meme, who always had good advice. She gifted me a Catholic burial plot (that she owned) to bury Mama in. This was so funny. Mama hated Catholics more than she hated Jews. She said they prayed to rocks (statues). Now she was to be buried in Catholic sacred ground. Meme talked to the funeral home. They agreed to honor the existing policy, so I was able to get a nice casket. David and I also bought a cement casket vault.

As soon as I got home from picking out the funeral details, the nursing home called. They said if Mama was not moved out the next day (January 31), they would have to charge me for the whole month of February and Medicare would not pay. It would be $4,000.00.

Diana's mom, Neva Jean Johnson

I got up the next morning and could not get David or Mark to help me move Mama's things. So here I was again, all 115 pounds of me, moving a recliner, triple dresser, TV, small refrigerator, and countless other things. I paid a nurse aide to help me load David's truck. Feeling furious, I knew my brothers would be waiting at my house to go through her belongings. They would be looking for family pictures. I loaded the pictures in a box and piled the food from the refrigerator on top of the pictures. I did not want the pictures. But the Little Red Hen had cared for her, paid for everything, sacrificed, and received no help. The brothers helped in no way, shape, or fashion, so they got no pictures.

As I anticipated, the brothers were waiting for me to get back home, so they could go through what was left of her meager possessions. I carried the food into the house with the pictures on the bottom of the box. I stored them in the attic with the other things I didn't want.

At mama's funeral I found out Gary's wife, Kim, was pregnant. This was especially troubling news because Kim had a severe heroin problem and was unpredictable.

A New Life

The minute Mama died, my standard of living skyrocketed up! I could not believe how much time and money Mama had taken up. I had three children, a husband, was working full time, but now I had oodles of time and money. In fact, I felt spiritually, emotionally, financially, physically, and psychologically free. This was a carefree freedom I had never experienced. I think it is quite sad that I had felt the heavy burden of responsibility all my life, from an abusive parent, and it took her death for me to finally feel free.

In less than four months after her death, I was able to save $10,000.00. It was the first time in my life I could actually see any long-term benefit at all from my work. I started to save money like crazy. In June, I was able to take the family on a fabulous vacation to Mexico. I wanted to make sure we went in June because the children were three, five, and eleven, and they still qualified for child discounts. On the airplane, five-year-old Melanie said, "If you take me on this airplane ride, and I get killed I will never forgive you". I worried all the way there and back home, because even though I love to fly, I was afraid that my young daughter was more spiritually connected to God than I was and knew the future.

The day I got back from Mexico I found out my maternal grandma Fearn had died. I went to Grandma Fearn's funeral but can't really remember anything because I was focused on my drug-addicted newborn niece, Ali. Kim had delivered the four-and-a-half-pound baby. Ali was in the throes of drug withdrawal.

To make things worse, Kim decided to put a beautiful polyester dress with a rough net underskirt on the infant in the hot, East Texas heat of late June. The miserable child was rubbed raw all over her chest and stomach. I stripped her down and was horrified by the tiny baby's difficulty breathing. The tiny child did not look like it would survive to me. She was struggling, with parents who were completely unconcerned and smoking. But I did not know what to do. My Aunt Maxine was the DHS Supervisor who took away children for a living. Maxine seemed to ignore the drug-addicted infant, as she had ignored the abuse my brothers and I had suffered. I am ashamed to say I was worried sick about the tiny baby and the drug-addicted smoking parents, but I said nothing.

Completing My MBA

If I wanted to run my own healthcare business, I knew that I had to learn how to become a better manager and an entrepreneur. I also knew that starting an agency meant I had to get it right the first time—I couldn't financially afford to fail. Going bankrupt was not an option. Plus, I've always been a person to widen rather than narrow my options for the future. I was working in the ICU at Riverside Hospital at the time, and one day when I talked to the head nurse there about my thoughts for my future, she suggested I get an MBA. That seemed the right thing to do.

Centenary College, where I applied, had a very tough admissions policy. I was scared about my admissions interview with Dr. Barry Richardson. I had read a book that was very popular at the time, entitled Dressed for Success. To enhance my chances of success, I followed every one of their guidelines to a tee.

My ex-husband Luther had married a woman from a wealthy family whose mother, Piper, had taken to dropping off large garbage bags of the previous season's designer clothing on my back porch. This beautiful lady threw out every single item from her closet every three months. She even threw out 14 karat gold jewelry. I never knew when I would come home from work to a large garbage bag of the most beautiful clothes in exactly my size. Most with the price tags still on them. They fit me perfectly! It was wonderful! They were all the latest styles from the most expensive stores. I would take the wrinkled, dry-clean only clothes to the cleaners, and it would cost several hundred dollars just to get so many of them cleaned.

When I went for the MBA candidate interview, I really tried to look like what I thought an MBA candidate would look like. I was dressed in a size four, black linen suit, with a short suit jacket with a peplum and a big wide black belt. I had my hair swept up tight in a French Twist. I carried a brief case with me. Even so, within the first two minutes of questions Barry had me in tears.

"Why don't you tell me about your high school graduation?" was one of the first things he asked.

That really got to me because I had to tell him that I hadn't graduated with my class. I'd dropped out of school my senior year to get a waitress job to support my family. I had earned my diploma by taking the G.E.D. More tears came when he asked me to tell me about the family I grew up in. But I was brutally honest. I told him about growing up poor, and without a father. I told him my mother had been alternately violent or absent, leaving me alone to care for my younger brother and that by age eleven I was pretty much running the household: cooking, cleaning, bill-paying, and grocery-shopping.

As I left the interview, I was certain I would not be accepted; they were selecting twenty-five students from over a hundred applicants. I could not imagine why they would select a poor girl with my background for this prestigious Executive Management MBA program. But that is exactly what happened. Imagine my surprise when I received my acceptance letter and found out I was the only woman accepted

Diana, Dana, Melanie, and Julia 1988

that semester. Out of twenty-five candidates!

Within a day of my acceptance of the MBA program, I received a call from Gary. I literally had never received a call from Gary before in my life, so I knew right away it was trouble. "How do you like baby girls?", he questioned. "I think they are the best thing on earth!" I replied, thinking about his sweet baby Ali. "Well I tell you what, if you want this one you can drive to Dallas

and I'll drive her to Dallas and you can either pick her up or put her in foster care. It's your call.". Yes, that was Gary all right, a real piece of work. He had just dumped his problem directly in my lap so his conscious could be clear. If the child did wind up in foster care, he felt he was completely off the hook. In his demented mind, he had done

Diana holding Ali Johnson, 3 weeks old

all he needed to do about the care of the tiny baby.

I agreed to drive to Dallas without asking David. As I hung up the phone, I knew David would not be happy. Mama had just died, freeing us up to focus on our family. I had been accepted for the MBA program. I was now taking a special needs baby, Gary's at that.

I drove to Sonny's house the next day to pick up Ali. When I arrived, the baby was so sick she could hardly breathe, but too filthy to take to the Emergency Room. I knew that nurses were mandatory reporters that would call DHS and possibly the police to take her away immediately in her current condition. I had to bathe her, wash her clothes, and scratch a huge patch of cradle cap off her head before I could take her to the Emergency Room.

The child was extremely allergic to cigarette smoke. Gary and Kim, who both smoked incessantly, had her on three medications to allow her to breathe. She had thick, green snot coming from her nose and her ears were infected. The child was also stiff as a board from the heroin she had endured in utero;

221

she could not bend her arms or legs. She looked more like a stiff, plastic doll than a real baby that normally have their arms and legs drawn up close to their body. I made Sonny go to the Emergency Room with me in case I got arrested for child abuse. We didn't.

I took her back to Sonny's, medicated her, and slept with her naked body tightly hugged to my bare chest that night (and for the next three nights) so the tiny infant would bond to me and become mine. She bonded to me, and me with her, almost immediately. I had to do physical therapy on this baby, bending her legs and arms every time I changed her diaper, until she could bend her arms and legs on her own, months later. The child's respiratory illness cleared up and resolved because she was in a nonsmoking home. I immediately changed her formula; she started to gain weight. The baby took only about two weeks to get completely straightened out. She was a joy.

The next day as I left Sonny's and drove home, I knew I had to make my husband a very good meal to make up for bringing home an infant. I placed the baby on a quilt while I went into the kitchen to cook. I heard her making a few mewing sounds then she was quiet. When I looked into the living room, David was holding the baby up to his face with the baby licking his face like a puppy. She licked him all over his face. When dinner was finally ready he said, "I think this baby may be more adorable than our babies." Yes, she was pretty smart.

My childrens' education and lessons became a strong focus that I wanted to develop. I sat down to write out a plan for each individual child to become well-rounded. I have always suffered with a lack of confidence over the silliest things such as not being a good dancer or not speaking a second language. I wanted them to have social confidence. I wanted them well-rounded in every area of life.

I focused on academics, but also on inspiring each child with opportunities to be socially comfortable, interesting, and versatile. I focused many of my lists of activities that I could do with them as they grew so that we could stay a close family. I wanted each child to have a lifetime sport such as golf, tennis, archery, or badminton. I wanted them to have the experience of playing softball at future company softball games, as that was very popular in Shreveport at the time. I wanted them to be able to dance, but not professionally, so I steered away from ballet and tap. I centered on cheerleading and gymnastics, as that would also help them to fit in socially in junior high and high school. I wanted them exposed to art, music, and foreign languages. I insisted they read books.

I did every craft you could do with a child. We sewed, painted, glued, baked, and entertained ourselves with endless projects. I had them spray painting anything I could find. David and I played T-ball with them when they were little, then later set up a badminton net in the backyard for two years. We played badminton and volleyball with them, trying to allow them many different activities that would work all their life. I taught them all how to cook.

I was shocked watching an old family video from Dana's College graduation recently, that I found time to travel to Monroe, Louisiana, cook all the food for her graduation party, and built a gingerbread house with the girls. It was Christmas, and I was trying to find some project to entertain them, but gingerbread houses are hard when you have a lot of detailed things to do, like throw together a party. But there we are all putting it together. Parties were my specialty! I could always throw one together in thirty minutes. The girls definitely acquired that learned task.

The MBA program at Centenary College was set up for working professionals. You took one class at a time for ten weeks straight; each class had a minimum of 12 hours of homework per week. After ten weeks you moved in to the next class. Another program requirement was that we study and work together in teams. I was assigned to a team with Tom Bickham and Joseph Turner. At age 32, Joseph was a delicate looking man with curly red hair. He was honest to a fault; neat and clean, and always seemed to know what he was talking about. Tom was 40, about 5' 10" tall and very quiet. He had an accounting background and was already qualified as a CPA, so he was a whiz with anything having to do with numbers. We all became good friends during that time, Tom and I especially so. At age 30, I was the most driven of all of us three.

I had an area of expertise for collecting outstanding money for the hospital that no one else wanted to do. I would run a medical review on a chart to find the places that the doctors failed to fill out then notify the delinquent doctors of what was missing in their charts to get the hospital paid. Often, doctors' claims for Medicare or Medicaid were rejected simply because they never finished filling out their paperwork. I went through tedious, 1500-page reports and made stickies to identify the missing parts then I had to get the doctors to document what they'd omitted. This allowed me to learn how to identify how to determine what was missing from something to complete it. This is a talent that few possess. It has allowed me in my life to create departments and businesses where none existed before.

One day, I got a panicked call from Joseph, who besides being my friend was the Assistant Administrator at Doctor's Hospital. Joseph tipped me off that Henry Evans, the Administrator (Henry was the son of Dr. Evans, the cigar-smoking surgeon/ hospital owner), was going to call me into his office to tell me I had to have sex with one of the doctors.

Julia, Melanie, and Diana holding Ali

I was frightened, but I had the good sense to call a lawyer. The lawyer advised that I purchase a voice-activated tape recorder that I put in my pocket to record the conversation. If the hospital fired me, I was to tell them I was not leaving until they copied every page front and back in my employee file, even if it was blank, including the outside and inside jacket of the file folder. That way, I would have a written record of my stellar performance reviews.

I did as I was told. I returned from Radio Shack with my voice-activated tape recorder in my pocket. Soon enough I was called down to the Administrator's office. Henry, speaking meaningfully, told me, "We have a team member who needs your special, personal support that only you can give him. We are a team here. You are expected to support the team."

Seriously, if I had not been tipped off I wouldn't have even known what he wanted me to do. I had no idea what "special, personal support" might mean. But I remembered the lawyer's advice. "How much are you offering me to leave?" was my very cold reply.

Words of Wisdom

It is very important to have good friends in life and to choose your friends wisely. Associations with good people are important. Romans 12:21 says, "Do not be overcome by evil but overcome evil with good." Proverbs 13:20 says, "Walk with the wise and become wise, for a companion of fools suffers harm."

Henry appeared surprised that I would play hardball so fast. I was expecting two weeks of pay, but right away Henry offered me 90 days of pay. As cool as a cucumber, I said, "I will wait for the check. I want every page, front and back of my employee file copied, even if it is blank, including the outside and inside jacket of the file folder. I also want a letter of reference and I will wait right here in your office until I have these." Even though I was freaking out inside, I managed to maintain total control of my demeanor. Henry complied with my demands.

I was out of the hospital, without of a job, in less than

an hour. I had a check for over $10,000.00 after taxes. They had included 91 days of pay, all my worked hours, my vacation pay, and my holiday pay. I took the check to the bank it was written on where I cashed it. I then deposited cash into my bank. That way, if Henry changed his mind, he couldn't cancel the check withdrawing my money from my account. He would have to sue me to get money back. I knew he would never be that foolish with witnesses and a tape recording.

I then went right over to Tom, who was an administrator at Bossier General Hospital, to cry about my situation. I cried make-up all over his white shirt that day. It turned out that a certain Dr. Wong was pulling a power play. In his sixties, he had told Henry he would pull his patients out of the hospital unless the Assistant Director of Nursing slept with him. He didn't ask for the Director of Nursing at Doctor's Hospital to sleep with him because she was married to a fellow doctor.

Later, Tom got Joseph on the phone and they discussed the whole thing. Shortly after I left Tom, Dr. Wong tried the exact same power play at with Tom at Bossier General. Even though Tom's Director of Nursing was in her fifties and obese Dr. Wong didn't care. That's because it wasn't about sex, or the woman involved, it was a power play to force the hospital administrators to do something unpleasant. Tom was so angry at what had happened to me that when Dr. Wong started his charade at Bossier General, Tom fired him.

To graduate from the MBA program, we chose a partner with whom to write a thesis—a business proposal for a viable business we might start up. Tom and I chose to work together on building a hospital. Together we researched demographics to demonstrate that a certain geographic area needed a non-Catholic hospital for women and children.

Tom did all the financial projections. When it came time to present our thesis, one of the humanities professors started questioning the numbers. Tom, a trained Certified Public Accountant, had an answer for every question. Finally, Tom got so fed up with the interrogations, that he burst out and said, "You're a total ass. What you are asking doesn't make sense. You are here questioning something you don't know anything about." To back him up, I took my hands off the table and brought them down really hard, to make a loud noise, and to show my anger.

After those interactions, I thought we were going to fail our MBA thesis, but instead, because it was so detailed and thorough, we got 100 percent. For over ten years after we left the MBA program, our proposal was the one the other students

were recommended to look at. What's more, even though I didn't realize it at the time, the demographic research and needs assessment that I learned how to do would play directly into my ability to place travel nurses in areas where they were needed.

Dana, Diana, Melanie, Julia, and David Wright; Christmas

Tom and I remained friends until he died. At age 45 he came and worked for me and we eventually built three hospitals together. He suffered from severe depression, which unfortunately turned out to be a prerequisite to Parkinson's disease. He died of end stage Parkinson's Disease. I'll always remember him as a great and loyal friend.

A Women Scorned

Five years had passed since I'd seen my future in the graph predicting the healthcare needs of aging baby boomers and I was working my plan. Get the MBA. Get a credentialing job, so I could learn how to credential healthcare providers for a hospital. Learn risk management, infection control, quality improvement, how to pass audits, and, generally, everything needed for the management of medical staff. It was no mistake I was pursuing the experience I was specifically seeking. My credentials might seem all over the place to the uninformed person, but I had a very specific plan for business success that I could not see failing. I was working my personal plan for future business success and making good progress.

During the months I was writing my MBA thesis, I read the jobs wanted ads in the paper every day and went on "practice job interviews." This was wonderful practice where I honed what became my exceptional job interview skills. On one of these "practice interviews" I found my next job as Chief of Quality Management at the VA Medical Center in Shreveport, Louisiana.

If I had not been in this exact opportunity of paid time off and working on my thesis, I would not have been able to wait four months for the VA Medical Center to decide to hire me or not. I knew nothing about Quality Management but studied up on the position and used all the right keywords in my many interviews.

I completed my Master of Business degree on May 4, 1991. On that same day I was inducted into Sigma Theta Tau International Honor Society of Nursing.

I had no idea what the Chief of Quality Management at the VA Medical Center did. Fortunately for me, no one else did either. I started that job with almost no knowledge of quality management, risk management, infection control, credentialing, home therapy, or passing external audits. However, I had accepted the position in part because I wanted to learn everything about how a hospital works: how to credential every employee, run external reviews, and handle sentinel incidents. It was an important stepping stone.

The VA was physically enormous. I had to park in what I call the "South Lower 40" and then walk almost a mile to get to the medical center. One day my dress for success outfit included a white dress with black polka dots, plus black patent leather shoes. In those days I wore a full slip too, underneath my clothes. As I walked from my car up the hill it began to rain hard. I hadn't brought an umbrella or a rain coat, so my dress went absolutely transparent with water! The first building I reached was the Environmental Department, or maintenance center. I appealed to the electricians, who lent me a hair dryer to dry out my hair and dress, and then went about the rest of my day.

I was one of the top people in charge of the VA. Above me

was the Chief of Staff and the hospital Director. Lateral to me was the Chief of Medicine, and the Chief of Surgery, both of whom also answered to the Chief of Staff.

My first day of work a guy named Daniel from Outpatient Therapy informed me about how things worked at the VA. "You protect your turf while respecting everyone else's," was how he put it. I couldn't disagree more. In my opinion, that kind of attitude isolates and divides people. You can't approach or reach people if they are spending all their time protecting their turf.

I had a lot of departments below me. I had to work with each and every one to get them into compliance. From day one, I made sure to thank people for whatever they did around the hospital. I was non-threatening and made sure to speak very calmly when I wanted things done, as if I was a mother reminding a child to brush their teeth. When I went to speech pathology, I knew nothing about what they did, but I tried to be upbeat and make appropriate suggestions. Because I was always in control and did a great job, the director would always give me another huge department—to which I'd say, "Thank you--I think."

I was there for 30 days when everyone realized that I was someone important and would remark, that I would succeed. I befriended everyone.

I soon found out that few people were connected or liked one another. So I set about very strategically bringing people together. For example, the medical and surgery departments hated each other. My solution to that divide was to I become best friends of the Chief of Surgery and good friends with the Chief of Medicine. I had a brand-new Ford Explorer. I could put everyone in my car and take them out to dinner: the two chiefs, along with the chief of psychology, the nursing director, and the Chief of Dietary, a woman who was a dietician.

Once people started getting along instead of fighting with one another we got more done and improved patient care.

Within two weeks of starting my job, the JCAHO had come to this giant hospital to perform an audit. I had negotiated in my interview that as a newcomer I could not possibly be held responsible for the outcome of the upcoming audit.

I found out in my first audit the power of distraction. Since I had no idea what we were doing, I kept light conversation with jokes flowing about anything except hospital quality assurance. Distract, distract, distract was my plan for the day! It worked beautifully. The two doctors from JCAHO were enchanted with the conversation about their interests of roses. I did a great job with the audit and had bluffed my way through a five-day audit without ever having to actually talk business.

I soon learned my job by studying everything I could get my hands on. At my MBA Program, Dr. Barry Richardson, The Dean of the College of Business, had said, "You can be an expert in anything in one week if you just study the process." This is so true. I was the keeper of all bad incidents, sentinel events, and lawsuits. In less than six weeks I rapidly became the resident expert in Quality Assurance and Improvement (QA/QI) at the VA Hospital.

We passed all external audits, whereas previously they'd failed. Soon the hospital pulled up to a higher level of functioning. If I walked into a section of the hospital and I smelled urine I immediately knew they were not taking care of their patients. The first thing I did was talk to housekeeping about how they managed and figured out with them methods by which they could keep things spotless. In the process, that created a working relationship we could draw on going forward.

I sat on every committee. I learned that most people who are in the committee meetings are busy and do not like to be there. The Chiefs of Surgery and Medicine in particular didn't like to do anything but see patients. Even though their attendance was required, they considered sitting on boards a waste of their time. They wanted someone else to do all the work. I volunteered to take the minutes for the meeting, in part because as the "little red hen", I understood that the one who takes the minutes gets to record them any way they want and make whatever changes they like.

While I was not officially in charge of departments other than QA/QI, I steered the meetings towards whatever results I felt would make the most impact for the hospital and the patients we served. I asked questions concerning topics I wanted, then recorded the minutes to reflect the outcomes that were best for patient care. Many times, people would pull meeting minutes from six months earlier and say, "Yes, now I remember that's what we decided."

Well, not exactly, that's just how I recorded it. Taking the minutes were a lot more work for me, but the patient outcome was more than I could have ever asked for. I impacted patient care positively at the VA. I only changed minutes so that it changed the facility from a poorly run facility to better run one that focused on Veterans.

The home oxygen program was a sham. A disaster. The external vendor to the hospital never showed up on time. He didn't fill prescriptions correctly. The care to these Veterans was deplorable. I was furious. But we were stuck with this particular vendor with no easy or obvious way to get rid of him. The VA had no track record of ever successfully replacing a vendor. So the next time the representative from the Joint Commission showed up at the VA I told him what was going on with the home oxygen program. He agreed to go with me to pay a visit to the home oxygen vendor.

We called ahead to arrange a meeting, but when we arrived at the vendor's place of business for our appointment at 9 a.m. He was not there. We called his home number and he answered, but when we got to his house for our appointment he was not there, either. We looked into the garage window and right away I saw where the epitome of poor care had begun. The oxygen tanks were laying on the floor as if they'd just been dumped from a car. To work properly, oxygen tanks are supposed to be stacked upright in a specially designed structure and kept orderly.

Now I had evidence. I wrote all this up. The Joint Commission Surveyor wrote him up. As a result, I got rid of a bad vendor who was giving terrible patient care and service.

I learned that when a little tug inside me said, "something is wrong here", I'm always right.

I decided we needed to credential the doctors on a regular basis. That way, we'd know if we had a doctor who could, for example, do heart surgery and cardiac thoracic surgery, and if an issue came up we could point to a list and say who was credentialed to do what. During the credentialing process, I discovered a doctor who had come from China had no paperwork because he was not licensed. I found a respiratory therapist who was an ex-con who had learned his trade in prison and falsified the diploma he hung on his wall. Even though he was the best respiratory therapist we had, we had to let him go because he'd lied and falsified his credentials.

So much of quality care was about paying attention to the small things.

When people in the OR began popping up with Streptococcus Group A infections, we cultured everything to try to figure out where the streptococcus was coming from until finally we found the source: the nurses, who were not wearing underwear under their scrub dresses! The infection was coming from vaginal droppings. In that case, my quality control measure consisted of making the nurses wear scrub pants instead of dresses.

Another time I noticed ants climbing up the glass container in which we kept lipids (fats) and getting stuck inside. Those lipids were going into an IV tubing and then into man's arm. It didn't take much more observation to notice that the ants were climbing in through the open windows. I put in an order for more air conditioning and a quality control measure to keep the windows shut. Ditto for the ICU, where I found fly's coming in through the open windows to lay eggs in people's wounds. In that case, I made sure the windows were nailed shut.

All the little things added up. We were able to monitor patient care through evidence-based medicine and documented results of reducing length-of stay and post-surgical infection rates. All the things that I did increased patient satisfaction.

On January 1, 1992 I was board certified by the Healthcare Quality Certification Board. This enabled me to make all Joint Commission decisions. I was now the board-certified expert.

I made a lot of friends working at the VA in Shreveport. Daniel in Outpatient Therapy had told me that within a few minutes of me being at the VA, he knew I was going to make it because I "looked like" I was in charge. I dressed in suits, wore one-inch, very ugly, practical heels that made a clipping sound

Words of Wisdom

This became my method of doing business for the rest of my life: keep conversation light, make them like you, and wait for them to bring up business issues. Being "Political" means being "Friends". For me it has always been a winning combination; just make friends with people.

when I walked my normal fast pace down the linoleum halls. I had every hair in place, the perfect seven pieces of jewelry, and carried a clipboard. You could hear me come tap-tap-tapping down the hall before you ever saw me. I did not creep around like all the silent nurses in their tennis shoes! I set out to be recognized. And I was.

While I was at the VA I developed a demeanor I have seen in many courtroom lawyers: I was pleasant and kind, spoke to everyone, talked light topics, but, underneath, I had a steel backbone that could be inflexible when pushed to the limit. I was seldom challenged. I spoke like I knew what we were supposed to do, with authority, and people followed! People just did what I said. This always surprised and amazed me. I think if you look the part, have the title, and act confident you do not get questioned.

I remember one time educating a group while repeating what I had read without a complete understanding of exactly how to

1) Collect the data for the Indicators,
2) Monitor the indicators, and

3) Tabulate the data.

I was very worried that someone would ask a question, so when I finished, I smiled brightly and said, "See it's that simple".

"Oh, yes!", they agreed, and no one asked any questions.

Within a year, I was presenting at conferences, representing the Shreveport VA on Quality Assurance and Quality Improvement. However, several troubling things happened that began to create an environment of dissatisfaction at the hospital. Slowly, I came to realize that those in charge were not handling responsibility as they should. I saw several serious problems completely dismissed.

The first incident had to do with the psychiatric unit. The two elderly physicians in charge were both extremely odd. One frequently referred to "Bob and Carol and Ted and Alice." He spoke in terms I did not understand, with confusing language that I assumed I was too uneducated in his field to comprehend. I would smile and nod a lot when he visited in my office. He finally brought me his book he was writing and asked me to edit it. When I looked at his writing I was appalled to realize that he was suffering from severe dementia. He wasn't talking over my head, he was confused. He was fixated on a 1969 comedy movie called "Bob & Carol & Ted & Alice." I was also appalled with the actions of my boss, the Chief of Staff, when I showed him the manuscript. He transferred this doctor, who was suffering from dementia, immediately. He just moved his problem, which I found out is common in the VA. I was very disappointed in this behavior and lack of fortitude to take appropriate action.

I had supervision over Infection Control, which was managed by a male RN, Jackson, who had hated the previous Chief of Quality Management because that person had tried to tell Jackson how to do his job. Jackson liked me as his boss because I knew he knew way more than I did about Infection Control. I just let him do his job. Jackson was over the AID's Clinic, which was a brand-new idea at the time.

Shreveport had been experiencing an unknown assassin who was shooting people from a bridge as they passed below in their cars on I-20. The weekend before, a 28 year-old cello player at the Shreveport Symphony had been paralyzed from a gunshot to the chest that had damaged her spinal cord. Jackson came to me and said, "I have an AID's veteran that claims responsibility for the shooting, but we can't call the police because everything they say in the AID's Clinic is protected information under HIPPA."

I flat refused to keep this hideous secret. I would not allow this dying veteran sharpshooter to murder innocent civilian people just because he was dying from poor choices he had made for himself. I told Jackson I would not keep this secret, even though he desperately pleaded with me to maintain confidentiality. I flat refused. Too many people had been hurt by this man's decision to kill as many people as he could before he died. I dismissed Jackson and called the police. I have never been sorry that I stopped this AID's patient from continuing his killing spree. I was never confronted by anyone about reporting this pervert.

A third incident that occurred was with a veteran that was admitted to the psychiatric unit after attacking one of the psychiatrists with a wooden cross, claiming that the doctor was a vampire. This was before being a vampire was all the rage of the 2010's. The veteran claimed that his girlfriend was a vampire. He claimed he killed her with a stake to the heart. I was called because of the severity of the incident, as I was in charge of all sentential events. I asked the veteran where his girlfriend was, and he replied, "I put her in the trunk of my car and it is parked in the parking lot outside."

I called campus security, took his keys and, to much sadness, found his young girlfriend in the trunk of his car. Just as the veteran confessed, she was dead after having been staked through the heart. She obviously wasn't a vampire, as her beautiful body was fully intact. I don't know why people don't follow up. The boyfriend had been in custody for two days before I was called.

While at the VA, I experienced so much peer support, recognition, and credibility.

The Assistant Administrator, Sam, was studying religion, but not reading the Bible. He was reading books about the Bible. I had never had any religious training of any kind. I never attended church until David and I were married. I was a relatively blank slate, so to speak. I decided that all fully educated people must read the Bible in their lifetime, so I started a religious quest with Sam. He and I used our 15-minute morning break to discuss religion and the books we were reading. (I also remember the delicious cat's head biscuits I used to eat on the break that cost 10 cents and were as big as your head.)

Words of Wisdom

You cannot get recognized creeping around holding your head down. You must be bold. Take up space. Do not sit with your arms and legs crossed, spread out and take up space. This is what a person in charge does. Look like the person you aspire to be, not like the position you are in. Work harder than everyone else. Put yourself out there.

I decided that Judaism was obviously the religion of my God, The Father Almighty, so I began my study there. I read everything I could get my hands on: I bought many Jewish books, including the Hebrew Bible.

But I got to a point in my studies that I had to decide if I believed that Jesus was the son of God. I did. That meant I had to find another religion other than Judaism. I then looked at the various Christian religions. Since Jesus handed the church over to Peter, and he was the first Catholic Pope, there was no other religion I could choose. I had to go with the religion Jesus started, not some other religion began by man. I had to choose a religion started by God and Jesus.

I was respected; the staff listened to what I had to say. I was the top female in command. The problem was that I was a nurse: as a nurse I was paid according to the nurse pay scale and not the male manager pay scale. The men under me were making twice what I was making; Sam was making three times my $40,000.00. Dissatisfaction was rising.

About that time a TV journalist was doing an exposé on the VAs across the country. She would walk into a VA's Quality Management Department, claiming authority under the Freedom of Information Act, then raid their offices. She would review files until she found something terrible, then make a TV show about it, ruining the careers of the people she crucified. She was striking terror in my Director's (my boss's) heart. He was terrified because he was only three years from retirement and he needed the last three years to make his highest retirement pay.

My heart felt that what the television host was doing did not sound legal. Whenever I listened to my internal Holy Spirit I never went wrong. I started researching Rules of Law. I found 3305. Under 3305, I had to give her any file under the Freedom of Information Act she requested by name but did not have to provide her with open access to my office files.

When I heard she was to arrive at the VA in Shreveport, I prepared for her arrival. Just to be on the safe side, I took the most inflammatory incident files and minutes and locked them in the trunk of my car. I then sent my staff home and locked my office door. I stood in the hall with a copy of Rule 3305 in my hand, my keys in my pocket, sucked it up, and looked totally in control.

The television journalist said,

"I have come to review your files."

"Of course," I said, "which one do you want?"

She became threatening, "I want to go in that office, you better get out of my way!"

I smiled and said in my most polite southern voice, smiling brightly, "I really want to help you. Under 3305, all you have to do is identify the patient record you want and I will hand it over."

She screamed in frustration. She did not get into my office. My Director was so over wrought that he was laying on the floor in his office having chest pain. I had avoided a sentinel event for sure.

The next day, my boss called me into his office, and said, "I have good news and bad news. I am raising you to the highest pay limits available for your grade and you will be "redlined" there for three years." The phrase "for your grade" was what really annoyed me. I had started my job a GS11.[4] I was being discriminated against for being a nurse! I worked hard, taking on more and more responsibility. Soon I was at the top of my grade. Now I was redlined! I could not get raises for three years!

I did the only thing a girl who respects herself would have done, I turned in my termination notice, on the spot!

He begged, pleaded, and refused to accept the resignation. I left his office furious and a woman scorned. As everyone knows, "Hell hath no fury like a woman scorned."

Tritek Medical Staffing

One day at lunch in the VA hospital cafeteria, I was joined by my friend, John Noles, Sr. As the political campaign manager for Edwin Edwards, Louisiana's colorful Governor, John was paid to run Edwards' campaign for two years of

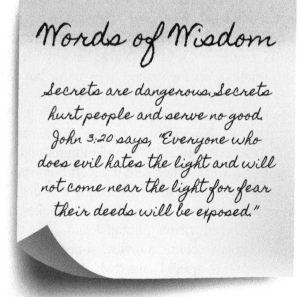

Words of Wisdom

Secrets are dangerous. Secrets hurt people and serve no good. John 3:20 says, "Everyone who does evil hates the light and will not come near the light for fear their deeds will be exposed."

his four-year term.[5] During the two years when Edwards wasn't campaigning, John, who had a master's degree, worked as a social worker. John was a most fastidiously groomed, most lovely man with good manners. John always complimented me on what I wore, and perhaps for that reason I unloaded my predicament on him. I told him how furious I was to be treated with so much discrimination for being female and a nurse. It was just humiliating, that I should work harder and make less than men who were under me and answered to me.

Like the knight in shining armor he always was, John came to my rescue. He said he wanted me to meet a friend of his, Owen, who had started a respiratory therapy agency that I might want to join.

When I first met Owen, I felt that little internal tug that meant something was not quite right, but for the next two months, John and Owen persisted. They called every week asking me to lunch. I told them I was not interested in coming to work in their new business. I didn't think that was my next career move. They would reply, "No, really, we don't want to talk about the business, we just really like having lunch with you." Then we would talk about the business.

I finally acquiesced and in 1991 I joined Tritek Medical Staffing full time. Owen had me sign a Confidentiality Non-Compete Agreement that said I would never have ownership of any part of the company located in Shreveport,

> **Words of Wisdom**
>
> Follow up is what separates success from failure. If you are going to manage your children or employees, you must follow up to make sure that they do what you tell them.

but that I would own part of any branches we opened.

My first day working at Tritek, I met Owen's wife, Aubrey. She was about forty years old and as I got to know her I saw her as someone who didn't give much thought to the consequences her actions might have on other people. Instead, she seemed to live for the moment and do things in ways that were convenient mainly to her and Owen.

The company was headquartered in Owen and Aubrey's formal dining and living rooms. Their respiratory therapy business was at only one hospital in Monroe, Louisiana, where they had 19 Registered Respiratory Therapists (RRT's) with four-year degrees working. The California School of Certified Respiratory Therapists (CRTTS) had just been approved to start teaching in Louisiana, but the Respiratory Therapy Board had declined to impose any differentiation between the duties of the four-year RRT and the one-year CRTT. Nursing had maintained tight control on the duties of one-year practical nurses. I could foresee that in one year their little business--with only one hospital, in an extinct discipline— would be gone. The solution, I saw, was to switch to nurse staffing. When I proposed my theory, Owen and Aubrey heartily agreed. Nursing is 73% of hospital staffing while Respiratory Therapy is 2%. We started nurse staffing that day. In one week, I had more nurses than they ever had Respiratory Therapists.

My job was to call hospitals, find shifts, then find nurses to fill the shifts. Sounds easy, right? But I could not get in the door anywhere. If the CEO could see me, he would always go to lunch with me, based on my professional looks alone. Louisiana men were gentlemen. The male CEO's always insisted on paying for lunch. I was not beautiful. But I was highly attractive, intelligent, professional, conversational, and fun.

My lack of classical beauty was a plus for the Directors of Nursing who did feel threatened by my looks. The DON's loved eating the free lunches that I provided. They loved the opportunity to discuss JCAHO with an "expert." My position at the VA, along with my certification in Quality Management made me the closest thing to an expert anywhere. At the time, I was one of only 28 individuals certified in Quality Management.

I soon devised a marketing plan. As a door opener, we would sell education to the hospital, and then back it up with staffing. There is nothing so valued in a hospital as educating the staff. The medical profession requires that staff be educated every year to maintain several certifications. Everyone must have their flare! It was always a problem for the DON to schedule the nurses to attend the required classes and still have enough staff left in-house to care for the patients. I proposed to solve both problems. I would offer the classes, and then register all their staff to attend my class. I would then fill the floors with my staff. This may sound grandiose and complicated, but it worked wonderfully. Besides, I don't do simple.

Every DON I called was thrilled to discuss how they could "develop" their staff! They were intrigued with my "solution" to taking care of the patients. I knew myself well enough to know that I am no teacher. I hate it. I soon hired a lady named Ashley to write, develop, and teach classes for Tritek.

Before long, the business was booming. I was successfully marketing back in the days when all marketing was done face to face and over the phone. I was obtaining about a 100% close rate--if I could get an appointment with the decision maker for the hospital. The biggest challenge was to identify the decision maker. It often took multiple calls to different departments in the same hospital to figure out who was in actually in charge of staffing services. Sometimes it was the CEO, or the DON, or the CFO (horrors), or HR. The CFO never wanted to part with any money and could care less about patient care. HR never had time to talk about staffing nursing (they really weren't nurses, anyway). The DON was like a drowning man looking for anyone to be a savior. Also, they always felt it was their duty to chew me out thoroughly before signing my contract. Every DON's management style was the same: have a strong offense to weaken the defense. They tried to get me straightened out up front, so we wouldn't have problems later. The DON and HR always hated each other. Hospital dynamics were, well, so dynamic.

Tritek flourished. I did not know I was so good at marketing. We moved to a new and bigger location, then an even bigger one. We took on more staff. We had a broader reach of staffing nurses and respiratory. Then Owen decided we needed to branch out. Although it would take me some time to understand, the problem was we didn't have any money. My job was not to worry about where the money came from, but to get the deal closed and the business booked. I was good at it. Too good. So, I kept growing the business.

We built an education company, MedEd; a clinic, MediKid Clinic; a Surge Protection Business that Owen's friend Ethan ran, and a home health agency. With Tom Bickham, I owned three psychiatric hospitals which were hospitals within a hospital.

As we grew the company, my salary grew. Our house on Patton seemed to shrink with four growing children. At this point in our marriage, David viewed our marriage as an autocracy where he issued orders and expected them to be followed without discussion. He expected a little "Yes" girl, but that is not the girl with the iron backbone he married. With David's gentleness, he did not have the authority to command quick obedience from me. I usually complied because his requests were normally reasonable. Although we seldom argued, when we did, I could easily counter any theory of his and persuade him to the validity of my views.

Melanie and Julia, 1990

There was no bedroom for Ali. She was four years old and had no bed. Dana was sixteen and she refused to share a room with a four-year-old that had to go to bed at 8:00 PM. We would put Ali to bed in our bed every night, so we could have the living room. Then move her to the couch when we went to bed. I wanted to move; David wanted to stay. One day everything came to a head when he was punishing Ali for "taking" Julia's pillow. He firmly said, "Go get your pillow." I wheeled on him, "She doesn't have a pillow, or a bed, or a room, or a chest of drawers, or anything except a cardboard box and this is just ridiculous! I refuse to live like this any longer, we make too much money to live this way!" After putting my foot down, he finally agreed to the move. Although we have never been separated for even a night, we had the same difficulties every couple faces when you take two fallen creatures and try to merge one life.

Our relationship usually went exactly like this every day. David never humored me. He never gave in to my small requests for other than the cheapest necessities. He never indulged me in any way. He is still this way. He fought me on every purchase every day of my life. At that time in our marriage, on a daily basis, I had to get so fed up with his treatment of me, that I was to the point of walking out, for him to acquiesce and agree to "allow me to purchase" anything I considered common sense and a basic necessity.

David and I are very different people. We have very different methods of relational reaction. The problem for me was that because I had to get to the point of divorce every day, for me to get what I considered basic necessities, it detached my feelings from him.

Ali Johnson 1990

At the time, I felt his behavior was a deliberate attempt to keep me at arm's length and avoid true intimacy with me. He was just being a financially aware person. As I became more successful in business and more assured of my decisions, he had a lack of trust in my decisions. It was always about money.

I have since grown to understand that David just thought he was being the boss. He felt if he gave in to any small request, it would lead to a larger request and undermine his authority. When in fact it would have done just the opposite. I would have given him the

Words of Wisdom

Good manners go a long way. You can get away with a lot with perfect manners.

honor that every man craves. David is a man of true honor. What I did was just get immune to his criticism. I ignored him completely. I hid money from him. I provided for my children as I felt was appropriate. I did not outright lie, I just hid my purchases. I never yelled or screamed at my husband. I just refused to follow his commands. I would just look at him and walked away from him when he was telling me one of the new rules. In those days there was always a new rule that I would not follow.

For a rule to work, the rule must be agreed upon by both parties. It took David many years to understand this. David had five sisters and he was used to making up long lists of rules and taping them in prominent places in his parents' home. I would just look at him when he started with the frequent "new" rule and walk away. I wouldn't say a word. I didn't outwardly challenge him. He would quietly ask, "You're not going to follow the rule are you." I would tell the truth non-confrontationally, but firmly and simply, "No". I would not be nasty or unkind, I would be calm, and through calmness and firmness comes the definition of stable strength.

Our poor marital communication continued until, one day, David just gave up and "decided to let me be the boss." David's decision to "let me be the boss" was a whole lot like what I would consider a partnership to be. Instead of announcing some decision or rule, we now discussed the situation and came to a joint decision on how our lives would be lived.

Dana, 1990

David remains a husband that never indulges me. He still doesn't come home with flowers or nice little things. But by collaborating on decisions and discussing them with each other, our relationship is strong. I began to pray every time we went to church that I would fall in love with him again. I asked God to let me love him without measure and that is exactly what I received. God answered my prayers, I received a faithful love without measure. I truly adore my husband and he adores me.

<u>1993</u>

Springlake

We had to move to a larger home. We found our home on Springlake Drive in the heart of one of the best subdivisions in Shreveport.[6] The house was a two story: a long beautiful brick with five bedrooms, two living areas, and two dining areas. The floors were actual brick pavers and I loved them. There was an old Chambers stove top that I adored. Everything in the house had been built in and was of the highest quality. I got a real deal on the house for $135,000.00.

We looked at over 70 houses. David would reject each one with no discussion. He would just say "No". We finally agreed on one, except when I visited it in the rain, I noted an area in the roof where the house had been added onto that pooled water. When I looked at the ceiling there was a wet spot. I could see where the owners must have been painting over the spot. The roof had been added on to form a pool that could not drain except into the living room. The roof was too expensive to fix. We cancelled the contract.

When the realtor called me about the house on Springlake, I went right over to see it. I loved it on the spot. There was another couple viewing the house at the time. I went right in and looked it over, then ran out to my car to call David. I was always ahead on technology, so I had a bag phone that worked in the car when no one else but movie stars had car phones. I called David and excitedly told him this was our house. He had to come right then. We immediately put a contract on the house and I was thrilled with it!

Our next-door neighbor was a Selber, of the esteemed Selber Brothers Store, that I had worked for when I was seventeen. He came right over to visit to tell me the "rules of the neighborhood." The first one was we don't mow our own grass. I was infuriated with the rules of decorum of the old south: no pictures of loved ones in the dining room, no nudes in the living room, pearls only until five, and then diamonds, flats or low sensible heels during the day then heels at night, and my dreaded "Who is your Daddy?" that started every conversation, so everyone knew who you were related to, because everything in Louisiana is political.

I thanked him. Since my new curtains were on order, I proceeded to tape aluminum foil over all of my windows just to drive this regimented old southern man crazy. I then hung baby pictures of my children in the dining room and a nude in the den. On Saturday that week, I put on my green, camouflage print bikini with white socks and high toped pink tennis shoes (it was the 90's) and mowed the grass. This was the first and last mow. My camo bikini always got the attention of men; they loved it. This was in the days before camo was common. When I wore it to the Elks club one July Fourth, I had drunks hitting on me with Julia on my hip and David laughing at my predicament. My camo bikini got my neighbor's attention too! He spent the entire time I was mowing hanging on the fence looking at me, trying to talk to me.

The move changed my business status in Shreveport. I had been negatively saddled by my past in business dealings. Too many people remembered the little girl, from the wrong side of the tracks, with the funny glasses, who was so poor she had no clothes. I basically did not speak at school from eighth grade until I dropped out, so no one remembered me well. But my lack of social status in a state that did all business by political connections made starting a new business difficult.

Living in Springlake gave me the right address and the right neighbors. I soon secured carpools with the right people. We took each other's children to the private Catholic school. Business meetings became easier to attain. During that time, I became one of only five private hospital owners in the state. I had always looked successful, but now I actually was successful.

The weekend we moved into the house on Springlake, Kim, Ali's mother, came to visit her for her fifth birthday. Kim was eaten up with jealousy over Ali's attachment to me. She pitched a fit for Gary to take her away from me. Gary came and got her. I had custody of her for eleven and a half months and only needed two weeks more to claim child abandonment in Louisiana. They knew the laws better than I did. There was nothing I could do but watch my precious baby leave, just to get abandoned in Houston with a stranger, because neither Gary or Kim wanted to care for her themselves.

Lisa, Another Abandoned Child

I had been living in Springlake briefly when the doorbell rang. Standing on my steps was the most forlorn looking sixteen-year-old girl with a mop of red curly hair. She was tall, skinny, and poorly dressed in terrible brown laced shoes like you see on a maid. "Hi, I'm Lillian and I heard you took in girls. I traveled from Georgia and I have had cancer" she said. I was shocked. My philosophy has always been to love everyone God sends you, so I opened the door and put Lillian in Dana's room to share. They had met each other somewhere. The entire time Lillian was with us, we never heard from her parents or received any financial support.

Lillian had not been in school in years but was the most brilliant girl I have ever met. She told me step by step of a pancreatic and gallbladder surgery she had seen on TV with complete recall. I got Lillian enrolled in school, began teaching her how to dress and groom, and worked on her college admissions. She was just so smart in so many ways, and so clueless in so many others. I told her she had to have one great recipe. I taught her to cook my spaghetti that my husband swears he could eat seven days a week. Lillian

> *Words of Wisdom*
>
> *Most people do not understand the power of a simple "No". Just say the one word and shut up. It is amazing the power the word holds. Faced with my cool firmness, David would choose to let the "new rule" go.*

lived with us the entire year and a half that we lived on Springlake.

I got Lillian accepted into college on a full ride. We were preparing to move to Arkansas and I wanted Lillian to go with us. She came to me one day and said, "I have been thinking, and it doesn't make any sense to me to get a college degree. I am afraid I won't be able to work to earn spending money and go to school because of the cancer. You earn less than my mother who is a naked table dancer, so I think it makes more sense for me to go dance naked on tables than go to college." My only reply was, "You have to get out of my house and leave immediately." I had too many sweet, innocent, little girls to allow an intelligent, teenage, naked table dancer to influence them. I had my daughters Dana, Melanie, Julia full time and Ali, Amy, and Tracy part-time. So many girls.

A week later Lillian came back to me. "I was raped last week when I got off work", Lillian complained. I replied stonily cold, furious with her choices, "Yes, that is part of your job now. You tease the men by your dancing; they wait for you in the parking lot. That's called cause and effect. Get used to it. That is going to happen every night." I felt she had thrown away a great opportunity for a good education with a family that supported and loved her, for drugs, prostitution, and the seedy side of life. I was furious with the decisions that Lillian made. When I think about it now, I realize that the problem with Lillian was that she didn't trust that I would continue to take care of her as I had. Lillian's mistrust of me made her make choices that would negatively affect her life for many years to come. She would lose her son and worry about staying off drugs.

Trisha, the Loss of a Dear Friend

Trisha had been suffering from progressive mental illness for several years and was rapidly deteriorating. She was in and out of mental hospitals constantly. She started looking physically stranger and stranger as she took more and more psychiatric medications that did not help her. She was becoming violent and a danger to herself and her children. She had taken up self-mutilation, frequently waking up at night and getting a knife from the kitchen. Her husband, Mason, could not sleep for fear of what she might do to him and the children. I was keeping the children almost every weekend.

Trisha thought she was the Antichrist. She would carry on about the number 666, making all kinds of farfetched associations that were ridiculous. We took her to every doctor, psychiatrist, and mental institution in Shreveport, with each one giving her a new diagnosis and new medications. There was no allopathic stone left unturned in our search for her cure. But her cure should have come in a search with God. I know now that she needed an exorcism. But Mason and I were not religious enough at that time to consider this as an option. The worst that could possibly happen occurred.

Trisha and Mason got a divorce. They truly loved each

other, but the mental illness was out of control. Medicine; shock therapy; nothing helped her.

Another day Trisha threatened to kill herself and the children, I stood up to her. She was the size of Mama and crazy. I backed her down, took physical custody of the girls, and kicked her out of my house. I put my foot down with Mason. I told him for the children's sake he had to get a divorce, get custody of the children, and get them away from her.

Trisha and Butch

Trisha retaliated by getting pregnant with a little boy from a man she would never name. She then married a man that was not the boy's father. It was the same man that threatened to rape me so many years before.

Trisha was 33 years old when she died tragically. I was in New Orleans opening a new psychiatric hospital at the time I received the news about Trisha. I

Words of Wisdom

Never follow man's rules, only God's rules.

rushed home to comfort her children and my children. It was truly one of the saddest times of my life.

1994

Sale of the Hospital

After the funeral, when I returned to complete the hospital opening, I was sleeping alone in a hotel room, when I started having chest pain. I was miserable, 33 years old, and alone. My best friend had died. Her young children needed me. I was successful in every business operation I started, but my partners were making business decisions that were ruining all of my marketing and sales efforts. I had to make some changes.

I have made my living off the poor management found in many hospitals and businesses. Many managers feel like they can say and do anything to their subordinates in the most hideous and nasty way. They feel the more aggressive they act, the more power they have. I feel truly sorry for these people. Because the opposite is true. By being a model your employees can look up to and emulate, people will follow your every guidance. They will strive to please you and anticipate your requests, doing them before you ask. But first, the manager must know what instructions to give every day.

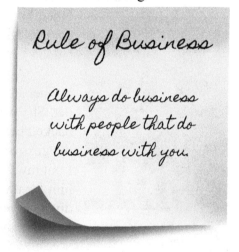

Rule of Business

Always do business with people that do business with you.

Throwing up obstacles to make someone's life or work hard or unpleasant just because you think you have a right because your role places you in charge is injustice. Injustice is perceived by everyone of every age. It has always been the one thing that has most infuriated me. Poor management does not yield the personal power that managers working for the good of the family, company, and individual can claim.

Unfortunately, Owen was spending money faster than John and I could make it. The problem with Owen was that he and Aubrey were partying hard on the company profits. In those days the IRS allowed a 100% deduction for meals and entertainment. Owen and Aubrey entertained a lot at Kon Tiki Restaurant. Almost every night, they hung out at Kon Tiki with friends who joined them for an expensive company paid dinner and drinks.

Even though we invoiced weekly, there was a six month turn around before we received any money from the accounts receivable from the hospitals. We paid the nurses every day and we did not receive the money from the hospitals for six months.

I was so focused on working hard to make money, that I wasn't following the money. I would get a check paperclipped to a piece of paper with a signature line for Owen, Aubrey, John, and me. I would sign the receipt, acknowledging that the check went out. My error was in assuming that if all four of us signed the check; it was actually put in the mail.

In July, everything started to fall apart. My first clue that something was wrong was the day I came in and found the 60 year-old accountant lying on the floor. When I asked her what was wrong, she wouldn't tell me but just kept screaming and crying. Eventually, I went over to her house and I learned what was really going on.

Owen wasn't paying taxes. Instead of mailing the payroll tax checks to the IRS, he'd hid them in a file in his desk drawer. When I finally found out, the debt was well over $120,000.00.

He'd also used company money to pay for his son's very expensive wedding with twenty attendants.

I quit on the spot. I had loved this job and my co-workers. Now over a hundred thousand dollars was owed to the IRS. Owen and Aubrey talked about how John and I were going to have to come up with a large amount of money as co-owners. Negativity reigned. Everyone lawyered up.

I produced the document Owen had me sign when I first started working for him that clearly stated I would never own any part of Tritek in Shreveport, which was the only location we had ever gotten off the ground. This document was signed and notarized by him as concrete proof I was not an owner and thus not responsible for the debt that he, and he alone, had incurred without my knowledge.

Tom and I had what was then called "disproportionate share funding" in the hospitals. If someone is on Medicaid and there are a disproportionate number of admits then the state will come in and pay $243 per patient per day. I could run things for less than that, which meant that we were making a profit. In May 1993, when I saw that the state was changing its policies, I sold my share of the hospital and sure enough, in December 1993, the state ended its disproportionate share funding so the hospital I had started with Tom closed.

While we were prospering, Owen had a habit of taking me to visit a crazy, old, rich Arab man named Abdul who sat in his office cluttered with what he considered supernatural items. Today, we would call him a hoarder, but back then I didn't have that label. Abdul had lucky rabbits' feet, elephants, four leaf clovers, and any other item that inferred good luck. All of it nestled in a pile of game trophies that ranged from small birds to a grizzly bear and some kind of unusual lion like creature and mixed with too many other things to figure out. He even had a coin-operated fortune telling machine that was an Indian Swami like you would find at a carnival. Whenever Owen asked for financial support, the Arab consulted a child's large plastic magic ball for answers. It was creepy and weird. I was always uncomfortable; I knew that Abdul only let Owen in to see him because he was entertained by my banter. He really enjoyed stringing Owen along, but never gave him anything. I knew he despised us both, but me less than Owen.

Owen sued me; I do not even remember what it was for. I went to Abdul to ask for his help to get Owen to drop his suit. Maybe one of those lucky charms worked, because I never heard from Owen again and the suit was dropped.

I chose to pay off the IRS debt with the proceeds I received from bank loans on our house. Against my husband David and Tom's advice, I had agreed to share profits on any sale of the hospitals with Owen, Aubrey, and John, because we were "partners." After the law suit, I had them sign over their part of the ownership in the hospitals. I received ownership and the mortgage of the building where Tritek was located. I had taken a second loan on David and my home to pay off the IRS while I waited on the hospital proceeds to be received. Tom buying me out of the hospitals allowed David and me to pay off the bank. We came out even.

I was able get a doctor to take over ownership of the clinic and the building. I was able to stay friends with Tom and John through all of this unpleasantness. Owen and Aubrey never saw me again. They continue to own a per diem staffing agency in Shreveport, LA.

All in all, it was nasty, bad business. It was worse than a divorce, as we fought over everything. I vowed to never have business partners again. And as of this writing, I have kept my vow.

<u>1995</u>

Moving to Arkansas

With the end of my exciting career at Tritek coming to a rapid close and the sale of the hospitals, the only business I was left with was being the owner of MediKid Clinic, a free clinic for Medicaid children. There were plenty of poor children in Shreveport suffering from medical issues. At the time of the sale, I had built the largest Medicaid clinic in the state, outside of New Orleans Parrish.

Words of Wisdom

Strong managers always have goals broken down into tasks, which are then broken down into steps. Do the steps.

David had worked for Swepco Electric Power Company from the day he graduated from college and would continue to do so until he retired at 55. Swepco had just sold to Central and Southwest (CSW). They were in the middle of a "fruit basket turnover" where they were sending every employee that CSW kept to a different location. David would have to move to keep his job with CSW. He got his first offer in Dallas. I refused to move to a bigger city. I did not want my beautiful children on drugs. To me, Shreveport was so terrible, I did not need a bigger city. I told him he could come home on weekends as it was only three hours away, but he turned the position down. The next position he got offered was the one he had dreamed about all of our married life. It was a return to Arkansas to be second-in-command at the Flint Creek Power Plant. David was ecstatic!

I agreed to a move, sight unseen, to Siloam Springs, Arkansas. It was a particularly good time as I basically did not have much of a job. Dana was in college; the children were good ages for a move. Life was ready for a relocation right then.

David told me to pick out any house I wanted. I selected an awful house on the Illinois River with twenty acres 15 minutes from town. The house was a mess. I thought I could remodel it to make it work. The water was a sulfur well. That alone should have been my sign to look further for houses, but I was an energetic, late thirties woman who was unemployed for the first time in my life. I loved the property.

David couldn't believe he was so lucky to have me select that property; he loved it too. I couldn't fix the house. I worked on it continuously for ten years. It always looked like a mess to me. Other people would come in to say they loved the décor, but I never felt I could get it right.

It was Christmas week. I always visited Sonny and Sue in Mesquite, a Dallas, Texas suburb. I had my three girls with me. I picked up Johnathan, age ten, and Ali, age six, from Gary, to keep them for the holidays. Each year I provided their Christmas. Life was taking a toll on Sonny. Sonny begged me to spend the night, but I had too many kids for their childless life. They had such a bad year, I did not want to add any further burden to them. I can't count how many times I wished I had spent the night. The next day, December 23, 1994, Sonny, my beautiful 47-year-old brother, had a massive stroke. He had fallen right after he had gotten out of the shower and lay on the floor of their kitchen all day, until Sue finally came home from work around 6:00 PM. When Sue found

Sonny, he was breathing his last breaths. Sue did CPR on him. Sue got him transferred to the ICU Unit in a nearby hospital. He was barely alive when he was put on a ventilator to breathe. He had a large brain hemorrhage in his head that had been bleeding since 8:00 that morning.

Dana

I felt I could not leave Dana in Louisiana alone. I was eight hours away from her in a different state. I couldn't see how I would get to her in one day if she needed me. She was only 18. I told her she had to move to Arkansas and go to school there.

That Christmas I was a walking zombie. I couldn't remember where I hid my Christmas gifts for the children that I had already wrapped. I had to take the presents I could find and divide them between Dana, Melanie, Julia, Ali, and Johnathan (Ali's brother). I was stressed out from running back and forth to Dallas and the upcoming move. This was the worst Christmas I ever prepared for my family.

New Year's Eve

Words of Wisdom

Always save every document anyone ever gives you, I mean everyone. If you really want to hide a document, just file a paper copy of it and delete the original on the computer, making sure that you overwrite the original electronic file. Everyone is too lazy now to actually look for a paper copy.

On New Year's Eve, the medical staff called a family meeting. Sonny and Sue had gotten a divorce, but still lived together. The hospital claimed I was next of kin. They were refusing to take Sue's direction. I was mandated to be at the meeting. David and I drove over to Dallas. When I arrived, the three doctors confronted Sue and me. They said they wanted to pull the plug to let Sonny die. I had never seen my sweet "Saint Sue" sister-in-law, get angry. But she was furious. God must had directed her words that day. She pulled herself up to all 4'11" as she said "This is MY husband. I want him any way God deems to allow him to continue to live with me. This is MY life, not yours, I want to take care of my husband all the days of his life. I will not have them shortened by you or your decisions that do not concern us. We are Catholic. We do not believe in mercy killing or abortion. Do not turn off that ventilator! I want my husband to have antibiotics and anything else he needs to survive." They looked at her and said, "That is very good, but you don't have a legal right to make those decisions, she does" and pointed at me. I had risen and stood at Sue's side, understanding the power of solidarity, before a board of life and death decision makers. "We are doing whatever she says, I will not go against my sister-in-law", I meekly said. We left the board forcing an end to the meeting, because if I had the power to make any decision then we were done!

After the meeting, David and I drove home to Shreveport, LA, to spend the last night in our lovely home. To our surprise, Dana had moved everything out of her room to run away to Dallas with a known criminal, Dylan. We were so exhausted, emotionally beat up, and depressed we just couldn't fight her. If she wanted to run away, we wouldn't chase her. Even if it was with a horrible criminal.

They took Sonny off the ventilator against our wishes. Glory to God! He started breathing on his own. He did not die. The doctors had told us he would not recover. They did not expect him to wake up. Sonny had always commanded me with a lot of hand gestures. When I was a child he was a teenager. He would snap his fingers, then I would know what he gestured. He had a way of making things fun. He made everything he wanted me to do a game, which was such a sharp contrast to Mama and Gary with their spiteful meanness. When they wanted me to do something, there was screaming and hitting. That's why I always loved Sonny

Rule of Business

My secret to a successful business is to work three times harder than anyone else.

the most.

I was sitting at his bedside the next morning. Sonny was snapping his fingers and pointing to the intercom. His eyes were closed. It was random. He would just suddenly snap and point, rest a while, then snap and point. Was my brother still in there? Was there a possibility that he was able to think? Then I realized the loudspeaker was calling for Leon to come to the front desk, Sonny's given name was Leon. The nurses were calling the CNA to come help them over the loudspeaker. Sonny thought they were calling him. He was able to hear and respond.

Sonny's progress was slow. He was transferred to the VA Medical Center in Dallas for treatment. He stayed there a year and a week before he was released to go home with Sue. Saint Sue worked all day to support them, went home to feed and care for the dogs, then she went to the hospital to sleep all night in a straight back chair with her head resting on the side of his bed. That is true love.

Siloam, Finally Home

We arrived in Siloam Springs on January 1, 1995. January 2nd there was an eight-inch snow. We had no boots, coats, mittens, hats or scarf's. I layered Melanie, age 13, and Julia, age 11, in layers of light clothing. I let them go out to play in this new experience called "snow".

We moved into a very old, dark, and nasty condo. It was so bad that David told the realtor who was leasing the property that the only way he would be able to get me to stay there would be if they shampooed the carpets. I guess he just overlooked the four-foot by three-foot hole in the living room ceiling that blew insulation all over the living area every time you opened and closed the door.

We didn't have a dryer. The children only had Louisiana

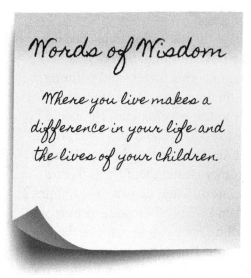

Words of Wisdom

Where you live makes a difference in your life and the lives of your children.

summer clothes. Shopping was limited in Siloam Springs. We had to wait until the roads were clear enough to drive to Tulsa to purchase coats and appropriate winter clothing.

With Sonny in the hospital and his future uncertain, Gary, who had never been stable, began calling me with terrible rage, poor coping ability, and acting out behavior. Gary and Mama could never stand any attention to focus on another person. They would act out until the focus was back on them, no matter how negative their behavior had to be. He went to Sonny and Sue's home. Gary tried to break in to steal Sonny's guns. He reasoned that Sonny was already dead. In his mind, everything of Sonny's would belong to him anyway, so he should take it right away. Mama and Gary never understood the concept of delayed gratification. He called me, discussing hiring a locksmith to break into Sonny's gun safe. I told him I would have him arrested. He could not understand that the community property belonged to both Sonny and Sue, as they had been together 30 years. Upon Sonny's death, everything would belong to Sue. In his mind, everything Sonny owned belonged only to Gary.

Gary was intensely crazy. I bought airline tickets so that Gary could send his children Ali and Johnathan to me for safe keeping. He was terrifying in his drunken, threatening rage. His distress over Sonny's illness was managed by staying drunk and taking whatever drugs he was using at the time. The children were much better off with me. He was a total loser.

Johnathan stayed with us for about two months then decided he couldn't stay away from Gary any longer. Gary worshipped that boy. Ali was content to stay with me until school

Words of Wisdom

The mother is the true spirit of Christmas. The mother makes the preparations, cooks wonderful dishes, buys Christmas, wraps the packages, puts up the tree and decorates, and does most of the work so that her family will have a wonderful Christmas.

ended, when Kim once again threw a fit. Kim had Gary take Ali away from me, so Kim could once again leave her with strangers.

Life in Siloam

I spent that winter and spring still managing the MediKid Clinic long distance, driving every couple of weeks to Dallas to check on Sonny, visiting him in the hospital. Then on to Shreveport, where I would do the books for the clinic and check on my employees. I would then return home through Little Rock to visit David's Mother, who was a recent widow. When I returned home, I nurtured the children, and remodeled the house on twenty acres.

Words of Wisdom

If the mother is not happy, nobody is happy.

That house on Old Hwy. 68 was a money pit. It was the worse constructed house. The previous owners bought everything randomly from salvage auctions. I didn't notice the lack of symmetry in the house when I looked at it before we bought it, but, afterward, I would literally stand in a room with my head swimming. Rod, my carpenter, would come in to stand with me. He could always figure out what was off in every room. We replaced half of the windows in the house, so they would be the same size as the rest of the windows in the same room. The bathroom drains had not been connected the entire twenty years. Under the tubs (two), the bath water had drained under the house, creating a swamp that was so dangerous the carpenters had to cut a hole in the floor to reconnect the drains that were never connected. There was a lack of sealed space in the house with openings under the house that went down to the outside. This allowed a variety of varmints to come up into the house from the open swamp below. I had to have the carpenters seal all the openings to under the house in every room.

There were three sets of sliding glass doors set up in the middle of a large living room to act as free-standing room dividers instead of walls. It was horrid. I had chosen the house. Half the time I lived there I could have kicked myself.

But the 20 acres of property had so many wonderful features. We were secluded with no close neighbors. The house sat on the top of a bluff overlooking the Illinois River. In the winter, Eagles would soar right outside our dining room window. The property butted up to the National Forest, so there were hills and mountains, streams and rivers, with an Indian burial ground right outside our front door. The girls and I canoed, hiked, spelunked, fished, and played on this beautiful property. When I finally got the house livable, we spent most of our time outside enjoying the property.

With that move our lives changed completely. We left living in the ritziest part of big city Shreveport, enjoying the country club and private schools with a group of really mean people. (They could not get over my background to accept me for the person I had become.) These former classmates always felt they were better than me. It used to amuse me, before we left Shreveport, to be snubbed in the grocery by a mean girl from high school who was now an unemployed, divorced, broke, poor, fat slob. As this was a regular occurrence, I would always try to go to the grocery right after work, so I still was dressed up in my suit and heels. It always made me feel better to be overdressed than underdressed when being snubbed. When they would snub me I would run over to get right in their face by being so nice saying,"

How are you? I heard you got a divorce. I am so sorry. That must be so painful for you. Are you working? How old are your adorable children?"

Real Arkansas Friends

I was living in a rural area where no one knew me or the children. Our less than suitable house was better than most of the neighbor's homes. I never went anywhere in Louisiana without my handgun and my concealed carry permit. Here people left their purses on the car seat in the parking lot of Wal-Mart. They didn't lock their car or house doors. Life was much safer and, for the moment, slower-paced. We were quickly accepted by a large group of real, true friends at both church and by the childrens' friend's parents.

Friends in Arkansas are very different than any friend I ever had in Shreveport. I would call my friends in Shreveport, except for Mason, fair-weather friends. Meaning they wanted to be with you if there was a party but if I needed something they were not available to me. But in Siloam things are different. Here we have real friends that have become family. When someone is sick they bring meals, keep your dog, help you with anything you need. People you don't even know do wonderful things for you. Even help start up a new business.

Our Catholic church family became our closest friends. The first thing that we noticed with the children was that they were so much happier and outgoing in Siloam. My little children that attended Catholic school were so quiet, shy, and appeared introverted. In Louisiana, my girls were just another pretty face in a schoolyard of beautiful little girls with long blonde hair and blue eyes. Our girls were not different from the other children. In Siloam, they looked very different, in a good way. They were academically advanced from the years of private schooling. They had been cheerleaders at St. Joseph's Catholic School, which allowed them the experience to make the cheerleading team when tryouts came up in the spring.

Julia was blessed by getting young, Mrs. Natalie Harris as her sixth grade teacher and Natalie loved Julia so much, she decided to be her cheerleading coach for the next six years.

I noticed a total change in the children within a couple of months after we moved. I was dropping a blossoming Melanie off at school. This once introverted child, got out of the car, jumped gracefully up in the air, doing the splits, known in ballet terms as a Grand Jeté. This was in front of the all the other children assembled for school in the morning.

David and my life began to focus completely on the children's activities. Our free time was spent going to church, youth group, extracurricular activities such as gymnastics, and ball games the girls cheered for. We were busy and happy.

Words of Wisdom

I would be so happy and smiley, forcing these nasty people to speak to me. I totally ignored their discomfort as I ignored the snub. I refused to let them get away with their bad behavior any longer. This is a trick that will work wonderfully well with a snob, or anyone who is trying to disrespect you. You can expect them to become so shaken by the total lack of acknowledgment of their snubbing or disrespectful behavior they start shaking. I always found it hilarious to make mean girls freak out by ignoring their bad behavior while acting like they were my best friend. Interestingly, my behavior actually made some of them like me.

The Criminal

After several months I had to go get Dana from Dallas. She had bought a husky puppy instead of paying the rent. Unfortunately, "the criminal" followed her to our home. "The criminal" had been raised in foster homes and then gone to jail where he learned to perfect his theft, lying, and many other techniques to defraud and misuse the law. "The criminal" convinced Dana to go with him to a "buy here pay here" car lot to write her check for a $1000.00 down payment on a car for him. She cried the whole time she was in the dealership, saying repeatedly she didn't have the money. "The criminal" said he would pay her right back. She knew "the criminal" didn't plan to pay her back, as he didn't have any money.

The *Best Buy Here Pay Here* car dealership gave him the title on the $7,000.00 car. He promptly drove to Dallas to sell the car to someone he knew for cash. Of course, he did not pay Dana back. The check bounced. The "buy here pay here" car dealership owners were particularly nasty people. They called ten or more times per day demanding their money back while threatening legal action. I begged them to sue him. By the time "the criminal" showed back up at my house, minus a car, I was so furious I was ready to kill him. Literally. I gave him a head start by telling him I was loading my rifle. I was coming down to my trailer that Dana was living in. I told him I was going to kill him. I wasn't kidding. I was that angry. I didn't have to go get my gun, Dana knew from my tone I was serious. She loaded him in her car. Then they took off.

Later she came back to say, "the criminal" and I are going to get married will you pay for the wedding?" I replied, "NO, but I tell you what I will do. I won't attend the wedding, but I will pay for your divorce. When he beats you up, I will come get you. But he can never come to any family function." She later told me that my answer made her decide not to marry him because she knew I did not believe in divorce. If I felt that strongly against "the criminal", then the marriage probably wouldn't work. I am always amazed when this child actually listens to me!

That was the end of "the criminal".

THE UNBELIEVABLE PLIGHT OF MRS. WRIGHT

PART FIVE

Founding a Company

The Right Solutions

When I left Tritek, I signed a one year Non-Compete Agreement not to start up a competing nurse staffing business in less than one year or within 100 miles. I honor contracts. After I got our house in order, I spent the rest of the year researching demographic data and looking for a niche market from which to create a business model.

I was looking for a nursing job and was shocked by the low wages for nurses in Northwest Arkansas. Four-year degreed nurses were making $11.00 per hour, which was not a livable wage for a college graduate, much less an experienced nurse. I planned to change that, which is exactly what I did. I wanted to build a community for both my in-house employees and nurses. I wanted this community to include hospitals, housing owners and managers, and families. I wanted all the people who worked for me to feel a part of this community.

My personal and business motto has always been: "I don't do simple, I only do complicated." But during this time I came up with my winning recipe for business success:

Diana's Winning Recipe for Business Success

1. Keep no inventory; nothing to store, dust, or depreciate.

2. Do not invest money in depreciable assets. (Buy used office furniture and cut corners as much as possible to give your employees more money.)

3. Sell something that everyone needs, is not going away, and has a high value.

4. Create value in your product through credibility, creative marketing, and impeccable service.

I wasn't sure what career path I wanted to follow in Arkansas. I went to Real Estate School, then decided not to sit the exam because I decided that I did not want to leave medicine. I went to Insurance School, then decided that most of my fellow students—with one glaring exception—were dishonest. I completed both courses.

The best thing about Insurance School was that I made a new friend, Anthony. He was six feet two, blond, twenty-five years to my thirty-five, a sweetheart, but a bit of a lost soul. When I told Anthony I was going to start my agency again, he said he wanted to rent a desk in my new office for $300 a month, effectively splitting the rent. Although he only stayed about three months, that was the deciding factor in my decision to open The Right Solutions, a per diem nurse staffing agency in 1996. I had $18,000.00 in cash for the startup and a $50,000.00 credit line, splitting the rent was a big help.

While waiting for the non-compete time restraint to end, I had spent the previous year writing a professional business plan, which was by now an inch thick. I took my business plan to Arvest Bank. My neighbor, a Vice President of the Bank (one of literally hundreds), looked at the book. His eyes bugged out because he had never seen a professional business plan before. Most of the "guys" that want to start a business just "wrote it on a napkin," the banker told me.

That started the banking discrimination I would endure for several years. One of the male loan officers always called my husband to ask his "permission" for me to access my line of credit. The same bankers had absolutely no idea of what I did in my business. They would reassign my deposits when I had deposit coupons made out correctly. These good old boys just knew I couldn't be making right decisions. After my years of hard work and strategic planning, I was incredulous to hear them say I was "so lucky" to just "happen to fall" into a good business. These bankers attempted sabotage at every opportunity. For example, they wouldn't renew my line of credit, even though I had no debt on it, in the hope of putting me out of business.

I wanted to change banks long before I did, but my husband

could not believe that our neighbors could treat me so poorly. He felt certain I was doing something to aggravate them. I was too busy being the CEO of a successful business to have time to devote to thinking about bankers. But every time I tried to discuss the discrimination I suffered for being a woman nursing business owner, I would get so furious I could barely speak.

As living well is the best revenge, I focused on growing the business and getting a banker that liked me. My next banker, Art Morris, is the finest man that ever lived and was a tremendous mentor for my developing business. What made the difference was that from the very beginning, Art believed in me.

Recent highway improvements had made the closed off area of Northwest Arkansas more accessible to surrounding larger cities. To travel from Siloam to Tulsa had been a curvy, arduous process 2.5 hours away until April of 1995, when Highway 412 was connected to the Cherokee Turnpike, making the 85-mile trip take about one hour. Simultaneously, the mountainous trip from Fayetteville to Fort Smith was reduced to 39 minutes from two hours by the opening of Highway 49. These highway improvements helped to fuel my idea, which was to essentially pull nurses from Arkansas and place them in Oklahoma. This was to make Arkansas hospital pay nurses a living wage.

I created application flyers to arrive in the homes of Registered Nurses in the Northwest Arkansas area on Saturdays because I knew that RN's worked every other weekend. Half of them would be home to receive my marketing flyer. I like to joke and say they all signed up, but they really did. From the beginning, I required my nurses to promise to work two sixteen hour shifts back to back. Even though they would have to drive to Tulsa, which was a difficult mindset for people who thought of Tulsa, which was not an hour's drive down the road, as being "so far away," by working two sixteen hour shifts they got five days off a week to be with their families. I paid their gas and hotel room and $24.00 per hour (more than double the prevailing wage). Everyone loved the program.

Just as I was shocked by the Arvest banker's attempts to sabotage my startup efforts, I was equally shocked by the tremendous help I received from another acquaintance. When I told Walter Gray, a local Siloam Springs businessman, about my new business idea, he helped me corner the staffing market in Tulsa. What he did was to call Tulsa area nursing agencies and pretend that he needed to staff nurses for a physician's office. The agencies--my future competitors—sent him contracts and pricing, which he gave to me. When I went to Tulsa, I severely undercut the competition.

Opening The Right Solutions

It was November 15, 1996. I opened my company in a dowdy, one room office in a strip mall where I could hear the married couple next door, who ran a nurse aide school, have sex. I bought three desks and assembled them myself. This was quite the feat, as I am not handy. I bought one computer and installed one of the first nurse staffing payroll systems available. I bought a three-person phone system. I bought the first combination fax, copy, and printer available. I bought a cheap Xerox copy machine, which proved to be one of my more prudent investments, as anytime it broke down I could call Xerox. They would send me a box to put the broken machine in then overnight me a new one. This was no small copy machine. Technically, I had only half of the dowdy, one-room office. Anthony occupied the other half with his insurance selling business.

I had bought a five-inch-thick directory of all the hospitals in the United States in a big blue phone book. The directory had all contact information, including the names of the officers' in the hospitals. I started working my business plan. I selected Oklahoma and Arkansas hospitals outside of the Northwest Arkansas corridor, within a two-hour driving radius. I called every person in both states. As before, when staffing Tritek, finding the right person was the tricky part. It took me numerous calls to identify the decision maker for each hospital. I sat every day at the phone making hundreds of calls, setting up appointments, then traveling to take the decision maker to lunch, negotiating contracts, and signing up nurses.

After seven weeks, I still did not have any business. Not even one shift. Finally, on New Year's Eve, Eureka Springs

Hospital requested my first shift. Anthony took the call. I had gone out to deliver holiday marketing gifts of popcorn to local hospitals. (I had bought the popcorn half price after Christmas). By the time I returned to the office, Anthony had staffed the Eureka Springs shift with an RN named Carrie. I was shocked and delighted! We were off and running.

Carrie had two little girls and a husband that didn't work because of a bad back. She was the family breadwinner who worked non-stop to provide a better life. I like to think that my very first staff had fulfilled my goal to make life better for my nurses. Because she worked for me, Carrie was able to save enough money to move to Texas, where she had an opportunity to make increased pay.

In the first month of the 1997, I continued to staff Eureka Springs Hospital, an unusual, tiny, eleven bed hospital located in an artist community in the Ozark Mountains. In 1997, their number one diagnosis was AIDS. The little, three-bed Emergency Room hosted a variety of very sick patients, so that winter they required skilled and trained staff. I would receive a call, then try to staff it. If I couldn't find anyone, I would throw on my scrubs, drive the perilous, curvy, mountainous roads an hour and a half away and work the twelve-hour night shift after working in the office all day.

That February, a terrible event occurred that propelled my business forward in a hurry. The only other agency in town that was at all similar to mine was owned by a young lady named Kelly, who specialized in staffing LPN's and CNA's to nursing homes. She would pick up her nurses, then drive them to their assignments. She was killed one night, as her car flew off a mountain road after driving one of her nurses to work in Eureka Springs. Her successful company closed overnight. This left her facilities scrambling for a replacement agency.

Within a week, I had nursing homes responding to my calls for service. I had no CNA's to staff. I had not marketed to CNA's or LPN's. I knew that RN's would bring their LPN friends and I had not planned on a CNA staffing model for my business. But when you have a new company with no business, CNA business is better than no business. I signed eleven nursing homes in two

271

months. Business was booming!

On a typical day, I was up at 5:30 AM fixing breakfast, packing lunches for the whole family, then getting to the office by 8:00 AM. There I would market, call my hospitals for needs, do the accounting and payroll, insurance and risk management, then credential nurses for work in the hospitals. Because this was an overtime job, I had no time to staff the nurses during the normal work day of 8:00 AM to 5:00 PM. I raced home to my husband and children, arriving home by 6:00 PM, after a 45-minute commute.

I cooked supper, washed laundry, and supervised the children's homework. I settled in to staff the nurses and CNA's from 8:00 PM to 11:00 PM. Everywhere I went I carried my cell phone, which was the size of a man's shoe, a pager, and a large, metal, rolodex box with all the nurses contact information. I took calls wherever I was. I was running the company from my car on the drive home. When I was at church, I returned calls from the vestibule. Every Thursday and Friday, the entire time I was watching the girls cheerlead at a basketball ball game, I staffed nurses on my phone.

On weekends, I was one of two youth leaders for our church's very active youth group. I worked every Saturday for six years on projects with the youth, in an effort to give my girls a good religious foundation. On Sundays, we went to church in the morning, then I taught the youth religious study at night.

When I couldn't find a nurse to work a particular shift, I put on my scrubs and worked the night shifts, usually a minimum of an hour from our home, but frequently two hours away. My easygoing competence won me many friends working in these short-staffed facilities. I went to work looking professional. I knew what I was doing because I am an excellent nurse with highly competent skills. The staff responded with favor to me. I recruited the nurses I worked with from the facilities, then sent them to other facilities. I then filled the positions they vacated with nurses I had recruited in the same manner. Every shift I worked created more and more opportunity. More nurses signed up to work with me primarily because they were treated poorly by their nurse manager, while I was kind and easy going, but, at the same time, professional and competent.

In March of 1997, Dana was attending college in Monroe, Louisiana and came home for a week for spring break. Since she didn't have any friends in Arkansas and had nothing much to do, she came to work with me. I told her to sit at one of the empty desks, long vacated by Anthony, who I am sorry to say asked me for a job, but I didn't have the resources to pay him. I truly wish I had found a way to hire him. But I wasn't even able to pay myself. I did not pay myself for seven years after I started this company. I have often felt like Jacob, in the Bible, who had to work seven years for each of his wives.

Every cent I made was plowed right back into the company to make payroll because hospitals consistently delayed their payment of invoices. I had to carry accounts receivables for months before any money came in, from shifts I had already paid the nurses for, at the time they worked. I had implemented a new policy of daily pay, thus making my staff even more eager to work for me, while increasing my cash flow crunch.

The phones were ringing off the hook by this time. I was frantically running around trying to do everything I could to meet the demands of the facilities and nurses. 19-year-old Dana was looking around. She spied a large bundle of resumes I had not had time to process. "What are these, Mother?" she asked as she picked them up.

"People who need work that I haven't had a chance to process," I responded, in between frantically returning hospital and nursing home calls.

Dana picked up the phone. She called nurses (without being told), then scheduled them to come into the office to complete their credentialing, so they could work. When they arrived, Dana, again without any training, processed the paperwork. When the nurses left, she had booked them for a full month's assignment of hours. In that one week, Dana doubled my business. That's when I realized I had to hire some help!

I applied for my daughter Melanie to receive a hardship driver's license at fourteen. Melanie is the most responsible person I have ever met. She has my personality. I needed Melanie to drive herself and her younger sister to school and activities while I launched the Company. David had a very busy job, worked long hours, and wasn't available to drive the children either. We lived back in the woods so there were no neighbors available to help. The hardship license was granted because David and I both worked in two different towns. The children went to school in a third town. That hardship license allowed me the freedom to launch the business into overdrive.

Just when I thought I couldn't do another thing, the Columbia Hospital Group located in Tulsa, Oklahoma signed my contract for thirteen hospitals. In four months, I had signed contracts on fourteen hospitals and eleven nursing homes. My first assignment with Columbia was a travel contract working weekends in the Intensive Care Unit. I also had no one to fill the 13-week travel nurse assignment at Doctor's Hospital, in Tulsa. So I staffed myself for 11-7 Friday night, 3P-7A Saturday and Sunday. I could not afford to lose this contract with Columbia. Basically, I gave up sleep for three months. I worked the contract myself.

I would work all week at the office then all weekend at the hospital. After working a sixteen-hour shift at the hospital, I would get off work at 7:15 Monday morning. Then I would drive an hour and forty-five minutes to the office in Springdale, Arkansas, with my suit and heels in the trunk of my car. I could get to the office by 9:00AM. I would work all day, cook supper (I still cooked all the meals at home), and packed lunches. I visited with the family, then staffed nurses and drop exhausted into bed at 10:00 PM, missing an entire night's sleep.

At the hospital, my pager would silently vibrate, letting me know a facility needed staff or a nurse was calling off. I often wondered what my colleagues thought when I frequently took my large satchel into the bathroom during the night when I had to return calls and then book nurses to work. But no one ever complained because I was working harder saving lives than anyone else.

I never just sat at the nurses' station doing nothing. I stayed in motion cleaning and taking care of my patients and other nurses' patients. All the doctors loved me. Once, I even had a doctor

PART 5: FOUNDING A COMPANY

insist that I stay over my 16-hour shift to assist him in a complex procedure on a critical patient. He ordered the ICU Charge Nurse out of the room for contaminating his sterile field. The dummy had waived her hand over the sterile field; to be honest, I was shocked by her behavior.

I had learned a trick to charge up my body: order the large breakfast at McDonald's and a large coffee, which I would eat on the way home in the car. The fat, salt, and sugar revived my metabolism and energy. This allowed me to get through the drive and the day even though I was exhausted. This works well for a hangover also, although I wouldn't personally know, I have just heard that.

On Friday, I would work all day as this was payday and our busiest day to book shifts. The nurses came to the office to pick up their checks and would sign them up for more shifts for the next week. Fridays were very big days. I developed an interesting trick for naughty nurses. When someone had bad behavior, I would tell them, "Okay, that's it, your name is going on the board!" I would write their name on the dry erase board in the office. The errant nurse would get very upset. I couldn't believe how effective this was to stop bad behavior in an adult. They would even drive over to apologize, then beg me to take their name off the board. The simplest discipline ever, and possibly the most effective!

Mardi Gras

During this time, I made good friends with the Staffing Coordinator, Renee, at one of the Columbia hospitals. By the time the thirteen-week contract came to an end, I was "promoted" to work as House Supervisor in the hospital, thus "giving the fox the keys to the hen house." As the House Supervisor, I had complete access and control of the hospital schedule. As soon as the other supervisors left, I would cancel my competing agencies staff off the schedule then slot in all my nurses.

When the day supervisors came back the next morning, they would check to make sure the schedule was covered, never realizing the staff had been completely changed out. When I had a few spare minutes, I visited with all the hospital employees on floors I was not working. I signed them all up to work for me, no matter what specialty or discipline. Business was growing by leaps and bounds.

Some of the registered nurses I staffed that year were Pat and Chris, both males, and then Nettie, Debra, and Cherrie.

My First Assistant

Six months after I opened, I hired the eighteen-year-old daughter of one of my LPN's. She came to work, and, like Dana, watched me run around trying to do everything myself. I was too busy to train her. She just jumped in with no training. Within a week, she was doing all the payroll by herself. Then all of the

Nurse Story:

Pat and Chris: Best Friends

Pat was straight while Chris was gay, but they were best friends. The problem with these two is that they would go to Tulsa, get to drinking, and call off from work at the last minute. When they did work, they were excellent. One day, Pat called to say Chris and he were calling off. I told him if you do this I am calling your wife and telling her you are not working but spending the night with a gay man.
He went ahead and called off from work.
Just as I'd promised, I called his wife.
The next day 6'5" Pat came into my office to apologize. I was standing on tiptoe, shaking my finger in his face when he stated, "I just have one thing to say!"
"What is it?"
"You are really scary when you're mad!"
I started laughing at the absurdity. Here he was a foot and a half taller than me, outweighed me over a hundred pounds, and I was the scary one.

Pat and Chris: Best Friends Continued

After his divorce, Pat worked for me for many years.
Chris passed away.
Pat's story starts as the child of a divorce in California.
When he was 15, his mother passed away. He lived
alone in the house for over a year, selling his mother's
things before DHS found him. His dad was remarried. His
stepmother, who he had never met, flew out to pick him
up. He adored his stepmother. He lived with them until
he was married at 27.
Pat's story starts as the child of a divorce in California.
When he was 15, his mother passed away. He lived
alone in the house for over a year, selling his mother's
things before DHS found him. His dad was remarried. His
stepmother, who he had never met, flew out to pick him
up. He adored his stepmother. He lived with them until
he was married at 27.

accounting. That relieved me tremendously. I was not a good payroll clerk. I had actually lost my entire payroll one Friday just before I printed the checks. I was so distraught when I had to send nurses home without their checks and re-enter the payroll that one of my nurses, Chris, went and bought me some vodka as a gift to calm me down, so he could get paid. I somehow managed to get everyone paid by 5:00 PM that afternoon. I still don't know how I did it. Then I went to work at 11:00 PM that night to work a double.

I was sad one day when my only employee, the wonder assistant, told me she had gotten mad at her brand-new husband and put rat poisoning in his supper. She loved him. What would she do to me? Once I realized how crazy she was I was terrified of her actions and had to let her go.

The Citation of Commendation

On November 21, 1997, one year after I'd launched my

nurse staffing business, I was having lunch at the Hammett House Restaurant with the Director of Nursing from Claremore Regional Hospital. We were seated right next to Joe Carter and Senator Stratton Taylor from Oklahoma, who were also having lunch,

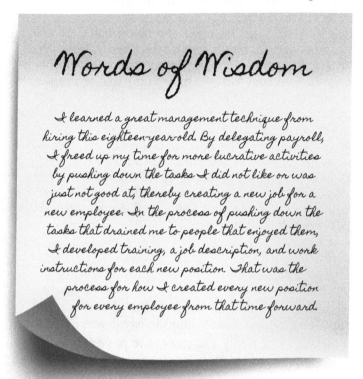

Words of Wisdom

I learned a great management technique from hiring this eighteen-year-old. By delegating payroll, I freed up my time for more lucrative activities by pushing down the tasks I did not like or was just not good at, thereby creating a new job for a new employee. In the process of pushing down the tasks that drained me to people that enjoyed them, I developed training, a job description, and work instructions for each new position. That was the process for how I created every new position for every employee from that time forward.

when, suddenly, Joe experienced cardiac arrest.

I had to think fast. Because Joe was a large man I knew that there was no way I could get him on the floor. The DON couldn't help – he was in a wheelchair after having recently fallen from a tree while hunting and had a broken right arm and left leg, both of which were in a cast.

In my most authoritative voice, I told the man sitting next to Joe, "On your feet soldier, get him on the ground." The red-haired man got Joe on the ground. In the process, all tables were thrown to the ground, ruining the restaurant's lunch crowds' meals. I was trying to loosen Joe's necktie because I saw it cutting off all air when someone handed me a pair of scissors. Once I got the

Nurse Story:

Rick & Pat Digging Up Mastodon Bones in Alaska

I sent Rick and Pat (male RN's who worked for me for years) together to work in Alaska. They had a contract to each work 72 hours per week. After the second week, I noticed they were only working 36 hours per week. Fearing that they would try to sue me for non-fulfilment of the signed contracted hours I called them to find out what was going on.

Pat told me that when they had gotten to Alaska everything was so beautiful that they rented a 4-wheeler. That led to exploring the area. They discovered they could tie themselves off with a rope to repel over the Baltic Sea. There they dug up fossils and bones of dead animals.

Then the packages of fossils and bones of dead animals began to arrive at my offices addressed to them. Many packages were delivered. I saved them unopened for when they arrived back in Northwest Arkansas.

They both came in to discuss what a great time they had repelling in Alaska. They made many memorable moments.

tie off I began CPR on Joe, as the DON directed. Fortunately for Joe Carter, that day in the restaurant, there were two doctors, two ICU nurses, and two ER nurses. The paramedics arrived with a defibrillator. We shocked him eleven times.

When the DON and I left the restaurant that day we both felt very depressed as we knew no one had ever survived that many cardiac shocks. Imagine my surprise when I received a Thank You card from Joe Carter about a week later. I then received a Citation of Commendation from Senator Stratton Taylor for saving Joe. That Citation of Commendation and Senator Stratton Taylor's letter hang in my office today.

In my business plan, I had projected I would close the first year at $790,000 gross revenues. I actually closed the first year at

$795,000, $5,000.00 more than I projected, which is an excellent proforma development or predicting.

The Family

Dana was still at school in Monroe, Louisiana. She was over "the criminal". Melanie and Julia were both very busy with their academic achievements and cheerleading. David was busy with his work. Ali was back with a stranger for the fall.

Gary and I had settled into what I called a "divorce agreement" concerning Ali's custody. I got her every summer (I would provide all school clothes and celebrate her birthday), every fall for a week (I would buy her a winter coat and more winter clothes), every Christmas (I would provide her presents and get her ready for the next semester), and a week in the spring (I would get the summer clothes and school clothes bought). All of Ali's medical and dental care was done during these visits. Often the small child reminded me she needed to be immunized for

Nurse Story:
Debra

Debra's story is sad. At 42, she had three daughters, ages 16, 14, and 12. One day she was scheduled to work in the Emergency Room in Tulsa, when she called off to say she was having chest pain. Her girls drove her to the family doctor. There she was made to wait her turn in the waiting room. She deteriorated. The girls threw her back in the car to drive to the Emergency Room in Fayetteville, Arkansas. She died on the way. The saddest part was that if she had been at the ER in Tulsa, they probably could have saved her. I went to her funeral.

Nurse Story:
Nettie

Nettie, RN, was an excellent nurse! She had twelve children when her husband left her. Her sister-in-law took a dozen of her children to raise; as both she and her husband gave up custody of the children. The youngest was a newborn. Nettie would say, "I would still be pregnant if I could find a sperm donor." Boy was I glad she couldn't find a sperm donor! Twelve children you don't raise are enough. She worked for TRS for ten years and was able to send her sister-in-law money from working before moving to Arizona permanently. Nettie always worked two jobs. She always said, "There is plenty of time to sleep when you are dead."

something or needed to go to a doctor or dentist.

Just as in many shared custody situations, Gary hated me with all the fury of any ex-husband. One of the problems was that I was his sister taking care of his child at his own request.

I figured out how to drive him completely crazy. Gary suffered from complete absorption and excessive love of his son. Whenever the boy was mentioned, I ignored the information about the boy to say something about Ali. He could not stand the lack of recognition for his son. The second thing I would say, whenever he stopped for a breath, while he was screaming negativity over the phone at me, was a line from the movie Overboard, "But honey, I love you!" This one line drove the man to distraction! Every time he took a breath I said this with the intonation of Kurt Russell, until he would hang up in frustration. There was absolutely nothing he could confront me for, I was being so "nice".

Running the Girls Out of the Heat

The company and the children grew. My philosophy in

raising my daughters came from a trick my husband did with his hunting dogs. When his female hunting dog went into heat he would take her out in the woods hunting and "run her out of heat". He had found out if he ran his dog hard enough she would skip her menstrual cycle. I used the same philosophy raising my girls. I tried to run them "out of heat" so I wouldn't have to fight them on some silly thing. I did every physical activity I could think of, to have them exhausted and worn out, while teaching them life skills.

My girls were growing up but spanned a twelve-year age gap. One day they were talking. They decided that Dana would wait to have kids until Melanie, Amy, and Julia were ready. This

Nurse Story:

Cherrie

Cherrie came into my office a broken woman. She had ambivalent sexual tastes and was experimenting with being involved with other women, which was not socially acceptable. She hadn't worked as a nurse in over a year, as she had been in a car wreck and injured her leg. She had spent weeks in the hospital recovering. She had no money, which was not socially acceptable. She had teenage children. Her self-esteem was shot. I sat down with her and heard her story. I begin to tell her the children's story about persistence, The Little Engine That Could. I would listen to Cherrie talk about her self-doubts, and then respond by saying, "I think I can, I think I can...". I told her that if she would take a shift, I would go with her the first time, so she could get her confidence back. She took a shift, then another, and soon she was working full time. She did so for years.

would close the age gap with children having cousins the same age. All the cousins could have a wonderful time together. Ali was a small child. I did not think she would grow up to get in on the cousin plan. But she did.

Queen Concordia

Summer in Tontitown, Arkansas brings the Catholic church's number one fund raiser: The Tontitown Gape Festival. This year was the race for the 99th Queen. As we were the only people in our church that were not from the old Italian families that founded Tontitown, it never crossed our mind that Melanie would have to run for Queen Concordia.

The race for Queen Concordia was not a beauty pageant. It was grueling work in the very hottest part of the summer. It was expensive to the girl running: gas, eating out, and drinks. The sixteen-year-old girl had to go to business after business selling tickets for a raffle on a pickup truck. The girl that raised the most money for the church was named the Queen. She got nothing for a prize except that she would have to purchase two evening gowns. The expensive part is that the girl had to spend up to sixteen hours a day selling tickets for a month. The girls raised thousands of dollars to support the church.

But in 1997, there were not three Italian sixteen-year-old girls. The festival required that three girls run for Queen Concordia. The ladies that decorated for the contest called to ask Melanie to run; we declined. The judges for the contest called us and invited Melanie to run; we declined again. The priest called us and requested that Melanie enter the race. I told him, "Father Corenti, I do not want to have bad relationships with anyone but if you require that we run we will win that race. You will have the first non-Italian Queen in 99

Words of Wisdom

Always look the part of the position you want, not the one you have.

years." Father was delighted with the attitude.

I developed a marketing plan for the most effective sales strategy for Melanie. You cannot sell tickets for a raffle to women for a pickup truck. They just will not buy them. I decided that we would hit all the fairs, carnivals, ball games, and any other venue where people were already spending money. There we would sell tickets. My child would wear a cute sundress with the Queen Concordia sash, to look the part of the Queen.

One of the girls running had lost the year before. She was running the second year in a row. I often wondered about the sanity of doing this. Her strategy was to sell tickets outside one of the local family-owned Italian restaurants. This restaurant was very busy, with people waiting in line to get in to eat, so this was a great sales spot. Accidently, David and I went to eat supper there. As luck would have it, we were seated in the window with the girl selling tickets right in front of us. She had her back to me. I started timing and counting her sales. I did this for one hour. I then multiplied the number of sold tickets by her time frame available to sell, (the restaurant was open from 5:00 PM to 9:00 PM, six nights a week, so she had 24 hours to sell per week) by the number of weeks in the contest. I came out with 8,510 tickets that she would sell. I now knew the number to beat! She actually sold 8,001 tickets, while Melanie sold over 11,000.

Melanie won the 99th Queen Concordia title. I still remember the first line of her acceptance speech, "As you may know my last name does not end in a vowel!" After the speech, Melanie was being interviewed by a news reporter. She was being filmed for the ten o'clock news. I was standing right behind Melanie. She had on the most beautiful Cachet sequined evening dress with no back. Since all my girls were skinny, fit girls with no breasts, we bought adhesive bra cups that taped separately on each breast. As we were standing there, with Melanie being filmed, she lifted her arm. The left breast cup flew out of her dress over her left shoulder. I caught it in the air and snapped it into my purse. When she finished taping, we both laughed like crazy. All I can say is that I am glad it was Melanie; my other girls would have been scarred for life, to have been filmed with bra cups flying. Melanie and I

Cancer Scare:
Stage 0

It was at the end of the Queen Concordia race that I went for my annual pap smear. It was positive for pre-cancerous cells of non-HPV origin. I was 40. I have been tested over 10 times. I have always been non-HPV positive, but the MDs kept testing me, as they refused to believe my cancer could be a gene.[20] It was cancer Stage 0.

Julia was on a softball team that traveled to Little Rock to play a game. I had been diagnosed with cervical dysplasia. I was forced to endure five different horrible procedures to remove cancerous cells. The last one had been the day before we left for Little Rock. The doctor just cut the entire end of my cervix off in his office. He packed my vaginal canal with packing. ("In his office" is code talk for "no anesthesia").

David and I drove down the night before to stay with David's mother, Pauline, before the big game. I woke up the next morning in a huge pool of blood. To my horror, I had hemorrhaged in Pauline's bed. I knew I could not go to an Emergency Room in Little Rock because "ER Doctor" means "the guy who flunked out of his residency program". I knew that he would want to examine, poke around, and still not know what to do. I called the doctor who had done the surgery. He said I had to be packed with seaweed to stop the bleeding. I could never get used to Siloam Springs hospitality. When the other mothers on the ball team found out I was ill, Camila immediately offered to keep Julia that weekend and bring her home Sunday. I had never met Camila, but we are friends to this day. I knew by looking at Camila she was a wonderful, sweet person who would truly take good care of Julia. We left her with a total stranger. David and I had to hope I could get safely back to Fayetteville before I bled to death to meet my doctor in the ER. It was risky, but everything turned out okay. That was the first time I had cancer.

thought it was hilarious!

Growing The Right Solutions

My office phone number was 1-800-98-Staff. Work continued to grow. I chose that number because I felt that 1998 would be my big staffing year. One day, a young man came into the office and interviewed for a job helping me with accounts receivable. I was having difficulty being both the marketing representative and "best friend" to the hospitals and then also having to call to get them to pay their invoices. Many times, I had used a fictional "boss" to encourage the hospital accounts receivables clerks to pay my invoice.

Isaac was perfect! He was not the nicest person. Instead, he was very direct. We got along fine for six years. He reminded me of my brothers. Isaac could work in collections to call on the invoices. I could continue to be "best friends" with the clients. I never mentioned money (another Louisiana No No). Within two months, Isaac was running everything in accounting.

In the fall of 1998, I hired a CPA named Jack. I was hoping to get invaluable knowledge about paying nurses across state lines, but Jack turned out to be a disaster. He was married, but in love with a waitress who worked down the street. I would look around and couldn't find him. He would sneak off; this was hard to do as we had a three-room office. He was never completing his work while running off to see the waitress. Mama always said not to mess up peoples' holidays, so I had to wait until the day after Christmas to fire him.

Isaac convinced me to buy a computer for every employee. Today that may be hard to believe, but then we functioned just fine with a rolodex and three ring binder. Actually, it was a lot faster to work manually than to enter everything into the computer. When we first started on the computers, no one in the office knew how to use the computer except Isaac and me. We had a total of six people working in the office when we decided to "network."

Designing Software

I could not buy software "off the shelf" because no shelf

Nurse Story:
Jane

As the year ended, a nurse named Jane came to work. Jane worked for me because she supported her two teenage children. Although her husband worked, he could not afford his expensive tastes in racing and buying cars. His race cars would cost over $100,000.00. Because Jane worked for me at TRS she was able to afford these cars and raise her boys.

Jane never spent any money on herself. She worked 72 hours per week, every week. Jane worked for TRS for years until her husband was injured racing cars. It was inevitable. She stayed home to "nurse" his broken body back to health, but he was never able to race or work again. Jane came and talked to me. She told me that she just needed to work 40 hours a week since the boys had grown up and her husband no longer raced. She took a job at a local hospital to support her husband.

existed and there was no software to buy. Instead, I wrote it. I had a red folder in which I'd written down a prompt system with numbered steps to tell everyone what they needed to do. For example, I'd figured out how to tell if a deal was incorrect financially, or if a nurse was overspending her budget on renting furniture, and we turned these steps into software. For years, Isaac and I would meet at the office Sunday nights to make design changes as needed, which we would then discuss with our IT team who wrote the code. We called the software program Travel Pro.

Per Diem to Travel

During this time, Mike, an RN, talked to me almost daily about starting a travel company. Mike wanted me to get out of per diem (daily staffing) and go into travel nursing. Never one to make a rash decision, I researched this topic for months, before I finally concluded that travel nursing would satisfy most of my issues and problems. I would no longer be land locked geographically, I wouldn't start each day out in the hole with no one scheduled to work, and I would increase satisfaction with both the nurses and the hospitals. As 1998 drew to a close, I decided to enter travel nursing.

One day, at church, the mayor of Tontitown came to David and me to tell us we needed to purchase 311 Henri De Tonti from him. I told the mayor that we didn't have the money to buy a four bedroom, three bath brick home and the purchase was simply impossible.

The mayor must have prayed hard because we somehow got enough money to buy it ten months later. He never put it up for sale on the market. We never saw or walked through the house before we made the purchase. It was a miracle because I would never have thought of buying the house if the mayor hadn't proposed the idea. We invested $18,000 renovating to make it into an office. We made the garage into a large meeting area and put in many doors. I loved the office and stayed there for 20 years.

I worked all night before the morning we were to buy the property. I met David in Springdale, Arkansas at the title company. They had already given the mayor his check before we got there (this would not have been done but he was terminally ill with cancer). The title company gave me the first page. This page did not match anything I had discussed with Arvest Bank. We called the bank, who never sent a representative. And so the day went. Another page would be presented, and nothing would match the agreement. At 4:00 PM, the clerk of the title company came in and announced that Arvest Bank had changed the paperwork minutes before I got there. She still had the changed copy. I furiously signed the paperwork with Arvest. I went early the next morning and changed everything to a different bank. I cancelled everything I had at Arvest and have never done business with them again. The president of that bank said, "we are not discriminating against you as a woman, we were just saying how "lucky" you were to have fallen into your business." I guess that eight years of education

TRS Story:

Hired Lynda to Design Travel Paperwork - 1999

I was friends with the middle school guidance counselor named Lynda. She came to work for me during the summer as she was preparing to pay for her oldest child's college. Her job that summer for TRS was to rewrite the entire per diem nursing paperwork to travel nursing paperwork. She did a fabulous job. Lynda finished the travel nursing paperwork, then made sure all the flowerbeds in the yard were in top shape. I have always appreciated her finishing the travel nursing paperwork, as the completion of this propelled me into travel nursing.

with a BSN and MBA was just "lucky." Forget about experience.

The "Supervisor"

I hired a manager for the Tulsa Oklahoma office. She worked alone, but one of her responsibilities was to tell the nurses the shifts that we had available. She got into the habit of referring to herself in third person as "The Supervisor." Then she got into the habit of announcing this vocally to everyone on the phone. "The Supervisor" is calling or "The Supervisor" wants this. She called the Tontitown corporate office one day to tell one of my recruiting employees that "The Supervisor" was calling and she better drop everything and do what she said fast.

I picked up the phone immediately. I explained to her that she was not the recruiter's supervisor. Just who did she think that she was? She replied that she was "The Supervisor" of the Tulsa desks and the chairs.

Dana Gets Married

Dana met Joshua "Josh" Graves. She fell in love. We tried to plan a wedding, but Luther kept making demands. He couldn't believe Dana was getting married. It had to be in May around his birthday. It was critical to her that he walk her down the aisle. Once he found that out, he made more and more impossible demands. He thought her wedding dress was too short for her beautiful heels (her favorite part of the wedding ensemble) and insisted that she

TRS Story:

Porn in the Accounting Software

Isaac and I came to work one morning to find that the man who worked all night for my company had accidentally downloaded porn into the accounting software, Quick Books. The poor guy had worked for hours in a failed attempt to remove the porn, but because he didn't have clearance to the password, he could not get in. Somehow, he had downloaded porn through a "backdoor" into Quick Books. The accounting team had come in to work and when they opened Quick Books, all they saw was porn. They too couldn't remove it. Isaac worked for hours with the Quick Books team to remove the porn. When he was finished, Quick Books was so impressed with his performance that they asked him to beta test Quick Books for them. As payment, they sent out jackets with their logo on them that wouldn't fit any American man, they were so tiny they were about a child's size 10 or 12.

take them off during her bridal portrait shoot. When she refused because she wanted her shoes to be photographed, he cancelled the shoot. Fighting furiously, he threw her out of the car, right into oncoming traffic on Stoner Avenue, a very busy street, in her wedding dress, with a seventeen-foot wedding veil and six-foot train.

She called me, hysterical, from a pay phone in Shreveport, but I was in Springdale, Arkansas, six hours away. I had no choice but to call Luther's alcoholic mother to ask her to go pick up her granddaughter. For once she honored one of my requests. I regret that we did not press charges on him at that time. Being from the wrong side of the tracks, there is an unwritten rule you do not get the police involved, period. The wedding dress had so much gravel and road rash on it that it appeared ruined, but somehow the cleaner made it look brand new.

After that, he flat out refused to walk her down the aisle. She decided she would not walk down the aisle without Luther. I decided that she and Josh needed to do a destination wedding. We paid for them to go to Jamaica and get married. I didn't have the money at the time for the family to go. They went by themselves and got married in Jamaica. It was sad for Dana, but she absolutely refused to walk down the aisle without Luther.

Later, when they got back, we had a lovely reception for them with a hundred family and friends. We did not invite Luther or his family to attend. Luther waited six months and insisted in having a "wedding" to impress all his friends in Shreveport, in January. They got married again in a big wedding.

The Lake House

We bought a lake house on Grand Lake. During the summer we boated, water-skied, wake-boarded, knee-boarded and swam. Much of my life I kept my girls in swimsuits. I bought five swimsuits for each girl every summer, which we wore every day. I was sick of women feeling ashamed of their bodies.

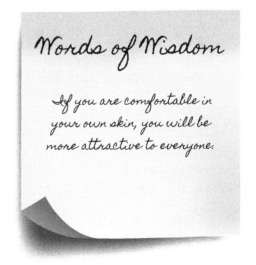

Words of Wisdom

If you are comfortable in your own skin, you will be more attractive to everyone.

TRS Story:
Robin the Recruiter

Robin, a CNA, worked at various nursing homes. One day she injured her back at the nursing home, so I went and got her. I drove her to the ER and stayed with her while she waited to be seen. She was treated and released. The insurance I had at the time requested that I bring her in-house to work.

In-house meant employ her to work for me as a recruiter at TRS. We all sat around a big table in the office, each with a rolodex, a three-ring notebook, and a yellow legal tablet. At first Robin just sat there and did nothing. She had the mindset of a servant who would not make eye contact with me, all the while saying, "yesums."

I realized I had to train Robin to be a person. I set her across from me and gave her permission to look me in the eye by telling her it was rude to not make eye contact. I told she was not allowed to call me "yesums"; call me Diana. I told her she was not a servant. I told her to get on the phone and gave her some nursing homes to staff. I told her what I tell all my recruiters: "Get on the phones or go home."

Immediately after that her behavior changed. She then went from being a servant to being a person and from a person she became a person you'd want to know. With only a 6th grade education she's one of the smartest people I've ever met. Robin has been with me over 20 years. She is my best recruiter to this day.

I wanted my girls to see me wearing a bikini, while not making excuses for having a woman's body. I wanted to change the general mindset to accept female bodies.

Dana and Josh

Dana and Josh were busy feathering their nest with puppy

dogs. Dana bought the tiniest little gray teacup poodle who later turned off-white. I did not like the name Emily. I did not want my granddaughters named Emily. I lobbied for the dog to be named Emily. Emily was just the perfect dog in every way. I loved her, and she loved me. She did not like being one of five dogs in Dana's household. I would "borrow" Emmy, who would spend the night like a kid would with their grandmother (because at that time all

Nurse Story:

The Nurse, Her Motorcycle, and Her Bulldog

I sent several nurses out to Chinle, Arizona to the Indian hospital so they could experience the Navaho culture and increase their income. One of the nurses I sent was named Luna. She drove a motorcycle and owned a bulldog. One time, when Luna got mad at another TRS nurse, she put her bulldog on the front of her motorcycle and drove the motorcycle through the hospital. She stopped at nurses' stations and knocked all paperwork to the floor while the bulldog barked and growled to keep staff back. Then Luna drove off on her motorcycle. Luna never called us for assistance and we never heard from her again! I was underwhelmed by this as throwing a few papers on the floor never hurt anyone.

I had was a grand-dog). When I brought her back, she would sit by the door to mourn for me when I left Dana's home. I offered cash for her time after time upping the ante every time. I was up to $2,000.00 at Christmas when Dana brought her over and said, "Here's your dog. You don't have to pay me!" She wasn't too nice about it, but I greedily took my baby dog. I learned to love the name Emily!

Melanie's Graduation and Going to OSU

Melanie is brilliant. Melanie has my sense of humor and thought the jokes we told each other were hilarious; other people did not get them. Melanie and I have the same taste in everything (a little gaudy). She spent every spare minute with me. She was my daughter that did not date. Melanie has my body exactly from the neck down, except she is tall at almost 5'8". She has David's face, only pretty and girlishly feminine.

Melanie graduated from high school as President of her class, Head of the Cheerleading Team, and second in her class grade wise. She gave the high school commencement speech. Melanie graduated with honors and a full scholarship from Conoco Phillips to Oklahoma State University. I had spent the previous fall turning my kitchen into a scholarship lab, writing 20 applications and winning nine of these for her to have a completely free ride. I have an MBA degree. I could barely complete the complex scholarship applications with all their requirements correctly. There is NO way a seventeen-year-old child has the ability to meet the requirements without help. Since her college was paid for, we bought her a brand-new Rodeo SUV.

Nurse Story:
Garth and His Mama

A male nurse aged 54 came to work for me, Garth. He always wore spandex, gym pants with suspenders, without a shirt when he came in the office. He worked, then went to the gym. He had never left home or married. Garth took a travel assignment. I received a call from his Mama. She thanked me for getting him to leave her house for the first time in 54 years. She was so happy!

Tulsa, Oklahoma Office

The company was booming. I was spending time running back and forth from my Arkansas office to my Tulsa office, trying to keep both offices producing. I was still working in the hospitals and had developed the policy of going to work with a new nurse on her first night to work, thereby giving her a good orientation while guaranteeing success. This allowed many recruiting opportunities for me.

Nurse Story:

Tom

A young man I had worked with in Shreveport, LA, applied to work as a nurse. This man was Tom. Tom's wife was an RN also. She suffered from a terrible drug habit. She was working for one of my hospitals where drugs had gone missing. I had to drug test her and the results were positive. I had to let her go. She was extremely unstable. She screamed and cried. I figured that Tom would quit, but to my surprise, he left his wife of 15 years, with whom he had children, and continued to work for me.

My company policy on hiring Registered Nurses was to take an application and background on everyone who applied until there was some credential that was just so negative I would not be able to place the nurse for work. So many nurses applied for work but did not go to work because of their background issues.

Trouble Arrives

In 1999, I was developing a new sales approach when a

young couple named Nathan and Hazel showed up in my office. They were both Certified Nurse's Aides (CNA's) who worked with another partner, Carla, and had started up an agency in the Harrison area. Because the accounts receivables in nurse staffing take so long to collect, their company had bounced their employees' checks for three weeks in a row. They had a payroll coming up they knew they could not pay.

"What sales volume are we talking about?" I asked.

"Three hundred," said Hazel.

"Three hundred is not worth my time," I replied.

I was not interested, but because they seemed so desperate, I made a business offer.

"This is what I will do to help you. I will pay your people, but I will invoice for the time, then collect the accounts receivable to cover the wages. I will not buy the company or assume any company debt, especially the unpaid payroll taxes owed to the IRS. I will take over the employees and the facilities. Every employee will have to come to work for me as an employee to allow me to do this. They will have to transfer their employment to The Right Solutions. I will hire you both to work as CNA's. Get your partner Carla on the phone to discuss it with her then let me know right now."

Nathan and Hazel didn't wait for an answer from Carla; they both agreed to my terms. Carla, interestingly, came back with a demand that I buy her fax machine for $90.00 as a transaction fee of effectively putting her out of business. Well, alrighty then. It was an absurd term in an absurd situation. I agreed to buy the fax machine.

We decided that I would come the next morning to Nathan and Hazel's house located in Harrison, Arkansas, to sign up the employees. I would pay them 60% of what they were owed for the last three weeks. As I drove over to Harrison, I was disenchanted with my decision to take on 300 hours, especially with the inconvenience it was causing me that morning. 300 hours of nursing aide work a week was only 7.5 employees. I could have kicked myself for making this deal for 7.5 employees a week. I knew that Nathan and Hazel were two of the less than eight employees. I felt sorry for the situation they found themselves in, as they were so desperate. 300 hours a week for CNA work at a low, billable rate. This was not a good business decision. I was wondering why in the world I was doing this, because I never made bad business decisions.

To top it off, Harrison, Arkansas, is the armpit of America. It is the home of the President of the Ku Klux Klan, which in 2015, was Thom Robb. Living there are a disproportionate population of low-income, uneducated, back woods hillbillies. These people have no teeth, because a disproportionate number of inhabitants of Harrison use methamphetamines and other illegal drugs. They believe that taking a two-week course as a CNA is a great career path for the rest of their lives. If you Google Harrison, Arkansas the leading headline is about a billboard advertising "WhitePrideRadio.com" which redirects to a page for "KKKRadio. com." Their football team is named the "Goblins." The racial profile of this town is 91.7% white, 4% Hispanic, and less than 0.8% are black.[7] These people are not racially or culturally diversified--as we say in Arkansas, their family trees do not fork.

Rule of Business

Always clarify what the terms of the deal actually are before agreeing to take over a company.

The median income for a family is $35,400 per year.[8] The majority of households are headed by single females with 25% of the population being children.[9] In my experience, the majority of the Harrison residents in the Nursing Aide profession were not nice people and were extremely rough.

As I pulled up to Nathan and Hazel's dilapidated, scary, pitiful home, I saw cars everywhere. I had brought my check book, some employee application packets, and a combination copy-fax printer. The smokers glared at me from the porch as I parked my car in the only place I could find—the backyard.

As I walked to the front door in my business suit and five-inch heels, Nathan ran out to meet me. "What is all this?" I said, shocked by the numbers of angry people waiting for me to arrive.

"These are the people that haven't been paid in three weeks. They are mad! I think if we don't pay them, they will kill us," he said in a frightened voice.

"I thought you said 300! That's less than 10 people! Who are all these people?" I asked.

"We did say we had 300 shifts," Nathan said.

I then understood. I had hard balled them because I thought they only had 300 hours because that was how we counted in my office. I talked in billable hours. But this company of CNAs talked in shifts not hours. This made no sense to me because there are eight-hour shifts, twelve-hour shifts, and sixteen-hour shifts. Their "300" shifts were all twelve-hour shifts. In other words, this acquisition effectively doubled my company overnight. I was staggered. I was glad I had not known the enormity of this undertaking until I walked in their door.

But first, I had to pacify sixty furious future employees.

I started addressing the crowd. They murmured and said terrible things, but having grown up in the ghetto, there wasn't a lot these hillbillies could say that I hadn't heard from the homies from the hood in Shreveport, Louisiana. "I will pay you 60% today. Then you will get a paycheck on the following Friday," I began. More grumbling from the crowd. "You don't have to come to work for me, you can just leave now. I will pay the people that do want to come to work for me."

The first nurse aide in line was a very short, heavy, poorly-groomed (as were they all) young woman with a very big chip on her shoulder. She handed me her time sheets and then demanded a check, refusing to complete the employee application. I refused to give her a check. Standing up, I loudly addressed the room. "I will pay what I can bill. I can only bill for my employees. If you want to be paid you will complete the employee application, if not, I will not pay you." I continued to stand. Talk about a standoff.

I soon had a packet of completed application forms handed to me. I quickly calculated the 60% and wrote a check. When the first person had a check in hand she was out the door to cash it. The rest of the people of Harrison signed up. The tension in the room cleared up with the expectation of receiving money after three weeks of bounced paychecks. Everyone got happy.

I knew I only had $8,000.00 in the account so I had to excuse myself to go to the car for more "supplies." I called the office and told Isaac to cover the account because all the employees were headed to a Harrison branch of my bank to cash their check. Most of the employees did not have checking accounts so they went directly to my bank branch for cash.

That turned out to be the morning half of the company. That afternoon we had another 60 employees show up to be paid. By that time, they had all been talking with the morning group, so the afternoon crew was a calm and happy group.

I immediately hired Nathan and Hazel to work staffing the nurse aides of Harrison, since they had done a great job. Initially, they worked out of their home, which was not a suitable environment for anyone (even them) to live in. This was abject poverty in Harrison at its worst.

Next, I rented an office in a small strip mall on Highway 62. The business next door was a sandwich shop that baked their own bread. It smelled wonderful when I first looked at the property, but I learned there are many reasons you don't want to be located next door to a bread baking enterprise. First, the smell makes you hungry all day. Second, you have to deal with the bugs and rodents that smell the bread.

The office in Harrison quickly became a disaster. We were broken into every other day even though I posted signs that said we had no cash or drugs on the premises. For some strange reason that I still do not understand, stupid people think that anywhere there are nurses, there are drugs. THERE ARE NO DRUGS IN A NURSE AGENCY, none, nada, zero, zip, zilch. There are no nurses either, despite the many times I have been told by a desperate DON to just send whoever is sitting there. I do not reach on a shelf, dust off a nurse, then send her to a hospital. It doesn't work like that.

The break-ins progressed until I moved the Harrison office

Nurse Story:

Gloria Broke Down, Cupcakes, and Childcare

TRS had a nurse, Gloria, who had a boy who was 11, a two-year-old girl, and a baby girl. She had a husband who didn't work but stayed home and babysat. She worked overtime to support her family. She would never book a hotel, preferring to sleep a few hours in her car to save the money. One Sunday, I called her about a shift at an Indian Hospital. She said she would go but didn't have a sitter. Gloria's husband was gone hunting with the boy. I told her to bring the girls over to my house, then go to work. Her car broke down on the way to work. My husband picked her up and took her to work. She called the on-call person, on a Sunday, to order cupcakes for her baby's birthday. She said any type of cupcake was fine, so we ordered a variety of colors on vanilla cupcakes (this was a year old baby). Here we were babysitting, repairing a broken car, and ordering cupcakes on a Sunday; talk about a full-service agency! Gloria complained Monday morning that she had wanted chocolate cupcakes with pink frosting. Talk about looking a gift horse in the mouth! We have a policy, now, against ordering or doing personal items for other people.

into the Regions Bank building on the second floor. The office was protected by armed security 24/7/365. To access the office, you had to call from the first floor of the bank to be allowed to gain access to the elevator, then be buzzed into our office door by our secretary. When I fired Nathan and Hazel, I hired an LPN named Kathy. I had no way of knowing at the time that Kathy would turn out to be my worst nightmare.[10]

Nurse Story:

Jenny and Her Dogs

Jenny was a RN who had three children and a husband that didn't work (this was to become a common theme with Travel Nurses). Jenny was homeless. Jenny also had two dogs. She talked a recruiter who staffed in my office into caring for her dogs, so she could work. This recruiter tied Jenny's Rottweiler to my picnic table. When she went out later to check on the dog, the dog and table were both gone, never to be seen again. As my recruiter was driving home with Jenny's Yorkie jumped out the rolled down window hitting his head on the pavement dying instantly. Both Jenny's dogs were gone on the same day. But the recruiter told Jenny, whenever she asked, that the dogs were fine.

Good thing for the recruiter, it turned out that Jenny needed to place the dogs, so she could move into a tent with her husband and three children in the woods in Oklahoma. She lived in the woods in this tent for several years. She got the phone company to run a line and nail a pay phone to a tree outside the tent so that I could call her for work. She worked as much as she could be staffed. All taxes due were always paid on time by both her and TRS. I wish she was as diligent about educating her children. She "home schooled" and was never at home. She worked for me for years.

A New Building

I began designing a building I needed to build in front of the house on 309 Henri De Tonti that became 311 Henri De Tonti. I wanted a place for my employees to gather at break times where they were protected from traffic and the dangers of being on a heavily trafficked road. It took me one evening to design the building I could afford. For maximum space with limited funds, I built a metal building that contained 7000 square feet. I reserved 2000 square feet as unbuilt space to design later.

TRS Story:

The Murder Conspiracy Attempt
November 23, 1999

The business and other issues with Harrison continued through the year. It was David and my anniversary. I had been on call at night for four years, without a day off. I told my second-in-command, a woman named Traca, that I was taking the night off. I would not be taking any calls that night, as David and I had plans. I told her not to call me under any circumstances. My arrogance almost got me killed.
Traca called and called me while I ignored her calls. I was determined to take the night off to spend with the man of my dreams. The next morning, I went to work to find that Traca had been calling me because a woman clerk had called to say that she had witnessed her bosses, Ruby, Selene, and Tina, borrow $5,000.00 from the bank, and then given the money to a man to kill me.

I began the hard work of getting permits, water perk testing, and hiring an architect to redesign what I had already designed. David and my best friend was a contractor named Jonathan Barnett so the decision of who to hire as a contractor was easy.

Conception to completion took a year and a half. It only took ten months to build the building, which was state of the art at the time. We always called it the "new" building, even years later, when it had become old.

The Murder Conspiracy Attempt
Continued

As I later found out, these three had come up with
a business plan to kill me and take over my business.
Luckily, the clerk's brother-in-law was an attorney, who
had informed the hapless clerk that she was part of
conspiracy to commit murder unless she informed me of
the plan.

I was furious. I called the woman who was the clerk in
their office. She put the office manager on the phone,
confirming the plan and the events as told. I ordered
the two women to drive to Springdale immediately
to meet with me. They claimed they had no money
for gas. I told them I would pay for their gas when
they arrived but that they must come right now. They
agreed.

Next, I called the FBI, the Springdale Police, and the
Benton County Sheriff. The police departments were
very sensitive to my situation because three weeks prior
another murder-for-hire scheme had resulted in the
death of two people. What had happened was this: a
couple had received a call that someone wanted them
dead and the caller needed to tell them about it in
person. When the couple opened the door, the caller, a
hired gunman, killed them both.

I immediately called David and told him to bring my
pistol to the office. David is an excellent shot. When
the two ladies arrived, I had my staff separate them. I
brought the clerk with the lawyer relative back into my
office where two Springdale Detectives--I'll call Barney
and Gomer for their expert police work--were hiding in
my bathroom. I also made sure that David and Isaac
were in the office when I questioned the ladies.

All of the people involved with this murder plot had
been in my office within the last month, signing up to
work as Registered Nurses. They had come to my office,
ostensibly to sign up for employment, but with the
ulterior motive of stealing my paperwork to start up their
own agency.

I had a complete employee file on each of the
conspirators with all of their identifying information,
complete with photocopies of their driver's licenses,
social security cards, nurse licenses, and banking

The Murder Conspiracy Attempt
Continued

information. I had information and phone numbers of their parents when they listed next of kin in case of emergency. The police arrested the three nurses, but did not hold them because the nurses, "didn't kill me." I was angry. Rule number one in situations like this is always get your control back. I obtained a copy of Barney and Gomer's police report. I wrote a letter detailing the murder-for-hire plot. I then sent the letter to every law enforcement organization I could find in Arkansas that could possibly come across my potentially dead body.

Once these were in mail, I looked into the conspirators' employee files. I called each one. I called every contact phone number, listed anywhere on the application, that led to any of their references or their relatives and said, "I better not get hit by a car, die of a heart attack, or get hit by lightning, because I have sent every law enforcement organization in this state a copy of the police report with a letter detailing what you have done. If anything happens to me, you will find yourself on The Geraldo Rivera Show, then prison for life." I didn't wait for a reply.

When I got to Tina's Dad, he started cursing me. He said I was lying about "his baby." He was the seed money for their start-up business. The next day, their business, which had been open for only a week, shut down permanently. They had a cute name, S.O.S., short for "Short on Staff, " and the logo was a nurse in a life preserver.

Interestingly, a year later, Ruby called to request a meeting with me in her lawyer's office. She had the nerve to ask me for $60,000 to pay for the $5,000 loan she had taken out to kill me. She wanted me to purchase her business, which existed in name only, except she wanted to keep the name. She had nothing at all to sell. She just had Harrison nerve to ask me to pay for her stupidity. I guess stupid just never learns.

While acquiring Harrison employees was a giant leap in the business, effectively doubling it overnight, the negative repercussions would follow me for years to come.

Drug Testing and Counseling

The hospitals that I contracted with required all nurses who routinely handle patients or medication to have routine drug testing. This was part of the contracts to do business with the hospitals. My attorney said all in-house employees must be treated "equally poorly" (as he called it) and meet the exact same requirements as the nurses.

In 2000, I had several people working at TRS that were what I called "questionable." Everything was being stolen every day. Employees came to work, and everything left the day before would be gone: light bulbs, toilet paper, scissors, rulers, staplers, white out, food and condiments, and all cash. It had to be a person who had a key and the entry code. I didn't know who it was, but the key requirement narrowed it down.

Everything came to a head when an in-house employee named Elaine got mad because someone had stolen the toilet paper. That morning she went to the store and bought more toilet paper but was furious because we had toilet paper when she had left the evening before—an entire case of 50 rolls. Elaine had a complete meltdown right then and there.

In desperation, I made everyone line up right then and take a drug test. If they wanted to stay on the job, they could not leave until the test was taken. I told the employees that I would not fire them if they were found positive but would provide counseling at my own expense.

One employee tried to get the secretary to give her some of her clean urine. I fired her for dishonesty. Another ran out the door without giving any urine for the drug test. She fired herself. Another tested positive then grabbed a stapler, raised it over her head, and threatened me if I fired her for testing positive. She was my second in command at 5'9" and 350 pounds.

By now everyone else in the room was watching to see how the scene would unfold.

I stepped right up to her. I have always suffered from thinking my 5'2", 115 pounds was as big as anyone. Because I came from an abusive home, I knew how to protect myself. I didn't back down, but said in a very strong voice, "Put the stapler down!". My angry, drug-addled employee stood down and walked out the door.

In the end, two employees tested positive. Unfortunately, one of the people who tested positive was Elaine who had been unhappy with the missing toilet paper. We never found out for sure who was doing the stealing, but as soon as those three women left, the thieving stopped. I never had any theft of personal property like that again.

In April 2001, Jonathan Barnett finished the new building. It was 99.999% done when we got hit by a spring downpour. Thunder and lightning pounded continuously. Then it happened. Lightning hit the old building with such force that the fireplace was blown apart, the light switch plates flew off the walls across the rooms and the trim around doors and windows flew throughout the building. The lightning crashed across all the electrical outlets and wires melting them. The old building was out of commission and could not be used. Fortunately, no one got hurt.

We immediately moved all computers and other equipment, which still worked, into the new building. We were up and running in 30 minutes.

It took nearly a year of work for the old building to be repaired. I had to replace all carpet. My first estimate for the repair of the fireplace was $18,000.00! The second repairman said he would pick up the bricks from the yard and charge me $100.00 to repair the fireplace. I went with the second repairman and he did a wonderful job. The worst part of the job was replacement of the electrical wiring as all of it had been ruined and melted. That took the longest.

The most wonderful thing about having been hit by lightning was that when I talked to the man who was replacing the carpet he asked if I would interview his young son in law, Bo Ramsey. Bo was twenty at the time, a self-taught individual, and I hired him immediately. He has a memory like an elephant and remembers every detail about the most minute changes. Under my guidance, Bo has written software. It is the best software available in the nurse staffing business, bar none.

Nurse Story:
Donna

Donna was the best RN I have ever met. She began her contracts by working in Kansas in March 2001 and worked for me for the next 15 years. She had very good contracts evaluations in California, New Mexico, Texas, Oklahoma, Arkansas, Alaska, Missouri, South Carolina, Virginia, and Louisiana. The entire time she traveled she never was written up by anyone at any facility. But like the women in so many of my stories she had an unemployed husband who was an abusive alcoholic that she supported. In addition to her husband, she traveled with Dina, her dog companion, who she dearly loved.

In the early years, we had to make sure Donna's apartment was close to a bar. Her husband would go there to drink when she was at work and didn't want to have a long drive home when he was drunk. Later he was incarcerated for DUI, so she had to work in California for a year so she could visit him while they were waiting for him to be released from jail. When her husband got out of jail Donna went to work in other states, but by then he had lost his right to drive. That meant we had to place them in an apartment next to a bar, so he could walk there to drink when she was at work.

Donna called us almost daily. I had her cell number in my phone. We were her family. Her husband was so bad her wealthy family had disowned her for marrying him.

One day Donna's recruiter called me to complain about Donna's woeful marriage. I understood Donna's position completely. She had to work overtime to keep cars that he constantly wrecked, pay his fines, and hire lawyers. TRS was good for her and she was good for me.

As a travel nurse with an increased salary, she was able to buy several trucks. She was able to remodel her home. She enjoyed her contracts. Donna had fun!

Donna Continued

She used the time she had on assignments to experience all that culture and tourism in the area had to offer. She built her resume with new experience and her travels.

She invited her recruiter, me, and her housing director to her son's wedding. This was a sacrifice for each of us as we had to drive three hours each way to get there and back. This took our entire Saturday. We brought a gift that was a decorative suitcase filled with wrapped gifts. It was big and impressive. Donna sat us on the first row in a reserved space. We really were her family.

Sabotage

Kathy, my Harrison manager, was a Licensed Practical Nurse (LPN), from Harrison, who had recently gone through a messy divorce. We hired Mary to work with Kathy as a clerk. After six months of Kathy working, I was completely fed up with the shenanigans in the Harrison office. The behavior of the nursing staff was out of control. I closed the Harrison office down, moving Kathy and Mary to the home office in Tontitown.

Later, in about 2003, I decided to fire every single person with Harrison's 870 area code because they were all such terrible employees. They were lazy drug addicts who never got to work on time if they went at all. They didn't bathe regularly and were dirty. They had horrible dental hygiene, and some had lost most of their teeth. Once I got a call asking if dental coverage could take care of a single tooth. This individual had only one tooth in her mouth to cover!

I was struggling with leadership of my office staff as I tried to get them to follow me as I planned the transition from per diem to travel nursing. When I make up my mind I am going

Nurse Story:
Jack, CRTT and Goldenchild, RN

Jack and Goldenchild (went by Goldie) had gotten married at ages 15 and 17. They had children young and raised the children. When they came to work for me they came to work together. Goldenchild was then 43, and Jack was 45. He was a Nurse Aide and she was a Burn Unit RN, which was an extremely rare nurse. Jack was the sweetest person; very courteous and kind, while Goldenchild was demanding, privileged, constantly upset and aggressive. She thought she was "Gold." Nothing we ever did made her happy while everything we did made Jack happy.

Jack was able to better himself working for TRS by becoming a Certified Respiratory Therapist Technician (CRTT), which mean he could earn a higher hourly wage. Jack obtained the mandatory year of experience and then for years afterwards traveled for me as a CRTT. Every few months Jack and Goldenchild would spend a weekend together and then they were off separately traveling the US. Jack stayed with me for years while Goldenchild worked a contract and then disappeared, working some distance away from Jack. She ended up working for all my competitors all over the United States, only to come back to TRS randomly.

Jack came to visit me after years of working to let me know he was able to pay off his home. He had saved enough for him to go in partnership with his brother and buy a sawmill. He planned to spend the rest of his days making boards from trees.

to do something, I cannot be persuaded otherwise. Traca, Kathy, Mary, and my other managers were flat out refusing to make the transition to travel nursing. They thought I was making a big mistake because we had the largest per diem agency in Arkansas. We were booking 10,000 hours a week. The problem was, we were only working half of them, with the hospital or the nurses calling off constantly. I added an employee to work nights, so that I had 24-hour coverage in the office to handle the volume of calls coming in. It had gotten to where taking call at night was impossible, as the on-call worker got no sleep. This was a very

Nurse Story:
Sophie Saves the Indians

Sophie was an older, religious RN from Oklahoma, who was delighted to go to work with the Indians in New Mexico. She decided that God would help her save the "savages." We were concerned about sending her because of her extreme religious beliefs, but she was so happy about going that we counseled her not to try to save anyone and hoped for the best. Sophie agreed that if the people she met showed no interest in religion then she would not pursue them.

Her first upset came when she was driving to work and hit an animal on the road. Most of us would repair the car and get over it. But to Sophie this was some sort of sign. She desperately mourned the loss of the poor animal.

Her second upset came when she became convinced that someone had been in her apartment and stolen her underwear. This story seemed ludicrous because Sophie was elderly and had poor hygiene. The nursing supervisor she reported her troubles to asked, "Why would anyone steal your underwear?" Sophie got so upset because she saw this underwear theft disbelief as a sign of religious doubt. She had to be driven home. Because we had gone out of our way to be kind to her, even finding another TRS nurse, Mary, to drive her back to Oklahoma, she saw this as a third sign, of God's love and kindness.

labor-intensive business.

Diana Wright, 2003

With per diem, I was landlocked, with a nurse only able to drive two hours to work. There were a limited number of hospitals in Arkansas, Missouri, and Oklahoma. I had them all. I was tired of coming to work every day with no one on the books the next day to work. We worked all day to have the nurses call off all night. Then my staff and I got up to do it again. I knew by looking at the demographics that the nurses were getting older. They needed the stability of a stable job, even if it was only for 13 weeks at a time. Thirteen weeks is more stability than a twelve-hour shift. But I could not get my staff to see the benefit of not re-working every day, or so I thought. The only person on board with me during this time was Isaac. I hired a young girl named Stella to work as a clerk to assist Kathy.

My first clue that things were not right was when Isaac brought to my attention in March 2000 that the copy machine had 8,000 more copies printed than it had ever had before. He had a graph of the copy machine usage for the last two years. That's why I loved Isaac. He always proved his point beyond a shadow of a doubt. Someone had made many, many copies of something. Isaac and I were perplexed. We had no idea what conclusion to make from this information. Or who had done this.

Diana Wright working, 2004

On April 24, 2001, I traveled with my son- in-law, Josh, to Wichita, Kansas to visit a hospital. He had been working for TRS for several years. Whenever anyone from the company travelled to a different town, it had become our custom to call the nurses that were working there and take them to dinner, lunch, or breakfast-- whatever the nurse's schedule allowed. At the time, I staffed many nurses in Wichita. Two from Harrison were sharing an apartment.

They had complained long and hard about their living conditions and we had moved them twice. I wanted to see their living conditions for myself, so I scheduled to meet with them in their apartment.

I knew when I showed up that was something was wrong; I had to get the access code to a gated community, complete with tennis courts, swimming pools, and beautiful landscaping. The apartment was lovely, brand new, and furnished beautifully. Painted a warm yellow, it featured granite countertops and hardwood floors. Very warm and comfortable. But when I started to talk to the two RN's, they were hateful and nasty, complaining about ridiculous, unfixable issues, that had nothing to do with the hospital or the job they were hired to do.

One of them told me she would be finished with The Right Solutions when her contract was done because she was going to work for Kathy's new company, Nationwide Nurses. I'd always told Kathy that we were able to staff nurses nationwide, but this company and its name—the first I'd heard of—was located in Harrison at a one-bedroom apartment owned by Kathy's ex-husband. The RN's already had a contract in place. I was aghast. Whenever I had tried to sell the concept of travel nursing to my staff, I had talked about my travel nurses traveling nationwide. Later, I found that Kathy had not only stole my concept and name, but also items from the office and plants out of the yard.

Five hours earlier, I had left Kathy sitting at my desk. By the time Josh and I drove the three hours back from Wichita to Tontitown, Kathy and Mary were gone. My Accounting Manager, Leah, was gone also. Traca was acting so strange and paranoid, it was disconcerting. She had herself so worked up knowing that she was betraying me, that she could not maintain calm in my presence. I had to fire her because her behavior was out of control. She immediately went to work for Kathy.

These women had stolen everything from my business that was not bolted down. They stole my phones, paper, pens, my files, my policies and procedures, literally everything. I took Stella, the new assistant out for ice cream. She told me everything she knew. Stella had only worked for the company for a month, was unfamiliar with our working methods, and didn't know they were using her to steal. Kathy was her boss. She had directed Stella to box things up and make the copies that Kathy had then carried out in her purse. Mary had dug up my Hosta plants out of the front yard of my office building to take them to decorate their new office.

The next day, I hired a private detective to go to Harrison to verify that the women were working there. They were.

A month earlier, I had hired a pregnant lawyer named Michelle as a corporate lawyer. I hired her for the sole purpose of re-writing the corporate policies I had written to make sure that they conformed to all branches of the law; state and federal. I got her cheap because she was unemployed and pregnant. She was one of the most expensive "cheap" things I have ever purchased. Hiring a corporate lawyer to work in my office was a big mistake. She made mountains out of molehills, as the saying goes, by filing lawsuits over relatively simple problems that I'd have generally solved by picking up the phone and talking it out with the person in question. When she came to work I had no law suits. When she left ten months later, I had twelve! In short, she wanted to establish her own job at the expense of the company good. As if to confirm her financial motives, one day she drove up to work in a new BMW. I asked her how she planned to pay for such an expensive car with a maternity leave and an unemployed husband. The BMW was returned as I preempted her plan for me to increase her salary to pay for the expensive car. It took years to get "Un-Michelled" by settling all the lawsuits she began. I would never have a corporate lawyer in the office again.

Michelle worked with the Private Detective and Harrison Police to have Kathy, Mary, and Traca arrested for theft and for breaking their Confidentiality Non-Compete Agreement.[11] When the police raided the Harrison offices, they took possession of every document that had The Right Solutions printed on it. The police took 19 boxes of documents and other stolen items. The police officer testified that he didn't get them all. The police had run out of boxes to put my materials in. Later, when Judge Mary Ann Gunn read the verdict, she said what had upset her the most was that Kathy's purse was filled with The Right Solutions pens, notepads, envelopes, and other small items with my company logo printed on them. She was just about hysterical about Mary digging up plants out of my yard. I was hysterical about the time it took to get a verdict and the business they stole from me.

I won the first court case for $265,000.00. They appealed. They won the second case, reversing my win. I appealed their turnover to the Supreme Court, winning for the final time in 2005. When they appealed, they were forced to place a surety bond, guaranteeing the first judgment awarded. That surety bond stayed in place until I won the Supreme Court's verdict years later and was awarded a judgment for $335,000.00, which I collected from the bond. I bought a building right down the street from the corporate office so we could expand to 159 Henri De Tonti.

Stella went on to become one of my favorite employees.

2001

Julia Graduates

It was 2001 and Julia was in her senior year. She was head cheerleader, president of the student body, and number one in academics. The principal called me saying, "Julia must have a phone." "She does have a phone in her car", I replied, confused, because in 2001, it was against the school rules for a child to have a phone in school. I had one that only worked in Julia's car when it was plugged into the cigarette lighter. "That phone only works in her car. She must have a phone that I can get in touch with her when I need her. She is important to what I am doing. She helps me with important events", he stated with authority. I was fully aware that she was indispensable to the school, my credit card showed numerous events that she bought things for them each month. Like a birthday cake for a teacher, or sandwiches for a luncheon. The principal pulled her out of class every day to act as his personal assistant, to do all the banking for the school, host all celebrations, and any number of other tasks he deemed necessary for her that day. "She is the only one I can count on", he whined. Boy did I know it! She would be gone after this year. Off to camp in the summer, then college the next fall. I came home to a clean house every day since the child was fourteen. I had never asked her to clean. Actually, I never realized that she was the one cleaning the house, until she fussed at me one day because I came in and cluttered up her clean kitchen counter.

That year was so much fun! We went to Julia's cheerleading games. I applied for twenty scholarships for Julia and received eleven of them. She got a full ride to college. She refused to look at any other college but the one Melanie was attending, Oklahoma State University. Julia had one goal. It was to get re-united with her sister, Melanie, as soon as possible. We enjoyed going to the celebrations to receive Julia's scholarships, even going as far as Dallas to accept one.

Life with Julia was easy and perfect. I didn't have to worry about her. We loved her boyfriend, Joe. His parents were our very best friends. They still are today. David and I had transitioned to one child so easy and really enjoyed spoiling Julia her last year at home.

Julia graduated number one at the top of her class from high school.

Amy, My Niece

That summer, Amy, my friend Trisha's child, was coming as usual to visit. We always enjoyed her visits. We hated to see her go in the fall. Ali was still coming every summer also. Both girls stayed all summer.

The fall of 2001 was the first time David and I had ever lived alone without children. The first week, Julia was at college, happily reunited with her sister, Melanie, we were without children for the first time in 24 years. David and I went to the mall to pick up something, then David pulled me into a jewelry store. "I want to see the biggest ring you have in the store", he told the salesperson. A large ring was brought out that was in my preferred emerald cut shape; my darling husband bought me the biggest ring in the store as a token of his love for me and the start of our life without children. His behavior was completely foreign to me. This was significant of how much he craved having me to himself alone.

But having me alone was not to be. In a few months, we received a call from Johnathan, Ali's brother. Ali was in trouble.

315

I must come get her immediately. Gary wouldn't tell me what the problem was. I got in the car to drive to Dallas, to pick up a petulant child who resented being taken away from her "best friends".

When I arrived at Gary's house I was greeted by Ali's best friend, who was also thirteen and seven months pregnant with her second child. I think this is child abuse of the thirteen-year-old. I was horrified. I got Ali out of the house in about an hour. Ali was furious about leaving Dallas. She acted out any way she could. I am grateful that I got her at thirteen, when her ability to act out was limited. Living in the middle of nowhere had its advantages. There was nowhere for a disgruntled child who had been neglected to go. If we had lived in a neighborhood, I am sure she would have hooked up with someone rather than stay at home with us in our very quiet home life.

When we got home, I removed all phones from the house except the one phone in the kitchen. Ali would take the kitchen phone and stretch the phone cord across the room to squeeze herself under the chair cushion of my big, red chair with her bottom sticking out into the room. The cushion covered her head as

Nurse Story:

Beverly, RN

Beverly, RN was a great nurse. She always received the highest compliments and hospitals asked that she return. For many years, she worked two seasons per year as a travel nurse and was home for the rest of the year. She was single, had grown children, and had a home she loved. Beverly was so wonderful that when I got severely sick, she came to my house for a month to take care of me after surgery. She truly was an angel.

she talked to her friends in Dallas.

I removed the computer from the house when I saw some of the emails she sent. I washed her smoke ridden clothing she had brought with her and was horrified by the demonic pictures and nasty sayings on her "school clothes". As I got the shirts out of the dryer, I was throwing them directly into the trash, when Julia saw the demonic shirts and said, "You cannot leave the devil in the house!" She carried the shirts half a mile from the house to dispose of them. I do not know what Gary was thinking, letting a thirteen-year-old girl wear a shirt with a pony on it that said, "You want a piece of tail?", or a picture of Satan. I was disappointed, expecting Gary to act like a responsible parent.

As the weeks went by, I tightened up on Ali with the Dallas friends. At one point, we got rid of the long-distance service for a month while going to a phone card she did not have access to. The purpose of my parenting was to allow her to move away from her Dallas influences, slowly allowing her to find true friends in Arkansas that were not headed for jail.

By the time a year had gone by, we were all living in harmony. Ali had all new good friends, a nice boyfriend, and loved school.

We were able to positively influence her, so that by the time she was old enough to be able to drive, she was used to being a productive part of our family, while following our rules. Ali was always a good child. She did not get into trouble. At Christmas 2014, Ali came to me and said that she and her husband went back to Dallas to meet up with her old friends. She thanked me for taking her at thirteen

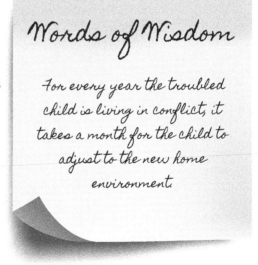

Words of Wisdom

For every year the troubled child is living in conflict, it takes a month for the child to adjust to the new home environment.

Nurse Story:

Johnny, RN

Johnny Frost, RN had an aversion to anyone calling her anything but "Mrs. Frost." I have an aversion to anyone younger than myself, in lower authority, requesting I call them "Mrs. Frost", while they called me by my first name. For that reason, I always addressed her as Johnny as she addressed me as Diana.

She dressed the part of a "Mrs. Frost." She always wore a starched white nurse's dress, thick white hose, and white nursing shoes. She wore a nursing hat pinned to her head. She looked as if she had stepped out of the sixties. Mrs. Frost was divorced, which surprised me as she was so prim and proper. She was well loved by all the facilities she worked with.

I was surprised when Mrs. Frost announced that she was going to work 72 hours per week in California. Her new boyfriend, a CPA, would live in her house and take care of her cat.

A year went by with nothing but the highest praise for her nursing skills when she called me furious one day. She accused us of not paying her for most of the time she had worked. I immediately pulled all her pay slips. We were paying her and had a copy of all her cashed checks. I faxed these to California.

As it turned out, the reason that she thought she wasn't getting paid was that the new boyfriend, the CPA, was cashing the checks himself. If she needed any money she had to "borrow" money from him. I tried to convince her to let me change the address on her checks, but she refused. She had not seen her boyfriend since she had moved to work in California. She had never been home. He was "taking care of things". In the end, he stole all her money, sold her house, and got rid of her cat--while she worked day and night! He really took care of things!

and caring for her welfare. All the Dallas friends had gone to jail and some were still in jail. Every one of them had a drug problem. Ali is not on drugs and she had never been arrested. Being a tough mother is hard, but so worth it when your children turns out just fine in the end.

The next year, when summer ended, Amy, whose mother was dead, decided to stay in Arkansas and go to college living with David and me. She had been working at the office every summer in marketing while pursuing a marketing degree, which she completed. With our own children away at college and summer camp, we had Ali and Amy living with us. We were back to being parents. Living with Amy was easy because she loved to do laundry. She kept everything in the house washed and put away.

Steady Growth

I was working as hard as the office staff could keep up. Most days I worked 10 to 12 hours, then picked up all supervisory shifts on the weekends. I had two long-term employees, Robin and Virginia, who had worked for me for years and were very hard workers. Robin was assigned to Oklahoma facilities and Virginia was working at Arkansas facilities.

I was focused on slow, steady growth. My weekly goal was to invoice out 20 billable hours more than the week before. Slow and steady wins the race, according to the tale of the Tortoise and the Hare. Most companies fail in their first five years. Mine was a new concept and it had taken off. Even so, I was operating on a shoestring. If I needed business cards, I made them myself. I had a friend with a card business who gave me her extra envelopes and I used those to mail my invoices. First growth is easier, but then the economy of scale changes because a business can't continue to grow at such a fast pace. Along the way, I'd had to create infrastructure, HR, and benefits.

My first year in business, I'd brought in $795,000 in revenue and in 1998, the following year I'd doubled that amount. I'd doubled it again the following year, and by 2000 I was heading a five-million-dollar company. Now it was 2001, and I'd brought in $6.5 million. Most important, I'd achieved the dream I had in 1985 when I saw my future in graph. The two lines—a nursing shortage and a rising population in need of healthcare—had come together in 2000 and I'd been there to capture the market. More challenges were to come, but I was on my way.

The Lawsuit with Georgian Court

We were still working with many nursing homes who only did per diem. Unfortunately, the majority of the nursing homes did not pay their invoices. Because I was focused on being completely solvent and out of debt, I did not pay myself a paycheck. I put all of the money back into the company to fund the accounts receivable, which were basically the nursing homes. Most hospitals paid their bills within 60 days. I took it very personally when a nursing home did not pay the bill. They were literally taking my check from me. This all came to head in a very dramatic lawsuit.

Georgian Court, located in Tulsa, Oklahoma, was a nursing home for which we had staffed many nurses and CNA's per diem. They were $129,000.00 behind on their bill and claimed they were going to file bankruptcy. Since my money was unsecured, they offered to pay me half the money to dismiss the claim. I could not afford to take only half payment for the services I had provided. The nurses had already been paid in full months ago and half payment from them would not begin to cover the expense.

All efforts to locate the person in charge or the owner of Georgian Court were blocked by shady business hurdles, but somehow, Isaac located a phone number for the owner, who happened to be a strict Mormon living in Utah. I called him and told him my plight about not having been paid.

He tore into me. "How dare you call me! You are nothing, not even a flea! You are white trash! Do you know who I am? You have some nerve calling me asking me for money!"

"Oh, I know who you are all right," I replied. I was furious. "You're the guy that doesn't pay his bills and expects other people to get stiffed in the process. I tell you what I'm going to do. I am going to close you down. I am going to take your pots, pans, bed, and your sign, and hang it in my office!"

I immediately filed a lawsuit against American Health

TRS Story:
Jimmie's Tuna

Jimmie first came to work for me in 2000. He was always on a fad diet of some kind and he worked out strenuously. He was in top shape. He decided that he needed to take in a certain number of grams of protein per day.

My sales were up, and the management team had performed well. We had worked for a goal of spending the week laying on the beach in Florida. It was a glorious week.

When we got home from Florida, Jimmie was getting sicker and sicker. Jimmie had decided that he would use tuna to get the daily protein grams. Jimmie began taking seven cans of tuna, add water, then blending the awful concoction and drinking it. I would gag just smelling it.

Jimmie thought he had contracted something in Florida. I told Jimmie I thought he had Mercury poisoning. I convinced him to go to the doctor right then. They drew blood. He had mercury levels that were so toxic that he could have died. To this day he stays away from tuna.

Care, Georgian Court, and all of the individual owners of the parent company of Georgian Court. If ever there was a situation where no one involved was who they said they were, this was it. These people had developed a master plan for swindling their vendors out of the money owed for services. They only paid half price for everything. The way they did it was by keeping all of the administrators in the dark at all of their facilities.

Bills were paid out of Salt Lake City, Utah. The vendor would complain, the corporate office would claim the check had been mailed, complete with a check number. The vendor would be satisfied for about a month. When the vendor complained again that he didn't get paid, the vendor would have to refile the original invoices because all the paperwork had been "processed and was not available" The corporate office would claim to the administrator that the vendor was trying to pull a fast one, causing the administrator to be angry with the vendor and think the vendor was lying. This would continue until the administrator finally figured it out who was lying and quit. Then the corporate office rehired a new administrator and started the process again. It seemed to be highly effective--until they met me.

When you file a lawsuit in Oklahoma, you have to go to mediation. I had hired two female attorneys out of Oklahoma City to represent me. These women showed up looking like your grandmother just dragged out of bed. Their hair was barely combed. This contrasted sharply with the super slick Mormon executives in their super shiny shoes, three-piece suits, and big watches.

We went to mediation. I filled four large tubs with files. Most of the file folders were empty but were labeled with outrageous names that insinuated I had knowledge of the dealings of the owners of Georgian Court. I wrote the outrageous claims that I suspected to be true about Georgian Court in size 20 font. I did not have proof. I was doing this to jerk them around like they had jerked me around. I labeled the outside of the file boxes with these claims, then I set the labels

Words of Wisdom

Never hire female attorneys as they want to make everyone happy. When I hire an attorney, I don't want a lawyer who wants to make the other side happy; I want a lawyer that will win for me.

facing the executives of the nursing home in the middle of the table with the list of "files" facing them.

The judge tore me up. He demanded that I settle the debt they owed me for $25,000.00 because they "didn't have any money." He said I wouldn't get a penny more in court! I was furious. "They can give me their corporate jet that's parked at the airport," I accused. The men looked scared. My intuition about their slanderous ways and the corporate airplane was making them nervous. I slammed my palms down on the table as hard as I could. I stood up, and then dismissed my team of shoddily dressed lady lawyers and went to court.

I told Isaac if he would help me beat the slimy weasels and collect the money, I would buy him a recreational vehicle. Isaac loved to go off for the weekend to concerts. His favorite band was Phish. Isaac started helping me prepare for court. He helped get the lawyers focused. I chewed the lady lawyers out and told them they better not show up in court looking like they did for mediation. One of the lawyers excused herself and the law firm owner took her place. That left me with a young research attorney who, unfortunately, was one of the most unattractive women. She wore no makeup with poor grooming and terrible clothes. But she was one great researcher!

This woman was flattered by the male attorney for the defendants, giggling and flirting with her. The only reason he came to speak to her was to read her notes. The stupid girl was so flattered she thought he was interested in her. I angrily turned her legal pad over where he could not read it. I called her out in the hall to counsel my counsel. She had to start acting more professional; he was not interested in her, just her notes.

The other lawyer was a bulldog and tore those men up on the stand.

I dressed carefully for court. I wore a white sweater set that was a mock turtleneck with a long gray skirt. I pulled my hair back in a modest ponytail. My goal was to look like I was the jury's Sunday School Teacher. The executives showed up in their slick, shiny, suits, flashed their diamond rings, and looked bored. When I was called to the stand I looked at the jury, not the judge, when I spoke. I humanized myself by giving a speech about myself every time I was asked a question. "I am a nurse. I own this company. I am only one woman trying to provide jobs in Oklahoma for many people. I have no savings. These people are trying to steal my money after they used the services."

Nurse Story:
Vicky, RN

One night, Vicky, RN, 43 years old, who lived in Jay, Oklahoma stopped by the office in Tontitown on her way to work to tell me that her 19-year-old son's girlfriend was poisoning her by putting arsenic in her sugar bowl. The girlfriend was living in Vicky's house with Vicky and her son. I thought Vicky might be exaggerating or making things up, but I handwrote a full incident report on paper and put it in her file to mollify her.

Vicky went to work. At the end of her shift, she decided to stop by Walmart to see if she could find any medicine to make her feel better. She never made it out of the store but died of poisoning at the Walmart in Fort Smith, Arkansas.

Police Detectives from rural Oklahoma came to my office and obtained the incident report. The police said her death by poisoning and the Incident Report I had written up in her own words were not enough evidence to question the girlfriend. These policemen had never seen Forensic Files, 48 Hours, The Closer, or Lieutenant Kenda.

The hospital thought we had sent them a nurse that died under mysterious circumstances on purpose. They pitched a fit and refused to pay for her last shift worked. It's a good thing my healthcare plan came with Burial Insurance--at least the girlfriend got something.

The Georgian Court Executives made outrageous claims. They claimed that they never ordered a nurse. They claimed that no nurses actually worked. To counter their claims, I produced hand-written orders from the administrator at the nursing home. I provided the faxes Georgian Courts had sent asking us for more staff. I produced time sheets of every nurse that worked there with the signatures of the administrator who had signed off on the time sheets. I countered every claim they made with the sweetest expression on my face.

One of the executives from Georgian Court took the stand and tried to imitate my address to the jury with his own plea that he was "just the owner of 17 nursing homes and money was tough." He would have never authorized the agency staff. He did not want them, so he shouldn't have to pay for them.

Then his ex-employees started taking the stand. They told horror stories: the wholesale food distributor had also been promised only half pay and had stopped food service altogether. On Easter Day, the nursing home had no food to feed the residents. The CNAs, the lowest paid people in any healthcare organization, had to take up a collection to buy eggs and bread to feed the residents three meals of eggs and toast! The ex-employees testified that the oxygen supply company had cut off service when they were paid half price, leaving the patients on ventilators with no oxygen (this causes brain damage). My competitors testified that they had accepted the half pay because they were concerned Georgian Court was going out of business. The electric company even testified that they tried to force them to take half pay to keep the lights on! On it went, with one horror story after another.

The terribly dressed lawyer had done a fabulous research job, including finding these woeful clients to testify. The actual testimony was so much worse than what I had made up for the file boxes.

When the jury went to deliberate, I took my lady lawyers to lunch. We did not even have time to get our food before the jury was back with a decision. I was suing for the $129,000 plus attorney fees which were $200,000.00, for a total of over $330,000.00. The jury awarded me the $330,000.00, then without being asked or petitioned for, they penalized Georgian Court for another $330,000.00. My award was for $660,000.00.

The next day I conferred with Isaac. Getting the jury to award me the money was only the first step. Georgian Court could appeal the jury's decision or flat out deny they had the funds. I was determined to find the money I was owed and to that end decided to garnish all of the bank accounts for their nursing homes. I knew Georgian Courts bank account and garnished it first. I looked up all 17 facilities, Googling the routing number for every bank in the town in which the nursing home was located. I then called the banks and told them I needed to deposit some money for the nursing home. I said the routing number correctly, then a made-up bank account number. Everyone corrected my "error" and gave me the correct account number, so I could "deposit in the correct account".

That day, Isaac and I sent out 45 garnishments to the 17 nursing homes. I had gotten so angry dealing with the attorney women that I was using my old friend and attorney, Lincoln Baker to chase the money. (He didn't have an Oklahoma license so hadn't been able to represent me in the case.) I had Lincoln trying to figure out how to garnish Medicare and Medicaid, when I received a call from the Georgian court lawyer: "We are prepared to offer you half of the award, if you accept the terms of our agreement. I can pay you today."

I told the lawyer exactly where he could go and hurriedly called Lincoln with the following instructions,

"Garnish the lawyer! He has their money hiding in his escrow account! Garnish him!"

Lincoln replied, "I don't think that is legal."

To which I replied, "Do it anyway and we'll clean it up tomorrow!"

Lincoln sent the Tulsa attorney (not the ones who had been in court) a letter with the intent to garnish his escrow account and the lawyer immediately caved. I had guessed my way into where American Health Care hid their money: in their lawyer's escrow account.

I collected every penny of the $660,000 from the lawyer's

Words of Wisdom

People hiding money "legally" often will hide the money in the escrow account of a trusted professional, such as a lawyer or CPA.

escrow account that day. Georgian Court closed for good.

Grandchildren

Dana got pregnant with our first grandchild. We were so excited. Within a few weeks she miscarried the child in January 2002. The whole family was thrown into the depths of mourning. Dana has always been more emotionally sensitive than the other girls and unable to function under extreme stress.

Dana had a pretty little poodle she named Annabelle that got lost one day and disappeared. Annabelle looked like a little white bunny rabbit when she ran a hopping little run. We hunted tirelessly but never saw Annabelle again. It seemed that Dana was suffering one loss after another to prepare her emotionally for the loss of a lifetime.

That summer we had all the girls home for the summer in our already crowded three-bedroom, three-bath house. Ali was being especially difficult at fourteen, so she had one bedroom and Melanie, Julia, and Amy were sharing the other bedroom. It was not an ideal situation. The girls had brought so many things home from college that we had plastic tubs of belongings stacked, one on top of the other, down the walls and hall of the girls wing of the house. It was crowded and uncomfortable.

I decided I had to move. The girls were all nearing college graduation, with no serious boyfriends in sight. I decided if all these grown women were not going to get married for several years to come, I would have to build a new house. David and I traveled to Savannah, Georgia to look at a building plan that Melanie had found in the Southern Living Magazine. The actual house was on Abberly Lane in Savannah. I loved the house, it was beautiful, and we decided as soon as we saw it that the house was perfect for us.

We hired Jonathan our best friend, to build the house for us. We bought land from Jonathan and James Barnett in an upscale subdivision that they were trying to get developed. Marilyn, James' wife, had named the subdivision Summerwood. Because their daughter's name was Abby, they had named the street Abberly Lane. So Jonathan built my beautiful home on Abberly Lane in Siloam Springs Arkansas. It took about 16 months to build our beautiful home.

2003

Isabella

Dana got pregnant again, on her anniversary, with the baby due in February 2003. We were delighted when the ultrasound showed a baby girl. Dana planned to name her Isabella Grace.

Dana went into labor on February 5th. The labor was long and hard, as she was trying to do everything natural.[12] After 26 hours of labor, at four in the morning, I convinced her to do an epidural. Dana had to have a C-section after 37 hours of labor. The baby was not doing well. The problem was that the staff thought the baby was doing just fine. I had cried myself sick after staying up all night. My judgment was not the best. I should've had the baby transferred to another hospital. Josh's mother took one look at the baby and started crying herself. The doctor told us that the problem was that we hadn't had a baby in a really long time. There wasn't anything wrong with the baby. But just looking at her struggle to breathe, I knew this wasn't normal. The baby also didn't sleep. But she didn't cry either. She just made eye contact with whoever was speaking, which made us feel like we all knew her. The night Dana and Isabella went home from the hospital. Our beautiful grandbaby girl died at home after crying for several hours.

The police had threatened to arrest Josh. We waited for the autopsy. We wanted to know what was wrong with our beautiful baby. The doctor receives autopsy results within days but withheld that information from our family for two months. The police were calling, trying to get ahold of the autopsy results, but we didn't have it. I finally got upset one day and called the Little Rock, Arkansas medical examiner, demanding the autopsy report, which

Nurse Story:
Cara, RN

Cara was a fantastic, conscientious, super traveling nurse who worked mostly in Labor and Delivery, Med/ Surg, and ER, but would float to other areas where she was experienced and trained. She worked for a total of eight years. The entire time she worked for TRS she was never given anything but the highest compliments. When Cara quit, she called me to thank me for the difference I had made in her life by giving her a travel nurse job. She said because I had provided her with her high paying job she was able to put her three daughters through high school and college and provide them each with a big wedding. She was able to pay off her house and establish a savings for her older years.

they faxed for a fee. The autopsy showed that the baby had a heart defect. The doctor never spoke to us again.

Our family was devastated by the loss of our first grandchild. There is nothing quite like losing a child. For the grandmother, that child ceases to be "grand", it just becomes your child, flesh of your flesh, child of your body, child that you lost. My "die before you cry" attitude dissolved into tears for months to come. I've never gotten over the loss Isabella.

Closing the Tulsa Office

Prior to 2003 and the Internet, to be viewed as a real business I had to maintain a physical place where all nurses could visit, drop off their time sheets, and pick up their checks. I still did daily pay. But times were changing. Now, according to the Internet, a business was real with only a webpage.

I had become tired of the work that daily pay entailed, and I wanted to move to direct deposit. I didn't want to do per diem or have to scramble in the middle of a nursing shortage for a nurse to work. When I got a nurse, she needed to work at least three months. Until now I had managed to employ both per diem and travel nurses, but now it made more sense to move into travel nursing only. Because of these changes, I closed the Tulsa Office and moved into Travel Nursing only.

Isaac's Demise

Isaac was my favorite employee. Every day I looked forward to going to the office to get to work with him. Every day we had lunch together. Every day he had a long list of items we had to go through. He prepared a list of checks I had to sign. He had lists of everything that we needed to take care of to run the company successfully. We were close friends; he and I met every Sunday night to work together, and throughout the years he'd regularly signed a non-compete, confidentiality agreement.

One day, in April, everything changed for me when Isaac told me about a company in Florida that was exactly like mine that wanted to hire him to be the president. When we went to lunch, he showed me a written offer he had in his glove compartment. Considering what I had suffered since having dealt with the lawsuit involving Mary, Traca, and Kathy, this was the most painful thing Isaac could do. I was very sensitive to betrayal.

Isaac had no intention of accepting the offer, but I assumed he was using it to press me for more money. That was what really got to me. If he had come to me and asked directly for a raise, explaining why he deserved one on merit, I probably would have given it to him. But it was the indirectness of what he did that hurt me, and the underhanded game he was playing. He immediately

Nurse Story:

Dr. Dave Smith

Dr. Dave Smith was an RRT with a PhD. He was very proud of himself and freely shared his assurance that he was great! Over his scrubs he wore a lab coat with Dr. Smith embroidered on the lapel. This caused many issues at various hospitals as they said he was impersonating a physician until TRS explained that he was indeed a PhD; it was primary source verified. He lectured at conferences all over the US for Respiratory Therapy. Dr. Smith was in great demand for speaking. However, Dr. Smith always walked the line of bad behavior. He bought a Mercedes car but never paid any of its payments. He was very evasive with TRS as he was juggling multiple women and never wanted anyone to be sure of his location. He was chronically short on money, begged to be paid early, (TRS doesn't do this), asked for loans on future money, and in general stayed in debt. He was married multiple times. One wife claimed he married her without being legally divorced from his previous wife. He was in a New Mexico jail for bigamy, but he told TRS he was in Colorado visiting a friend. The angry wife posted a web site with a list of accusations.

Through all this he performed well for TRS. He took good care of patients while he worked for TRS for about five years all over the US. He was never written up. He went to work as scheduled on time. After his contract was over, he would disappear for weeks. When he reappeared he would go back out on assignment. When he left TRS he was working to get into politics in California. His Twitter account shows that he was recently re-elected for public office. He was very colorful in everything he did.

lost all credibility. If he had been only an employee I would have understood, but we were as close as close can be, someone I thought I could trust completely. When he betrayed me exactly like the Harrison trio, I was a woman scorned.

That afternoon, Isaac sent me out to get something from his car. I took the letter of offer of employment from his glove box and made a Xerox copy, then kept the original, which I still have in my bank safety deposit box to this day.

Isaac had access to everything in my business. He had devised most of the procedures for how to do things around the offices. He had developed software with me and our programmer, Bo. He had helped me set up all the bank accounts with passwords. He knew all of the access codes to everything in the building; he was the holder of the keys; he was one of my closest friends. But I could not experience another theft by a crucial employee. I knew immediately I had to let Isaac go.

I went to Bo, told him about the situation, and had him put a key stroke capturer on Isaac's computer. I did not speak of this situation again until New Year's Eve, eight months later.

I told two of my managers about the situation at the time it occurred. Because I never spoke of it again, one of them assumed I was doing nothing about it. He got so disenchanted with what he perceived as my lack of action, that he quit. No one could ever have been so wrong about my lack of action.

To replace my manager, I hired Ryan, who was one of my greatest treasures. Ryan's great ideas propelled this company into the 21st century. Ryan had previously worked as a recruiter for another staffing company, then had become a staffing coordinator for a group of companies. In the beginning it took a while to get used to his communication style—he was not direct but danced around a subject. We used to say he talked like a girl. He was an interesting mix of personality; a guy who loved cars and motorcycles but was also sensitive to fashion and interior decorations.

The very first thing Ryan did was to have the recruiters work with only with the nurses and separate the account managers to work with only the hospitals. Previously, the recruiters had

Nurse Story:

Maxine's Wedding, LPN

Maxine was married to a Pentecostal preacher who had sex with her 6 times per day. His sex usually took less than a minute with no thought to her needs. She came to work for me as the Credentials Manager after she had gotten a divorce. When she was married she weighed close to 500 pounds because her first husband liked big girls. When she came to work for me she had reduced to 250 pounds, half of her former self. She was truly an underdog.

She was in her late 40's and single when she met her husband to be, Barry, at the laundromat. He looked and acted like a little troll. He was short and very thin. He was probably one of the least attractive men I had ever met. After a short courtship, they decided to get married.

My second daughter, Melanie went with me to the wedding as my date. Several of the people from the office were sitting on a row in front of us as we took our seat. There was a very old, deaf woman sitting behind us who narrated everything in detail. This had me giggling immediately with her inappropriate comments and her booming loudness. Maxine's soon to be stepson stood in front of the packed church awaiting the nuptials when he unzipped his pants and began rearranging his junk, tucking in his shirt. "What is he doing? He is not...yes, he stuck in his hand... What is he doing? I cannot believe he has his pants unzipped!" She had me laughing so much, as she was very loud, that I tried to hide my face in Melanie's long blonde hair. I was sitting very close to Melanie with my body shaking with laughter as the old woman continued to narrate.

The wedding march began as the Maid of Honor processed out. It was Maxine's own daughter who was

Maxine's Wedding Continued

married to a Pentecostal preacher. She had her bridesmaid gown pinned on the OUTSIDE of the dress as a protest to the lowcut bodice. Next came Barry's daughter who had a girlfriend. She kept inappropriately rubbing at the dress and squirming around as it chafed her body as the packed church watched. Through this all the old woman narrated loudly and I laughed.

When they processed out both his daughter and son ran to change into their jeans and T-shirts. We sat in the church and listened to Barry's daughter scream as she took off her pantyhose. His son rolled all his clothes in his belt and swung them around his head. Both appeared to be on drugs.

As we processed out to attend the reception, I was confronted by the gay significant other of his daughter. "Where did an old woman like you pick up a beautiful girl like that?" She asked in an accusing and hostilely aggressive tone. "I grew her in my belly, delivered her, and raised her. That's how I got her." I replied. I would not back down to this drug addict.

As we walked into the beautiful reception Maxine had done all the work herself. She was known for her cake baking and icing the cakes with fondant icing. She had made the seven bride's cakes for herself. They were all iced with fondant and laced together with ribbon. Each was a different flavor. She had made a chocolate cake covered in chocolate dipped strawberries for the groom's cake.

At the reception, I was "chosen" to help her daughter serve the cake as she cut. The extremely overweight daughter was cutting the cake Maxine had made with such care, so thin I had nothing to serve but a small pile of crumbs. I refused to serve the small pile of crumbs. I told her to slice them bigger there was plenty of cake, so they would have a "slice of cake". This did not make the daughter happy as she had plans to eat the remaining cake after the reception. With four cakes remaining, she was worried that there wouldn't be

> ## Maxine's Wedding Continued
>
> *remaining cake after the reception. With four cakes remaining, she was worried that there wouldn't be enough cake left over for her.*
> *Maxine divorced Barry when she got suspicious of him and ran a background check. He had told her she was wife number three, but she found out she was actually wife number eight.*

worked with everyone, but Ryan's initiative freed up the recruiters to work closely with nurses. That change doubled the company.

Between the time when Isaac told me about his offer from Florida and the time when he finally left, I purchased a spiral notebook with 3 x 5" cards that I used to write down everything to which Isaac had access. I had to be completely in charge of my company again, and part of that was to figure out how to capture all the pertinent information. After eight months, I felt like I had captured all the codes, passwords, and everything else that I needed to make a clean break from Isaac.

That New Year's Eve, I paid all my employees to take the day off at great financial expense and I got my friend Jonathan to replace all the locks. I had my alarm company rework all the alarms. I had a concrete company reinforce the concrete parking protection in front of the corner of my building that housed my computer servers because Isaac had always said, "if somebody wanted to wipe out our business all they'd have to do is drive a big truck through the corner of your business where the servers are."

I called Isaac. I told him he was dismissed. I told him I needed the return of my recreational vehicle and all of The Right Solutions belongings in return for his vacation, time off, and two weeks of pay. I was expecting Isaac to retaliate in some way, but he had way too much class for that. I have never had an employee that I hated to see go as much as I hated to see Isaac go, but he gave me no choice.

The DHS Child with Hemophilia

Dana got pregnant again on her anniversary in May. This gave us a baby due the exact same day that Isabella was born. Her heart was broken. She just couldn't get over the loss of Isabella. Dana signed up to be a foster parent. She wanted a baby as soon as possible. She couldn't wait for Alexander[13] to be born in February. In August, DHS called her about a baby boy with the most severe case of hemophilia a child could have. I told her on the phone, all the way to pick him up, for her not to get that baby. She took him anyway. He was a tiny, little, beautiful blonde with blue eyes. His story was so sad: he was from a family of seven children; six boys and was the second to youngest, and third with hemophilia. But his mother had dealt with hemophilia all of her life. Her brothers had both died from it. She was used to starting an IV on a baby to give them the life-saving medication that would stop her child from bleeding to death. We had no idea what to do with this child. The pediatricians had no idea what to do with the child. Dana, Jay, and I raced the baby back and forth to Little Rock, to Children's Hospital, on a regular basis.

The person that knew how to deal with hemophilia the best was the marketing representative that sold the blood clotting concentrates that provided us with the life-saving treatments known as replacement therapy. Replacement therapy or clotting factors requires that the child be stabbed with a needle to run an IV that prevents hemorrhaging. Every time the baby started localized swelling in what was an obvious bleed under the skin, my normally calm hands would shake. I just could not get the needle in the tiny vein. You cannot stick him without causing another bleed. We took him to Children's Hospital to have a subclavian port put in the child's chest. It was a horrific procedure. But at least now we had a way to administer life-saving medication to this child when he got bumped in the most normal way small children do.

He was not an easy child. Dana was an inexperienced mother. She expected way more than this delayed sick child could give.[14] After Alexander was born, we decided he was best back with his mother. So, we reunited him with his mother and her other children. TRS provided them with furniture and clothing. I

Nurse Story:

Sheryl, RN

Sheryl was a very good nurse and the people she worked with loved her. She worked day and night, received accolade after accolade on the wonderful work she did, and never received any negative write ups.

But her home life was a mess. She was interracially married with a husband who did not work. He stayed home with their multiple children. She would not go to certain states because of the "built in bias against black people," that she felt was present in those states. She refused to even stay for a night traveling through the states she selected. She would drive all night to get through them. This was very unusual thinking to me as black people live in every state.

Sheryl was always short of money. I loaned her money time and again which she always paid back. No matter how much she worked she never had any money. Sheryl lived in squalor. She and her husband did not clean up. They moved when a place they were living became uninhabitable because of their refusal to clean up. Finally, we moved them in a motel as the options became fewer and fewer. The motel maid came in and ran for her life as the room was completely damaged. The cost to repair the room was more than it would have cost to stay in the room for six months.

We were unable to find her a place to live so she returned to her home state. Sheryl was a very good nurse but a very bad housekeeper. Sheryl and her husband decided to start their own agency; I wish it had been a success.

provided a van. I would really like to say this turned out to be a beautiful story of a mother taking care of her child, but his parents separated. They gave all their children back to DHS. He was adopted by a sexual child abuser who was convicted and sits in jail at this time. His adopted mother maintains custody of him. My heart was broken. I loved this child so much.

Professionalizing the Nurse Staffing Industry

In 2004, I was asked by the JCAHO Board to sit on a committee to develop the Healthcare Standards for all nurse staffing agencies. Prior to this, there had been no regulatory bodies that ensured that this was a professional business. I always said that people staffed from their basement in their underwear. I joined the JCAHO board to pull the nurse staffing industry into professionalism. I had two goals that I wanted to achieve. One was to crosswalk the standards so that if a nurse was reviewed at the agency level she would not have to be re-reviewed at the Hospital level. I achieved this. My other platform was to develop rules for review. I theorized that the criteria to be reviewed by JCACO was for an agency to have 10 nurses working. I achieved this. Days later I decided that we also needed a rule that an agency couldn't operate unless that were certified by JCAHO. I achieved this.

Unknowingly, I had effectively created a barrier to entry for new agencies. They had to be certified to work but they had to have 10 working to be certified. In 2018, I was told by a JCAHO representative that nurse staffing agencies had fallen in number from 4,000 in 2003 to 160 in 2018. Interesting.

The Preferred Office Copy Man

In February, I called Preferred Office. I had bought their most expensive copier, but it wasn't operating as described. When their repairman arrived, I pointed to the message written on large letters on the copier: "Must be repaired by a trained repairman," and asked if he had in fact been trained. A discussion ensued about my concern that he'd voided the warranty of my ridiculously expensive copy machine. The repairman yelled that I knew nothing of copy machines or how to run a business.

I ordered him to leave. He refused.

I furiously slammed my office door so hard it caused everything on the walls to fall on the floor. I overhead paged all men to the copy area: Stat! to force the repairman to leave. Finally, I called the police to immediately assist us and filed a report.

Nurse Story:

Doris, The Nurse with a Brain Bleed and Hole in Her Stomach

Doris was a wonderful ICU Nurse. She went out to work in New Mexico with the Indians for the cultural experience. While she was there she suffered a brain bleed. While she was sick and recovering TRS stayed in touch with her constantly. It took her months to recover, but she did.

When Doris was well she went back on assignment as an ICU RN at Banner Good Samaritan in Arizona. One evening, Doris transported a patient to the ER and the on-duty nurse said Doris didn't look well and recommended she should be seen.

It turned out that Doris had an area the size of a dinner plate over her abdomen that was not perfused with blood. Doris had previously had stomach surgery to reduce her stomach for weight loss, which had caused skin to sluff away over the abdomen. Because of this hole she was in ICU as a patient (not a nurse) for many months.

Doris had two big dogs in her apartment. TRS called her apartment owner who went over and got her dogs out of the apartment. TRS located someone to care for the dogs while she was ill. They kept the dogs almost a year while Doris was ill. When Doris was recovered TRS reunited her with her two big dogs.

Nurse Story:

Brenda Hospitalized
Then Reunited with Dogs after 1 Year

Brenda, RN was a fantastic nurse. She worked several contracts and was always asked back, the highest compliment. In January, she had a stroke at the apartment she lived in. She called TRS in her very severely ill state and we were able to get an ambulance that got her admitted to an ICU at a hospital about 15 hours from TRS.

While she was in the hospital, she had two dogs that her landlord turned out on the street. The dogs ran off before another nurse we had called could pick them up.

She was in ICU for the entire year on a ventilator. When our Aetna insurance was exhausted she was extubated and discharged from the hospital that same day. There was no stepdown for her, no rehabilitation, nothing but a rude goodbye. The insurance company has refused to competitively bid insurance since. That was 12 years ago. That was the only claim we had that year, but we have never had Aetna since. I do not feel she received the care she should have and let Aetna know.

TRS was there for Brenda. We made sure that she got home to her family across the county. Best of all, we found her two dogs and reunited them with Brenda.

Naturally, I called the disruptive repairman's boss. This is where Preferred Office messed up. They only half-heartedly apologized. I immediately cancelled their contract, and immediately had them pick up the ridiculously expensive printer and the other 10 copiers I was leasing.

Later, some of my employees said that the way I handled

Nurse Story:
Chrissy the Drag Queen

In February, Chrissy, RN, joined the TRS family. She was about 6'5'', weighted about 350, and had an Adam's apple. She dressed in a long top with capri leggings, no matter the weather. She wore her long hair parted down the middle and pulled back by plastic baby barrettes. There was no makeup. She was a shocking sight.

Chrissy was a very caring nurse. We tried to send her to areas where her off putting appearance was not an issue. Such as Eureka Springs Hospital where the number one diagnosis at the time, AIDS, predicted a tolerance for cross dressing. There she was one of two nurses that gave the patients excellent care.

Chrissy went to San Francisco, California. She was able to fit in well there and made many friends. She cared for many patients. Chrissy received a commendation from the hospital on her great patient care. We never saw her back in the office but would talk to her to place her on assignment. Chrissy moved to California. She continued to wear those creepy plastic baby barrettes.

this situation gave them respect for my decision making as I came off as very strong in the face of adversity. Preferred Office calls routinely to see if they can come back in; we always decline and ask if they have read our file.

BusinessMAN of the Year

In April 2004, I received a letter saying I had been selected as BusinessMAN for 2003 and President Bush would officiate at a ceremony. I did not believe the letter. I asked Josh, my 6'5" son-in-law, to accompany me to Washington, DC where the award would be given. I didn't ask my husband because I didn't want to be embarrassed in front of him if the award turned out to be phony. (I didn't care what my son-in-law thought.)

Nurse Story:

Ann, RN in Alaska and Her Thieving Boss

Ann, RN, accepted an assignment in Alaska. She accepted the position as the Interim Director of Nursing. She started her job there expecting the best.
Ann ordered new bedspreads for the facility. They disappeared. She soon realized that money was also missing. In fact, there was nothing available for the patients. Ann audited many records trying to figure out who was actually taking and receiving the missing funds. She discussed the missing money numerous times with her boss. He was extremely interested in her progress in finding the criminal. At no time did she report this to TRS.
When Ann finally realized that her boss was the culprit, she called TRS in a panic as he had been by to see her just minutes before. TRS immediately moved her to a safe place where her boss could not find her.
We had to wait several days to bring Ann home because of an Alaskan storm. When TRS was finally able to get her out of Alaska we called the Tribal Police to report that the boss was suspected of stealing hospital funds. A full investigation was completed that found him guilty. He was the person responsible for hiring and paying Ann. Another person was appointed to take his position at the hospital, but Ann would not go back, but was paid in full by TRS.

Imagine my surprise when I was hosted by Senator (then Congressman) John Boozman. Then I found out he had recommended me for the revenue I had brought into the State of Arkansas and the number of people I employed. The entire experience was first class and very nice. I wore a little pink suit and pink heels and had my hair perfectly done. I was 44 years old and the only woman in the room—wherever I went the men thronged me. They seemed more interested in what I looked like than in what I'd done. I had my picture taken, received an award during the day, and in the evening, President Bush officiated with an official dinner and speech. Everything the letter said turned out to be true.

The only problem was that the speeches seemed to go on for hours, and I had to go to the bathroom. That's when I found out that although the men's bathroom was inside the security clearance, the women's bathroom was outside the security clearance. In Louisiana I was used to "potty parity," but apparently that was not the case in D.C. To go to the bathroom, I had to walk down the hall and down several long corridors. Once I found the bathroom I had to stand in a long line with other women because there were only two stalls. Then, to get back in to the award room I had to be rechecked by security, which meant rescreening my purse, with its lipstick, brush, wallet, and re-x-raying my person.

Josh and I visited the Smithsonian. I was still wearing my heels and my hose, but was literally dripping with water from the heavy, sideways rain. When I finally got inside the museum, I had to take off my shoes and empty out all the water. The people in the museum had a meltdown. One of the docents called the guard and the supervisors came over as if I was stealing a painting! Everyone seemed to be freaking out that I was in my stocking feet. But this was my

Words of Wisdom

It is OK to mess up, everyone does. If they interact with enough people, what separates the good businesses from the bad businesses is how problems are resolved.

first time at the Smithsonian and I made sure to see what art and artifacts I had time for.

Melanie's Graduation

Melanie graduated from college with a degree in chemical engineering. I had told the girls if they graduated from high school with grades good enough to get a full ride in college, I would buy them a car. And if they graduated from college, I would take them to Europe on a trip we entitled," Eating our way across Italy."

Dana's baby had a horrific bleed. He wound up in Children's Hospital almost dead. He was in the hospital for two weeks. The whole family had spent time sitting at his bedside in shifts. As soon as Melanie graduated from college, she went down to Little Rock to stay with him until he was able to come home.

As soon as he was home, Melanie, Julia, and I left for Italy. We had the most glorious time traipsing across Italy. We started in Venice, traveled by train to Rome, then backtracked to Florence and Pisa, finally ending up back in Rome. The reason we had to be in Rome on Wednesday was that we had tickets to Pope John Paul the second, Wednesday Papal Audience. We had no idea what seats we had until we arrived. We found out that the Bishop of Tulsa had included us as guests in his personal group, sitting on the stage with John Paul! For a devout Catholic, like myself, this was as good as it could possibly get! I felt so blessed to have this opportunity.

Melanie spent the summer with us. Her last summer as my child. She had to start a new job in July in Houston as a chemical engineer for Conoco Phillips. She was engaged to Clint. They were planning on getting married in November. Clint was working on his doctorate degree in chemical engineering at Rice University. As Melanie left the lake house, where we had spent our last weekend together, we both cried as she drove out of the driveway to start her new life as an adult. My baby says she cried all the way to Houston when she had to leave her mama. Although she's a success and a beautiful mother herself, it still makes me cry to think about her leaving me that day.

Julia spent her summer trying to take as many hours as

she could to graduate in December. Taylor had asked for her hand in marriage. I had told him that I cannot give her away until she graduated from college and turned 21. After I told them that, Julia hurried up to graduate from college in three years. They got married six months after Melanie, when Julia was 21.

Melanie's Wedding

We finished the house in September 2004. Our beautiful daughter Melanie married Clint in our home six weeks after we moved in. I had ordered furniture months in advance, but when it came in my expensive table was broken. It'd had taken months to receive the table and there was no time to order another one before the wedding. I needed a table to put the bridal cake on, so my sweet husband built me the most beautiful table, then stained it to exactly match the stain that was used throughout my new house. I love that table so much. It is a token of true love and my most prized possession.

Aunt Julie's Wedding

David's sister Julie had gone through a terrible divorce. She had a new boyfriend Bob and they wanted to get married. With the whole family coming in for Melanie's wedding, Julie called and asked if she and Bob could get married in our home the day after Melanie. Of course, I agreed.

The day of Melanie's wedding could not have been more beautiful as a late November day: it was 75°, sunny, and just beautiful. We had 200 guests in our home that we fed a lovely turkey dinner, drank champagne and danced into the night. When everybody had gone home, David and I picked up the party remains, swept the floors, and got ready for the next wedding the next day. I had a caterer, Camila, who had taken care of Julia many years ago, cater Julie's wedding. Jonathan's father Ray Barnett married Julie and Bob in my living room as all the family members looked on. It was a beautiful November weekend with two beautiful family weddings.

I stayed on a no carbohydrate diet from the age of 17 to 45. I had not had birthday cake, Christmas cookies, wine with dinner, a piece of toast, or a roll hardly in 28 years. But I had managed to maintain a perfect size four or less. With my grief, I decided at 45, it was time to add a few carbohydrates into the diet, especially in

Nurse Story:

Patti's Home Destroyed By a Tornado

Patti had traveled with TRS for many contracts when Hurricane Katrina hit New Orleans. It destroyed her home and all her belongings in the home. Patti said she could live without everything but her family photographs. She was heartbroken about losing her pictures.

TRS sent one of our own to the ruined home site. For days the person looked through the ruins of her home finding her pictures as we removed the ruined household contents. Finally, after concluding that all the photographs had been recovered that could be found, we brought the damaged pictures to a local lab, who restored the pictures for Patti. She was so thrilled she cried.

the form of wine. I allowed myself to gain some weight, with the goal of not getting into double digits in clothing.

My business persona was to always be perfect. My hair was perfect, my suit was perfect, my shoes were a perfect match for my suit, my makeup and jewelry were perfect, and my weight was perfect. It gave me the edge in business and gave me the personal confidence to make the right decisions, day in and day out, that continued to propel my company to the next level of success. When I looked completely put together, other people believed I did have it together. (Well I really did have it together, but this is what helped me put that face forth to the world, so no one ever questioned my authority.)

Morning Meeting Database

In March 2005, I had bronchitis and was extremely sick. So sick that I had to stay at home for a week. On Monday, Tuesday, and Wednesday I had a recruiter call me about a problem with a nurse that we had missed because we had no tracking system. By Thursday, I had developed the Morning Meeting database, to solve future problems and score 100% on external reviews.

The Morning Meeting Database became a software tool that I trained all my people to use to record any problem we had with anyone. They were instructed to record any instances in which, for example, a nurse didn't like her housing, or a medication error occurred, or timeliness was a problem. There was a penalty for my people if they failed to enter a problem.

We set about recording all the problems that the Joint Commission needed to know for performance improvement and quality assurance. The database also allowed us to see if a nurse had repeated problems with a facility. We could press a button to see a graph that showed if someone was an outlier. We could create a pie chart that showed the exact number of medication issues at a particular facility. No one else in America collects this degree and kind of data about their nurse staffing. When everything is categorized it's very clear whether a problem is attributable to a nurse, to the hospital, or to TRS.

Morning Meeting Database

The database also allowed us to locate the root cause of problem and figure out a solution. At one point we recorded seven instances of patient-on-nurse assaults at one facility and none at other facilities. My nurses at the Oklahoma

Words of Wisdom

Look like the job position you aspire to, not the one you currently have. Dress better than anyone else. You will feel better and have more confidence in any business situation. When facing a negotiation, wear black and red. Black and red signify power and sex, giving you the upper hand without saying a word. When you want someone to know you are angry but maintain control, wear red. If you want to exude truth and honesty, wear gray and blue together. Black is appropriate for every day wear and says, "I work hard." Brown is a loser color. I know many people love brown, but for business never wear it!! Ever!!!)

facility where the assaults occurred had all claimed workers compensation, which was running up my insurance costs. I called someone at HR in Oklahoma to talk to them about what was going on. It turned out that one particular guy who was physically large often came in on drugs and got angry, beating up the nurses. After my call, this particular patient was no longer allowed on the premises. The facility hadn't figured out what was going on until I brought it to their attention. We fixed that!

Every employee was trained in using the database so that

TRS Story:

Joe Shadowen Death

Joe and his wife had owned a convenience store for 20 years before they had children. Joe had eaten all his meals there for 20 years. Everything was battered and fried. One of Joe's stories was that one day he wanted a salad and grilled chicken breast, so he went to the grocery and purchased some raw chicken. He wanted something healthy. He gave the raw chicken to the women who cooked. When his food was ready they had battered and fried the chicken.

His 20 years of eating battered, and fried food caught up with him as he became diabetic and lost part of his foot. He had high cholesterol. At 51, he had to have four stents put in his heart. He had heart disease. His health was wrecked in his early 50's because of such a poor diet for many years.

Joe worked as the Recruiting Manager. He came to work in the downturn from a job as a contractor building cabinets and installing windows. When things picked up, he left TRS and went back to being a contractor. Joe and his wife were married 20 years when they decided to have a baby boy, then two years later their daughter was born. At the time of Joe's death, the young children were only 8 and 10. Joe was 54.

Joe went to the grocery just down Highway 412 from our office at 10:00 AM. While filling his car with gas, which was running, he sat in the driver's seat and suffered a heart attack. His body fell to the side and he lay there unseen all day. When he didn't come home from work his wife went looking for him and found him deceased in his still running car. This is a learning story of what a poor diet will to your life. Joe was loved by everyone he worked with.

TRS Story:

Jan Loses Her Car

One day, Jan came out of work and could not find her car. The whole office was helping her look and her car was nowhere on the TRS lot. The police were called. By the time they showed up, the lot was almost empty. One quick look told them there was no car.
They did what every mother does. They asked her where she saw it last. She told them that she got gas at lunch at a gas station two doors away. They got in the car and went to the gas station. There was Jan's car, still running. Jan had taken her car to get gas at lunch, left it running, went inside to pay, then walked back to the office leaving the car running at the gas station all afternoon. Jan is always fun!

there was no problem with putting in an issue that should not be there. There was only a problem if the

Jan, RN and TRS recruiter

issue had not been put in the database. Every morning select staff would review all issues and assign them to someone to handle each one individually. Then with a push of a button everything required for Performance Improvement was printed off and placed for review in a notebook. This revolutionized my business! No longer did issues get forgotten, there were no more hurt feelings. Nothing fell through the cracks ever again.

The first thing an External Auditor would ask for was our Performance Improvement Book and when we slid the 8-inch thick book over to them they immediately changed.

We have scored 100% on every JCAHO audit since 2005. No other hospital or agency has done this ever.

TRS Story:
Jimmie's Tuna

Jimmie first came to work for me in 2000. He was always on a fad diet of some kind and he worked out strenuously. He was in top shape. He decided that he needed to take in a certain number of grams of protein per day.

My sales were up, and the management team had performed well. We had worked for a goal of spending the week laying on the beach in Florida. It was a glorious week.

When we got home from Florida, Jimmie was getting sicker and sicker. Jimmie had decided that he would use tuna to get the daily protein grams. Jimmie began taking seven cans of tuna, add water, then blending the awful concoction and drinking it. I would gag just smelling it.

Jimmie thought he had contracted something in Florida. I told Jimmie I thought he had Mercury poisoning. I convinced him to go to the doctor right then. They drew blood. He had mercury levels that were so toxic that he could have died. To this day he stays away from tuna.

In April, I had an External Surveyor come audit us from Arizona. At that time, we faxed the nurse profiles. None of them were sent by email. The surveyor changed all that when she stated that to be competitive we had to start emailing nurse profiles. We had one company email. After talking to the surveyor, everyone was issued their own email address. From that time on we never faxed a profile again.

When we connected everyone, my oldest employee accidently mistyped Google's name. This was the first time anyone "googled." She was immediately inundated with porn that she could not remove from her computer screen. My IT staff had to come over and clean it up. The moral to this story is "Don't mistype the name 'Google.'"

Dana would not allow me to keep Alexander. I had "stolen" Emily from her and Jason adored Mimi, so she decided to keep Alexander to herself.

I was working very hard, developing a corporate growth plan, and propelling my company forward to success. I sat on the

Nurse Story:
Abby the Soldier's Wife

Abby was a true soldier's wife. She was proud to be supporting a man who was giving his life to his country. She worked as a travel RN for TRS with their two small children. She never missed work and was highly regarded by everyone who met her. She was a stoic; strong and honest. She traveled with the children for two years before her soldier husband came home. Abby was able to save most of her money while her husband was away. Finally, when the man to whom she had given her heart was home, he was a broken man suffering from PTSD. But she continued to travel with him. She felt that the traveling was good therapy and everywhere they traveled she found someone to treat him. For almost two years he continued to suffer from PTSD.

As time went by, as they traveled from place to place and he cared for the children, he was able to adjust to regular life back in America. Finally, Abby felt that they were ready to go back home. It was time for her oldest child to start school. Abby's husband was recovered to the point he was able to return to work. She remains a part of the heart of TRS. We have always been proud to support the armed services and our veterans.

Joint Commission board, which was an honor. But it took a lot of time traveling back and forth to Chicago.

Julia's Wedding

In April, Julia was getting married to Taylor. Melanie said it was going to take at least two years for Taylor to become "Wrightized" and accustomed to our ways. He would have to learn that when we told him something, we didn't change our mind.

The week of Julia's wedding, Dana miscarried again; she had to have surgery. I wound up with a 14-month-old Alexander, who weighed 35 pounds, and didn't walk, sitting on my hip the entire week of the wedding. I was running around in my heels, pulling together a home wedding for 200 of our closest family and friends, with this large baby on my hip.

At this beautiful wedding, we had a Louisiana shrimp boil. By the end of Julia and Taylor's beautiful wedding, Alexander was my baby. Julia and Taylor left to live in Houston where Melanie and Clint[15] were.

Julia had worked for me since she graduated from college. She was going to continue to work for me from Houston. Julia and I had a wonderful working arrangement. We could play good cop, bad cop without missing a beat. Whenever someone wronged us, I would cry out and demand justice; Julia would apologize while asking the person in the sweetest voice to make the situation right. She always got her way.

Dana bounced back from this miscarriage with less trauma than before; we were just glad that the baby had not been born alive and then died. Isabella's death had put many things in perspective. To this day we all still grieve losing Isabella. All the babies living and dying and being sick stressed me to no end.

Amy and Chad's Wedding

Amy and Chad decided to get married at Christmas, December 17, 2005. Her colors were pink and red. I went with her to buy the wedding dress and bridesmaid dresses, sent her invitations, made her a long red aisle runner, decorated the church, and prepared all the food for the 400 guests' wedding.

I was lucky as Melanie and I were driving through town when I saw someone from the city decorating the reception hall for a Christmas party. I immediately pulled in my car. I asked if they could leave all the Christmas decorations in place for the wedding, so they would have plenty of time Sunday to remove them when they would not be exhausted. They had to finish the party by 10:00 PM and we had the hall at 10:30 PM. They even had several trees they had put up and decorated. The evening before the wedding, I coordinated the cleaning and decoration of the reception hall. They had left all their dirty plates and cups on the tables. We quickly cleaned up the mess and swept the floor.

The day of the wedding I got up early to prepare all the food for the wedding. The step-mom did nothing, but the step-aunt and step-grandmother worked beside me. It was time to get ready for the wedding but in my rush to do things, I had forgotten to buy myself a dress for the December wedding. (The original wedding date had been August, so I bought a summer dress to wear to that.)

TRS Story:
Jan Loses Her Car

One day, Jan came out of work and could not find her car. The whole office was helping her look and her car was nowhere on the TRS lot. The police were called. By the time they showed up, the lot was almost empty. One quick look told them there was no car. They did what every mother does. They asked her where she saw it last. She told them that she got gas at lunch at a gas station two doors away. They got in the car and went to the gas station. There was Jan's car, still running. Jan had taken her car to get gas at lunch, left it running, went inside to pay, then walked back to the office leaving the car running at the gas station all afternoon. Jan is always fun!

My wife-in-law, my ex-husband's wife, Katie found a dress I had bought years earlier but never worn, it was beige and perfect for a mother of the bride dress.

As we left the reception there was a light snow fall that was super romantic.

The step-mom had to ruin my perfect night when she came to my house after the reception to give me an unwrapped golf mug with the .50 cent price tag still on it as a thank you gift. I have never golfed in my life. I immediately prepared to throw it into the trash. My second child asked for it to go into a Christmas gift basket she was preparing for her father-in-law.

Second JCAHO Survey

It is easy to remember the exact date of the second JCAHO audit as it fell on Valentine's Day 2006. I anxiously awaited the audit as I had written the software for the Audit Screen that printed out the Performance Improvement with a push of a button. JCAHO had a 45-day window during which time they could arrive to audit us. Previously, they had come for a visit on the last day of the 45-day period. We were always ready.

The auditor did not arrive until after 2:00 PM. Her plane had been delayed by weather.

Early that morning two auditors-in-training showed up. They began the audit. The first thing they tried to poke holes in was my Performance Improvement. "How do you determine the indicators?" one asked certain she stumped me.

"I take one standard deviation away from the mean and that gives me the correct number."

She shut up quick. She had no idea what I had just said. This works in an audit every time. They looked at the Performance Improvement manual. They flipped pages. They didn't know what to do or say. One was extremely belligerent and tried her best to intimidate me, but she was not intelligent. I deliberately spoke to her in complicated language until the real auditor, whose plane had been delayed, showed up later in the afternoon. I had written every book required for the audit. TRS has scored 100% since I wrote the program and trained all my people. That day was no exception.

TRS Story:
The Fire Chief and His Wife

Tontitown had a new Fire Chief. Sean was 6'3", buff, a real man's man. He was big boned, burley even. He worked out and had muscles. He hunted, rode Harley motorcycles which he loved so much he had tattoos of Harley's all over his arms, and had named his daughter "Harley". He loved fire arms, football (actually anything with a ball) and had named his son "Heisman". He was a paramedic and a fire fighter.

He came for the annual visit to review the Fire and Safety Manual, review the fire extinguishers and see if we had any physical plant issues that must be resolved so they wouldn't start a fire. We had no issues.

Sean enjoyed the attention he received from me and my beautiful assistant Maureen so much that he came every day after that. He would randomly show up and stay for hours every day and spend MY time strolling through my building looking for something out of place. He was auditing me daily. He was a major time such. I couldn't tell him to stop coming as he had the authority to close my operations by repealing my Business License.

For months he took to dropping in for my weekly Friday lunch, so he could eat with us uninvited. Then he took to speaking with my employees. He would lecture about gun safety, motorcycles and safety on the road. Nothing that nurse recruiters need for their jobs. He was always at my office. He liked me way too much. I had to figure a way to get rid of his unwanted attention.

Then it hit me. I would hire his wife and that would slow him down from constantly auditing me.

I called his wife Alice and offered her a job, which she gladly accepted in credentials. She came to work on time and was a fantastic worker. She worked with the nurses getting their paperwork done so they could go to work. We loved her kind personality and demeanor. My plan worked perfectly, and we never heard from Sean again.

Recession-Proofing TRS Healthcare

In March of 2006, I attended the Staffing Industry Analysts Executive Conference for owners of staffing companies. This conference was a world of information, contacts, and singlehandedly brought the staffing industry to a higher level of respect. Alan Beauleiu, one of the country's foremost economists, delivered a compelling talk predicting the trends that pointed to an economic crash in the year 2009 or 2010.

I had just bought four acres next to the airport in Siloam Springs, Arkansas to build an office building. I had hired a contractor and had just started discussions with an architect. I was looking at a $2 million building project. Alan told me all the reasons why I didn't want to do that, with the economic crash looming in my future. I came home from the conference to pull my building project, after reviewing the demographics myself. I knew Alan was absolutely correct in his predictions.

To this day, Alan Beaulieu and ITR Economics are my favorite source of information to predict economic trends. Because of that one conference, along with my own research, I was able to make decisions in 2006 that would carry my company to success through 2012.

I had never spent much money in my business. I spent all my money growing my business and on employees' salaries. My philosophy was to buy used goods as much as possible. My business itself had no inventory; I required very little supplies. I would never have started a business that had inventory, because all of your money is tied up, sitting on the shelf. Then you have to dust it, manage it, test it, pack it, ship it, and then you still have to wait for people to pay their invoices. With a nurse company, I knew I could make money at any level. I already had. I could shrink or grow the in-house staff if needed to always stay in a profitable margin.

I started talking about debt and recession at every Friday lunch meeting. I wanted my employees to know about what was coming in the future. I encouraged them to pay off all their personal debt. I hosted Dave Ramsey[16] classes to teach them how to pay off their debt. This became a normal part of every week's discussion, as I talked about what was coming in the future.

TRS Managers

The company continued to grow, while we continued to do very well. 2006 was a growth year. But even though we were growing, I started doing what I called, "buckling down the hatches." I looked at every expense. I cut everything I could cut; I made sure that all my personal and corporate debts were paid off. David and I never went out to eat during this time. We rarely bought anything. We saved, scrimped, and saved some more. We were able to pay off everything that we owned, even our mortgage.

Then I found out that my Chief Financial Officer, Jeri, was stealing from my company. I had learned a long time ago because of the previous lawsuits, that it wasn't good business to fight someone in a civil suit; it just ran up your bills. I went to the Washington County Sheriff's Department and had Jeri Freshwater Pumphrey arrested on criminal charges, convicted, then sentenced to 40 years in prison .[17] This woman had stolen over a million dollars from my company. I was only able to clearly prove $60,000. She directly wire-deposited the money into her personal bank account. Her sentence was commuted down to 10 years, God knows how, because I don't. Of that 10 years, she only served two and was released

Words of Wisdom

Don't spend money. If you spend money you don't have money. Never make payments on anything, except a building or house. You cannot get ahead paying interest payments.

Nurse Story:

Jessica, RN, Labor and Delivery Nurse

Jessica was a Labor and Delivery nurse. As was so often the case she was the main breadwinner for the family. Jessica had five children, a husband that stayed home with the children, and was seven months pregnant. She took an assignment as a 7-7 PM, Labor and Delivery staff RN. They readily agreed to give her the needed time off for the new baby to be born. Jessica had her newest baby at the same hospital where she worked.

After a few weeks of recovery, Jessica went back to work as she was the only income earner in the family. Her husband was a very heavy man. The first night she went back to work, her husband was sleeping with the tiny new baby boy when he rolled over in the night, asphyxiating the newborn.

I was very distraught. I paid for the funeral and all expenses for Jessica from my personal funds. (Unfortunately, I have personally paid for many, many funerals. With a lighter heart, I have also paid for many weddings.) I wish I could say there was a happy ending, but she and her husband divorced, forcing Jessica to care for the children herself.

Later, Jessica took a full-time job as a Labor and Delivery nurse. Jessica lost her babysitter, but she could not bear to look at her baby's killer. She realized that she could pay for a sitter.

Words of Wisdom

Moral to this story is that a man or woman must have more to offer than sex and babysitting. They actually have to do something.

on good behavior to steal from other people, while paying me $400 a month in restitution.

During this process, I met

two lovely people, Vicky and Loy Hoskins, who had also been the victims of Jeri's theft. They were able to prove $80,000 in theft. She pretty much got off with all of it scot-free; however, she is paying them $300 a month.

April 1st Cruise

To motivate my TRS Recruiters and Account Managers we always set a goal to achieve a certain amount of sales to work towards. We always had a trip as the award. This kept the atmosphere fun and happy. We won a cruise. I took all of my employees. It was scheduled to leave from New Orleans on April 1, Easter

Words of Wisdom

If your stomach hurts when someone comes in the room, that is God's method of letting you know that person is doing something evil to you in some way. (My stomach always hurt when I had to be working with Jeri.) Avoid civil suits, remember criminal suits are free. The state pays for the lawyers.

Sunday. Before we boarded the boat, there was an Easter Parade in front of the hotel. The women wore beautiful hats and everyone on the floats threw out beads. We had a fabulous time then boarded the boat. We went to Mexico and had a wonderful trip.

Ali Graduated

Ali graduated from high school with a 3.8 grade point average and a scholarship for Arkansas Tech college in Russellville. Ali spent a lot of time having lunch with Pauline. This was a win-win situation for both Ali and Pauline, because both of them loved to go out to eat. Ali would drive, while Pauline would pay. They both enjoyed each other's company and Pauline went so far as to tell me one time that her two favorite grandchildren were the grandchildren that were not her grandchildren. She really

Words of Wisdom

Ways to know that someone is stealing from you: they come to work early and stay late, come in on weekends, never take a day off, are the perfect employee, and everyone loves them. They take on more and more work. They never let anyone help them. If you want to confirm somebody is stealing from you or your business, make that person take a two-week vacation and have someone you trust fill in their place, preferably not one of their friends. The very best way is to just come in on a Friday at closing to tell them not to come back for two weeks. Change the codes on the alarm system to make sure they don't come in to work all weekend.

enjoyed and loved Dana and Ali.

When we returned from Mexico, I spent the rest of the year developing the company, to close as many sales as possible, to grow as large as possible, before the coming decline in 2009. I had my corporate growth plans in big, black, three-ringed binders. I looked at them all day every day delineating tasks, marking off tasks, while reaching goals.

The Nursing Vow

When we were young nurses, my girlfriend, Joanie, and I

Cancer Scare:

Cancer the Second Time

In October, my OB/GYN found a tiny white lesion, during a routine gynecological exam. The lesion was about an inch from my lady parts on my panty line. He did several biopsies. I was traumatized by the "in-office procedure", which is code for "hurt like hell". I went home, climbed into my big recliner, and was having a pity party for myself when my husband came home. He kneeled down in front of my recliner, wrapped his arms around me, and held me tight for a couple minutes. Then he said, "The pity party's over. It's time to get up, go out to dinner, and move on with life." I felt so much better with him just recognizing I needed a few minutes for a pity party.

The biopsy came back positive for cancer. I had surgery; the cancer was like the tip of an iceberg, the deeper the doctor cut, the further it was. He wound up cutting a wedge section completely out of my lady parts. When the pathology came back, the tumors were Stage III. My doctor immediately referred me to the only oncology gynecologist within a 100-mile radius to where I lived.

The financial year at TRS had been phenomenal. The managers had earned a special trip to Disneyland. If they had children, they could take them. At the time I had a very young crew of managers. Needless to say, everyone had a wonderful time. The third day I was there I received a call that I must return as soon as I could I needed another surgery as my first doctor did not get it all.

My new doctor was not sympathetic: he said, "you should be so happy to have a lady parts facelift for free, because your insurance is paying for it, when all the other women have had to pay for it out of their pocket." I was pretty horrified, because up to that moment I never knew that women would actually pay to voluntarily have that horrible surgery done to them. It hurts so bad, all I could feel was punished. My second surgery for cancer was scheduled January 8, 2007, after the New Year.

had vowed to do what we could to bring the term "nursing" to a more professional nomenclature. It always seemed that the name "nurse" was inappropriate for a professional person with a four-year college degree. It was offensive to me and most of my for colleagues, that a profession should be named the same thing as "suckle a child to the breast". The very name "nurse" pulls the profession down to a blue-collar level and sexualizes the career as soon as the name "nurse" is mentioned. It is no accident that sexy nurse costumes are one of the top sellers on the Internet. Notice there are no sexy lawyer costumes. The term "nurse" puts a sexual thought in the mind of most men as soon as they hear the word "nurse". The nursing profession is looked down on as most people do not consider the high level of education that most nurses have. I call them healthcare professionals.

Implants

May 2006 brought one of the greatest blessings I've ever had in my life, with the birth of my first sweet, little granddaughter, Elizabeth. Elizabeth is such a joy and so smart!

In July, I was suffering as the implants in my breasts had become hard. I had these implants in place for 15 years. I read an article just before going into surgery that said that many of the implants had mold and fungus growing inside of them. I told my doctor about this. I asked him to send my implants to a laboratory for testing; he thought this was silly. When he did the surgery, he didn't have to send implants out to test for mold and fungus; they were completely black. I had felt sick for several years, been to many doctors, and didn't know what the cause was.

When I woke up from surgery and was told the situation, to my horror, the doctor had replaced the breast implants. He took fresh implants and placed them in cavities that had held mold and fungus covered implants. I was sure that the new implants were contaminated, even though my doctor assured me that he had rinsed the cavity out completely. I was too sick at that point to have the implants removed. I had suffered some brain damage, possibly from the release of toxins when the cavity was opened, or more likely, from too much anesthesia, with a lack of appropriate monitoring. No one could tell I had suffered the brain damage except me. I had relied on my memory as my greatest business and personal asset. My father had a photographic memory; I had a semi-photographic memory, which I felt like was so much better, because I could forget things that I just didn't want to remember.

My immune system was a wreck. I was terribly, terribly sick. I was over sedated and didn't wake up for three days after surgery. My poor, sweet David

Diana, Joan Elizabeth (Joanie), and Joan

sliced his foot open on a piece of glass. He tried to get me to help him; I couldn't wake up. He had to call Dana to come over to babysit me while he went to the hospital to get his foot sewed up. We didn't have a bandage, a piece of gauze, or any type of medical covering for a wound in our house.

Christmas with the Wrights

Christmas at my mothers-in-law was always a big, happy time of all of her children, their spouses, and her grandchildren gathered together at her house. Pauline would always over buy gifts for everybody. But, as she had aged, Pauline was finding it increasingly difficult to provide holiday meals for all the relatives. I had taken several years earlier to cooking pots of Creole cuisine: gumbo, red beans, rice, and jambalaya to serve to all of David's relatives, cooking and transporting these to Little Rock.

By the time Christmas was over each year, Pauline was always worn out and sick. But after Christmas 2006, Pauline had pneumonia and was very, very sick. So sick she had to be in hospitalized. It never crossed my mind, the entire time I was married to David, that Pauline's care would fall to me. But that's exactly what happened.

The night before I was to go in for my second cancer surgery to my lady parts, my sister-in-law drove Pauline to my house from Little Rock to recuperate from pneumonia. None of my sisters-in-law offered to care for their own mother. David and I took care of her until she died in 2010.

2007

Making TRS Financially Secure

2007 was a growth year for TRS because I pushed, pulled, and did everything I could think of to close contracts. I knew hard times were coming. I knew that we would have a downturn in 2008. I was determined to position myself so that everyone's job was secure. I planned not to lay off anyone, and when the time came, I was able to keep to my plan. No one lost their job. This was no accident but done with great intention.

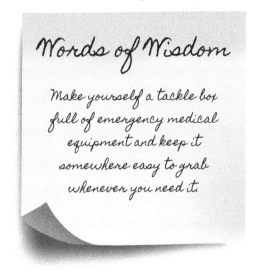

Words of Wisdom

Make yourself a tackle box full of emergency medical equipment and keep it somewhere easy to grab whenever you need it.

I wrote a Corporate Growth Plan that I carried everywhere I went. I developed it to help me remain totally focused on what I felt was most important to keep the company healthy and secure everyone's job.

I developed a new way of closing contracts. I have never cared for phone time. I care about results. Phone time is one way to determine if an employee is not performing. It proves nothing. Someone may have great phone time talking to their friends and close no one. I needed results! I needed to close contracts. We went to a more stringent qualification process that became more time efficient for the facility by prequalifying their needs in terms of departments and scheduling.

In an effort to close more contracts I began to accept housing oddities. We placed nurses who traveled with extremely hard to place animals like horses, cows, and even a chimpanzee. One horse or one cow was hard enough to find a place for, but we had an RN who traveled with an entire farm. She had two horses, one cow, several cats, and a dog. She had a husband who didn't work and two teenage boys. We were able to find her a farm to rent for three months while she worked.

The RN who traveled with a chimpanzee had to be placed 45 miles from a city inhabited by many people. We were able to find a trailer outside of Shreveport, LA. This chimpanzee wore diapers and was treated as a child. He ate at the table and slept with his owner.

We dealt with other oddities. TRS had travelers who traveled by unusual methods. We had an RN who only traveled long distances by hot air balloon, and only if it was not raining. He insisted on working at a large facility to access public transportation for the shorter travel distances. After my assistant checked, we found out he had lost his driver's license.

We had multiple RNs who traveled exclusively by boat. These travelers had to be placed by a body of water and their travel path had to be connected by bodies of water. One boater carried a moped with him to take him to the hospitals.

One major problem we ran into was the feral animals in New Mexico. Nurses placed in New Mexico were warned before they left not to take in the feral animals. But feral animals were everywhere. As soon as a nurse left her car they were swamped by feral animals. The kindhearted nurses could not ignore a hungry animal. They took them in, in droves. All the houses we rented had fenced yards, which we found odd. It seemed that every yard had a fence. The nurses began keeping the feral dogs inside the fences. They left food out on the porch for the cats. The hospitals began complaining about the numbers of feral animals kept by the nurses. The nurses felt they had to save whatever they could.

TRS had many nurses during this time who refused to travel unless they were housed where they desired. TRS also had nurses who desired proximity to casinos or to Hooters Restaurants. Most of these people wanted housing within walking distance so they could drink and walk home. We had many nurses that loved Casinos; however, the nearby housing was limited as most Casinos are on Indian Reservations. Despite these challenges, we did an amazing job.

Our one male RN who had to be near a Hooters Restaurant started out as single. Then he found male friends who traveled with him as long as they were all housed near a Hooters Restaurants, so they could party together. This lasted long after the economic downturn.

We had one outstanding RN that I had known in Shreveport, LA. He worked ICU, ER, and as House Supervisor. He bought a travel trailer. Soon he had a girlfriend he met on assignment. He would travel with her, but she wanted to work with another agency, any other agency. She unfoundedly hated me because I had known him for years.

Imagine how hard it is to place someone living with a girlfriend who traveled for another agency. To make things more complicated, he found another couple to travel with, only the woman worked for TRS. Then he found several other TRS girls. TRS fondly referred to all of them as his "harem." His girlfriend came to work for TRS for one assignment then the other girls "disappeared".

My old friend came to have lunch with me. I listened to the stories of his life. He wanted to ask his girlfriend to marry him, but he didn't have enough money to buy her a diamond ring. As I have always been in the habit of picking up jewelry at reduced prices from nurses, I had a diamond ring to give him to ask for her hand in marriage. I swore him to secrecy; he could never tell her the ring came from me.

I always have to laugh to think of someone who hates me (without reason), wearing my ring as her wedding ring!

The Company Cruise, My 50th Birthday, and Courtney Gets Hurt

My company achieved another sales goal! We were all going on a company paid (I paid) cruise. As fate would have it, I was having my 50th birthday on the boat. I was given a beautiful birthday party by my staff, a commemorative book of pictures and $250.00. I had no wallet with me, so I put the cash behind my room key as I had it in a case to hold the card around my neck.

David was still working his job, so he did not go on this cruise. I was exhausted as I had been working non-stop. I was recovering from a hard Arkansas winter and bronchitis. My roommate was my third daughter Julia. We had decided as soon as we got to Cozumel we would go to El Cid Resort to lay in the sun and have a senorita wait on us. I hoped the sun would heal me. We walked from the boat to El Cid Resort.

Julia and I had a fabulous time at El Cid. We had been there many times. As Julia and I were laying out my phone rang twice with a long number I did not recognize. I didn't answer it. Julia's phone rang with the same long number, but she did answer. It was my son-in-law, telling us several of my employees had been in a motorcycle wreck and I needed to go to the hospital immediately. We ran to catch a cab for the $5.00 ride to the hospital.

Julia and I arrived at the spotless, white hospital. I was surprised with the cleanliness. Courtney, and one of my other employees, both beautiful blondes, were being seen in the Emergency Room. They had both been riding the motorcycle when they were involved in the wreck. Neither had ever driven a motorcycle before and had the accident as soon as they started riding in the congested, wild traffic in Cozumel.

Another of my employees and her husband were present at the hospital as were the Mexican Police. The police wanted the full price of the motorcycle paid immediately or they were taking

My in-house employees raising money for cancer awareness, 2007

everyone to jail.

Courtney had a broken ankle that was cut wide open and needed to be sewed up. She had a laceration across her forehead that also required stiches. She had road rash everywhere and her back was embedded with glass. Once I arrived, she was immediately taken to have a CAT Scan of her brain to rule out a brain bleed. She was quickly back to the white room.

While she was gone, the police became more aggressive and belligerent. They demanded that we give them the money they requested, or they were taking everyone to jail. I did not think Courtney would survive in jail. We were able to pool all the money we had to make the amount they requested. All I had left of the $250.00 birthday gift was $204.00 as I had spent $35.00 to get in to El Cid Resort and $5.00 for the cab ride to the hospital. I saved $6.00 back for the cab ride back to the boat, and quickly handed over the rest of the cash.

Courtney's ankle and forehead were sewed up, but the broken ankle was not adequately cleaned. They did nothing about the road rash or the back full of glass. My other employee had a laceration on her knee that was sewed up. The scooter had $2000.00 worth of insurance for the riders, but when the two injured girls used that up, they were immediately discharged from the hospital.

I threw the girls, Julia, and myself in a cab and we returned to the boat. My care and concern were for beautiful Courtney. I wanted her to stay beautiful. I wheelchaired her onto the boat, and we stopped by the boat doctor's station and got dressings for her wound. I put her in my room. I called for Jan, RN to come help. We had to strip the glass from her body. It was extremely difficult. We had to lay down gauze and physically pull it hard, drawing fresh blood, to remove the glass and road rash from Courtney's back and front. Jan took the back and I took her front. For the next few days we cruised back slowly. I had to let Courtney lean on me as she hopped to the bathroom. Neither of us ate much. She became more and more septic. My bronchitis returned.

I called her parents to meet us in Galveston as soon as we got off the boat. Courtney needed to go to an American hospital.

As we were getting in line to get off the boat a woman asked, "did she get hurt in the war?" I laughed as I realized that some people might really think we actually put our wounded veterans on a cruise boat to get home.

Courtney's parents met us and assumed her care. She had to have surgery on her broken infected ankle; they tried without success to repair the lacerated forehead. From that day forward, I have recommended that people refrain from renting motor vehicles in foreign countries. Now I mandate it with a signed document.

TRS Story:

Jan and Robin (Two Recruiters)
Share a Ride to Work

Jan and Robin began riding together to work to save money. Being with Jan was always fun as she has funny things to say and do. She is extremely intelligent. She is like an absentminded professor. What she said and did was always absentminded and fun.[21]
I always told Robin that she was the smartest person I knew. Robin had more common sense than anyone else. Jan was talking to Robin. "I feel really sorry for that poor recruiter whose got 15 nurses on assignment coming off contract that will crush her numbers," Jan said. Robin looked sideways at her to make sure it was not said as a joke because the 15 nurses coming off contract were hers. She was the poor recruiter with so many nurses coming off. But to have that many nurses coming off every month Robin had to keep her working nurses' numbers high.

Nurse Story:

Cherrie, RN

The RN I had worked so hard on in 1997, to give a broken young woman something to live for, became a Priest ten years later. I met her for lunch at a local hospital. She was working there that day. As a Priest (I was afraid to ask in what religion), she visited patients and prayed for them. I didn't ask if this was a paid or unpaid position. She was doing the best she ever had. I was surprised to see such a big improvement in her self-esteem. She was self-confident and comfortable with herself. She was a successful person.

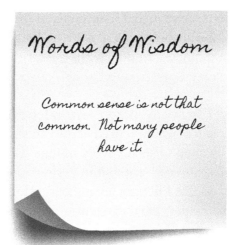

Words of Wisdom

Common sense is not that common. Not many people have it.

David Retires

David retired from his job as a Mechanical Engineer after 32 years. This was a huge deal as he counted down his time left on his job for years. Every time he brought this up, I would beg him to quit.

I had a big retirement party for him. We had a beautiful Dr. Seuss cake that was tilted and multicolored. There was not a Dr.

Seuss theme, but I just thought the cake was fun. After the party in June, we took a trip to Hawaii to celebrate his retirement. His retirement was hard to pinpoint as he had 5 weeks of vacation he took, then came back to work on his birthday, then retired.

Because he was off, we traveled a lot that summer. We went to Colorado in July. We visited Melanie's in-laws' cabin. It was very rustic. There was no electricity, no gas heat, and no bathroom. I spent one night and wondered how Melanie and her mother-in-law stayed two weeks.

In August, David started at TRS in the accounting department. We had spoken for years about what I wanted him to do. I wanted him to get the mail, open all the letters then deliver them, and deposit all checks. I wanted him to sit in the accounting department.

David and I had always kept our money separate. After the first few weeks, he received a monthly account letter from a bank. He asked if that was "real". It was. I dug through my drawer and gave him all the information I had on it. After that many more bank accounts came in and I surrendered those also. He then spreadsheeted all the accounts. They were no longer "mine" but were "his". We combined our money after that.

Our Anniversary

David and I went on a European trip for our November 22nd anniversary since he had retired and I had survived cancer a second time. We wanted to spend every minute we could together. We started the Rick Steves'[18] trip out in Paris, France and traveled through Germany where I bought an authentic German wool cape from a second-hand store. We then went to Switzerland where we hiked through the Alps. This was absolutely the best day we have ever had. Everything was crisp and clean. I had two silk jackets and no coat. I put on every piece of clothing I had brought, my long underwear that I had brought to sleep in, corduroy pants, two pair of socks and boots, two pair of gloves and a scarf, and a cashmere sweater.

After the extremely cold Swiss Alps we went to the balmy heat of Venice, Florence, and Rome Italy. We enjoyed this first trip more than any we have been on since.

It seemed that the downturn brought out the unusual behavior of the nurses. Or maybe we had more tolerance for them because of the downturn.

TRS had a great year. We celebrated our success by everyone going on a corporate cruise. We tried to celebrate our successes. We finished 2007 the best we had ever done financially since TRS began.

*Julia and Taylor
at David's Retirement Party, 2007*

2008

The Third Audit

As always, TRS was ready for the audit. Once again, JCAHO was sticking to their 45-day audit window. I was concerned as I sat on the JCAHO Board and was scheduled to be in Chicago on the day I was to be audited. But everything was as complete as I could possibly make it. I even called JCAHO and tried to get them to change the date.

Again, they waited until the last day of the 45-day period. Maureen, my assistant, conducted a stellar audit. The third JCAHO audit scored 100% because of Maureen and the software for the Audit Screen that printed out the Performance Improvement with a push of a button.

Pauline, David's Mother, Moves to Siloam

Pauline kept talking about going home to Little Rock. But when I took her to the doctor, she refused to take off her coat and put down her purse. She didn't weigh 90 pounds keeping on the coat, shoes, and purse. She couldn't take care of herself and was weak as a kitten. I had to ask her to stay each month, for another month, because she was just too sick to go home.

Nurse Story:
The RN and his Mama

We had another fantastic RN who traveled with his Mama. He had many requirements for the sake of Mama. The housing had to have one low step and two bedrooms. Mama was in her eighties. When they were traveling on their way to their housing he always made sure that Mama had her own hotel room. She loved to travel.

He had completed over ten successful contracts when we housed him and his mother in Oprah Winfrey's beach house. It had a beautiful open balcony bedroom that overlooked the beach. The only problem was that it started to rain. And rain. He had agreed to the house as he felt that he could sit on the porch, smoke, and watch the waves. During those days of rain, he was forced to stay in the nonsmoking house, open the bathroom window, and smoke out the window. He insisted on being moved immediately. Because he needed to smoke he insisted on leaving this beautiful house.

He traveled as long as he could travel with his mother. She told us that traveling was the highlight of her life. She enjoyed everything about it. She loved staying in the exotic locations, eating out, staying in hotels, and staying on perpetual vacation for several years before she died. When his mother died he quit traveling.

Each time I asked her to stay another month, she was delighted. I really didn't want anybody living with me and David long-term, as we have had so little time in our lives to be alone together. I couldn't believe my luck when I found Pauline a house to live in, located close to us, that met all of our requirements for her to live by herself. It was a beautiful, lovely three-bedroom with two handicap accessible baths, granite countertops, and dark wood cabinets. Pauline was still driving, so the house had to be flat with no entry stairs, and a carport with no center pole, so she could pull her car in easily.

I flat out refused to help Pauline sort through her 30 years of living in her house because I was still so sick. But I didn't have to; my sisters-in-law stepped up and took over that job. Pauline took her clothing and her jewelry but wanted nothing else from the house. I offered her everything, but she wouldn't take it. She wanted to start over with all new furniture, new linens, new dishes, new towels, and new appliances. She wanted everything to be all new for her brand-new life. So, she got it. However, neither one of us managed to get well until summer.

We started a new chapter in our life with the addition of David's mother, Pauline. David would go by and pick her up every day after work to bring her over to our house, where we would eat dinner together and visit until about 8:30 PM. I would take her back to her house for her to go to bed. I rapidly was able to put some weight on Pauline, so that by the end of the summer she was weighing about 135 pounds. Pauline was very happy during this time.

Grandbabies

About a month later, Dana announced to the family that she was pregnant again and due in September. A couple of days later, Amy announced that she too was pregnant and due in September. Amy developed gestational diabetes, so we were learning how to manage her diabetes. Julia lost a baby that January. It was very sad. Dana was pushing Jay in the wheelchair and developed a uterine bleed that obliterated any site of the fetus, which made the doctor suggested a D&C, which we declined. Melanie disappeared off the face the earth for several months. She didn't talk to anybody, she didn't return phone calls, she didn't text, and we couldn't figure out what was wrong with her. When Melanie finally resurfaced, she was four months pregnant and also due in September. To this day, those girls claim that my trio of predicted September babies were a result of a drunken Christmas party at my house.

Cancer Scare:
Cancer Surgery Again, Pneumonia

On January 8, 2007 I had a repeat surgery that cut another wedge section out of my lady parts. I can say I really did have a facelift down there, with the first surgery making me look 25 again, and the second surgery making me look just five years old.

Pneumonia is a highly contagious disease. I got home from surgery to my oldest friend Joanie, a nurse practitioner, and Ali, there to take care of me and Pauline. It didn't take me very long managing Pauline's breathing treatments with her coughing to contract pneumonia myself, in my weakened condition. So now we were both sick with pneumonia, on top of my third surgery in six months. My immune system was shot. Neither one of us could shake the pneumonia. When I thought I couldn't take another day of sickness, Lexi and Emily, my and Pauline's two little poodles, came down with it too. Even though I was sick, I took very little time off from work.

Words of Wisdom

The boss always has to go to work, no matter what! This is so they can insure that their employees have work to do, so that everybody has a job. It is not up to the employee to ensure they have a job, it is up to the boss to ensure employees have work. If an employee doesn't have 40 hours a week of work, you will lose your employee, because they will seek work elsewhere to support their family.

More Babies

The babies just kept coming. We had births, we had miscarriages, and we had more births. I had never gotten over losing Isabella. Her death haunts me to this day. It seemed that there was always a crisis with all of the babies and the births and the pregnant mothers. We had two placental abruptions, one where the mother bled out and had a stroke from blood loss, the other where our baby boy lost every drop of his blood. If he hadn't been born at Women's Hospital in Houston Texas, with a doctor that made very rapid decisions, he would not have survived. He stayed in NICU for 8 days.

My girls had terrible C-sections. Dana lost her uterus from one. We had two babies that failed to breathe at birth and had to be resuscitated. I had girls with gestational diabetes and severe sciatic pain, who could not walk. Girls had severe Braxton Hicks contractions for months.

As the mother to my girls and Amy, I was always taking care of a girl who had just had a baby and was sick, or a girl who had a broken heart from losing a child. Or a girl that was pregnant and needed help. My head was swirling as I moved from birth to birth.

Our grandbabies were all beautiful. They were also smart. Most of all, they just loved being with each other. My little boys, from the time they could talk, would say, "I only wanted to be with my cousins. My cousins are my best friends."

Elizabeth and Sawyer had a special relationship. Sawyer was always gentle, calm, and kind. He acted very much like David. Elizabeth is a little carbon copy of me. She is sweet as pie 99.9% of the time, but that .1% she will take somebody apart verbally or physically, dust her hands off, get up, put that sweet smile back on her face, then snap right back into being sweet as pie. Elizabeth and Sawyer get along perfectly, just like David and I do.

We've had such a string of boys that are all close to the same age: Sawyer, Jack, Sheppard, Carson, Beau, and Summit. We had these six boys in three years that love to play together and keep each other entertained. It's so much fun to watch this pack of little boys run around hunting bugs, snakes, and lizards, while thinking up games to play. Having had girls all my life, I have really enjoyed having the boys to have a view of what the little boys are like.

My girls and I at Amy's baby shower

Christmas with the Wright Family

As Christmas rolled around, I tried to think of memorable things to do with the family that just didn't focus solely on gifts. We decided to have an ugly lamp decorating contest with our family. It was so much fun. Pauline found the leg lamp, from a Christmas story, and won the contest. As my sisters-in-law were visiting, I devised a contest for them also. My sister-in-laws love hors d'oeuvres that are "crap on cream cheese", meaning putting anything on cream cheese and serving it with crackers. So, I decided to have a crap-on-cream-cheese contest. Everyone brought their favorite crap on cream cheese and we judged it. It was so much fun. Then to make things even more memorable for this very straight-laced family, I made them all put on ugly Christmas sweaters I had been saving for years and we went to a Chinese restaurant where we had a "walk off" in our Christmas sweaters, straight out of the movie Zoolander. Afterwards we sang Christmas carols including the famous "Tis the Season to be Jolly" from A Christmas Story, complete with lyrics of "Fa ra ra ra ra, ra ra ra ra." Everyone had a really fun time and it was a Christmas to remember. Every Christmas I try to have a really fun Christmas cocktail. All my daughters were married, except Ali, so it was a very adult Christmas, with just two little babies that belonged to Dana and Jay, and 14 adults enjoying wonderful meals and fabulous Christmas cocktails.

Foreseeing the Downturn

My entire work focus was to grow the company as big as possible, so that we had some extra financial bulk to weather the downturn that Alan Beaulieu had predicted. I had the company in complete sales mode with every word, action, and directive focused on getting the company as big as possible, as quick

Nurse Story:

The Rose and the Warlock

Bill was a Licensed Practical Nurse, (LPN), who was over 50. He lost his license while on assignment as he did not do his Continuing Education Units (CEUs). Because he was a wonderful nurse, I brought him into the office to train as a recruiter assistant under Robin, my oldest recruiter.

It was National Nurses Day, May 6. I stopped at a florist to get each of the nurses who worked in-house for me a beautiful yellow rose. I gave everyone, including Bill, a rose as a gift. Bill was so touched he was teary. This was a man's man. He did not normally become emotional. No one had ever given him a flower before!

This simple act made Bill confess his life story to me. He finished by telling me was a full-fledged warlock. I had never met a real-life warlock. I asked him several questions feeling more and more scared. I smiled brightly, terrified, and said I had to go.

I went back to my desk to call a local hospital chronically short of staff to inquire about openings. Since Bill could work in many areas he was a valuable LPN. They hired him on the spot. Within one hour I had Bill at the hospital to work as permanent staff. I removed Bill without creating awareness in my staff that we had a warlock on the premises. I remained kind to Bill. I sure didn't want to be on his bad side. After several years Bill called me. He was living with his son in Alma, Arkansas. He was terminally ill and was dying. We had a nice phone conversation in which he told me how much I had affected his life. He enjoyed traveling, he was glad he got to know everyone at TRS and he thanked me for finding him a permanent job. But what touched him the most was that no one else had ever gifted him with a rose.

Words of Wisdom

Keep your friends close and your enemies closer.

as possible. I wanted to take advantage of every opportunity available, before the recession started. I had incentives for everyone in the company.

I wanted every employee to have the opportunity to create a fabulous memory on a great trip with their spouse, and bond with their company family in a fun environment. With my own family I tried to make events as fun as possible so that each person enjoyed the holiday or trip. In my home, the mother is responsible for everybody's holiday and vacation happiness. I found this to be true in my corporate life as well. We had a cruise out of Galveston set as our goal, with cash prizes for the steps leading up to the goal.

I did not regret pulling the building project in 2006 because of the predicted recession. I needed every dime I had to be able to get through the recession, without laying off any of my employees. With all debt paid off and accounts receivable collected, I had the cash needed to weather the storm.

As we entered the last quarter of 2008, I had the best sales and revenue I had ever had. We finished 2008 and entered the first quarter of 2009 with a roar!

TRS Healthcare

Meanwhile, I spent my time working, developing, and correcting processes. I went through every process we had, correcting and streamlining the company, one department after another. I developed computer processing plans with my IT Director, Bo, that sped up the company nurse profiles. We created a competitive advantage over other companies' submissions with our proprietary software. We streamlined our paperwork and website. We rewrote all policies and procedures. We developed and perfected our work instructions. We retrained all of our employees to meet all of the new processes. I was gearing up my company, because I knew that in 2011 the tide would turn, staffing would pick up, and I needed an entirely trained and motivated group of experienced employees to seize the moment to double our company.

Sure enough, when April 1 rolled around, we began the same very slow decline that all the other health care facilities and agencies experienced in 2008. Our competitors began to experience losses in the last quarter of 2008, so by the end of the first quarter of 2009 the staffing industry was in an uproar, as was the rest of the country. These were difficult times for business.

I spent considerable time talking to each of my employees in-house and the nurses in the field. I pledged allegiance to each employee and told them if they stayed with me, I would stay with them. I guaranteed no layoffs and I kept my promise. I laid no employee off from work! Not one single one! Some of my in-house employees got scared when all the other employers were laying people off, and they actually quit to draw unemployment, which I fought bitterly; however, President Obama was mandating that anyone who applied would receive unemployment benefits for three years. It still does not seem right to me that someone can quit a perfectly good job and decide to be supported by my tax dollars, instead of working. It was interesting that the employees who voluntarily quit and left their jobs left nothing for the other employees to do when they left.

I told my nurses and allied staff if they would stay with me, I would guarantee them work first and would not hire any other nurses until they had a contract. Eighty-five of my nurses agreed to my pledge. I created a loyalty program that paid them more money as they completed more and more hours worked. Each time my nurses achieved a new loyalty level, they received a pair of TRS logo scrubs, a TRS logo lab coat, and their choice of either jewelry or money. I kept my word with my nurses.

I had a strict guideline that I tried to maintain where no facility accounted for more than 4% of accounts receivable; that way, if that facility went bankrupt or quit paying their invoices, we could survive. I had several hospitals and one vender management company file bankruptcy during 2009 and 2010, which cost me such a small amount of money in each case. While I hate to lose any money, they were small accounts none of them caused any financial problems for The Right Solutions.

The Hall of Shame

I started a "Hall of Shame" for my competitors that filed

bankruptcy. I would post their bankruptcy filings and the notices on a wall outside my office. As the years of 2008, 2009, and 2010 drew to a close, the wall was becoming full.

When Business Goes Down, Marketing Goes Up

I developed a facility marketing campaign to increase The Right Solutions "marketing touches" to hospitals. I bought the latest, greatest copier available that would print, copy, bind, and print on items. We wrote a magazine called The Right Times and published it each month in-house and mailed it to facilities nationwide. We received a lot of feedback from the magazine. Every month, I wrote a recipe and many articles.

My graphic designer, Hunter, and I developed a mail campaign that we did in-house to gain recognition in the hospitals. We sent out holiday-themed "gifts" to the decision makers at each hospital, to keep TRS on their minds. We put the items in unique and unusual mailing envelopes. We sent gifts in tubes, mylar envelopes, and odd-shaped boxes. We received much feedback. Some of our marketing projects were big hits and others bombed.

We sent out diamond paper weights for our current clients, complete with a little book that detailed suggestions of what to do with the diamond that were very funny. Potential clients were sent lumps of coal in a lovely jewelry box with their name listed on Santa's Naughty List. This included a coupon for the diamond if they booked staff. The hospitals' staff loved it.

For Valentine's Day, we sent out a "Secret Admirer Kit," where the nurse recruiter could blow up a big heart on legs with the words "Secret Admirer" scrawled across it. The kit came with several valentines they could set out over several days to make their co-workers jealous, and a hotline number to call if they wanted to receive a phone recording that romantically proclaimed how much they were loved. This was a big hit too.

But on Halloween we bombed big time. We ordered candy filled test tubes that were larger than we expected. We got some plastic bones, gum eye balls, and vampire teeth. We put this in an interesting, clear, plastic, rod-shaped mailing tube with a picture of Hunter wearing the vampire teeth and a black cape. We pretty

Nurse Story:
Lily

Lily was a full blooded Cherokee. She had four sisters-in-law that had all worked with TRS as Certified Nurse's Aides (CNA) in 1999. None of them could ever understand the concept of getting to work on time as they felt it was 7:00 until it was 8:00. Timeliness was never a priority for Indians. Except Lily. She understood that when a shift was booked as 7AM to 7PM, you really went in at 6:45AM. Therefore, she is the only one who had worked for me at TRS for all these years.

Lily became a nurse the hard way. She was a CNA, then became a Licensed Practical Nurse (LPN) in 2000, then traveled as a Registered Nurse (RN) beginning in 2003. Lily traveled all over the U.S. as an RN focusing on cultural experiences that she would not find in her home state of Oklahoma. She visited other Native American Indians such as Apache, Sioux, and Navaho. She traveled to Alaska where the Indians there are referred to as Eskimos. She visited California, Texas, North Carolina and too many other states to mention here. She expanded her world, and mine too, for 19 years! She is staying home currently as her husband is on a donor list for a new kidney, but she calls once a month to let us know she is alright. She did what she said she would and was always at work on time. She has had the same recruiter, Virginia, for the entire time!

much ended up offending just about everyone at every facility. The Indian facilities had a religious conviction about body parts being displayed. Some people hated vampires and thought it was terrible taste for us to have a vampire on our Halloween gift. Some people thought the test tubes were sex toys.

As the phone complaints came in I had them all directed

to me. I told each and every one of them the same thing I always tell people who complain. "This is the first time I've ever heard a complaint like this; you're the only person who has complained. I am so sorry! I am so glad you let me know, so I can take care of it. But do you need a nurse?" Really? Really? It didn't cost them a

Words of Wisdom

Always be a "foot deep and a mile wide" and "not have all your eggs in one basket." Be diversified in business, actually in all economic decisions. If you have only one client and that client gets mad at you, you will be bankrupt in one minute. But on the other hand, if you have many clients, every client is a small fraction of your business. While you never want to lose a client, there are few to no repercussions from the loss.

dime, if they didn't like the gift, couldn't they just to throw it in the trash? There are a lot of people out there with really dirty minds.

Arkansas Business Executive of the Year

In 2009, I received one of the biggest recognitions of my career when I was named the Business Executive of the Year for the State of Arkansas.

I had no idea what the award was all about. I had been nominated by an anonymous party and received an invitation to come to Little Rock for the gala event. I looked at the roster of potential winners. The men on the list were a banker, a mortgage

Nurse Story:

Markus

Markus lost everything in Hurricane Katrina. He was desperate to find housing as he had nowhere to go after the hurricane wiped everything out. We placed him on assignment as rapidly as we could as a Registered Nurse. He came to us a very sad case. The trauma he suffered was palpable. You could feel his hurt. As TRS provided stability and focus for him he came back to his normal self.
Over the course of two years, he was able to save enough money as a travel nurse to move to Mississippi and buy another home in the south that was far from hurricanes. Marcus was a strong nurse that had the wind knocked out of his sails, but he was able to recover and become the strong man that he is today.

broker, or an insurance agent—they all were the member of many, many, organizations and sat on many boards. All I had done was to create an insanely profitable company from nothing to multi-million-dollar status. The men had received their nominations for a job working for a bank or insurance company, but they had never built anything of their own. No wonder they had so much time to sit on so many boards; they were not the one responsible for growing their companies. When I looked at that list of nominees and read their biographies, I thought there was absolutely no way I could be the Arkansas Business Executive of the Year.

I was invited to a luncheon before the event, with all of the other 80 people nominated in any class, for any of the many awards that would be awarded later that night. But the Arkansas Business Executive of the Year was the top award, the most coveted recognition. It signaled you were the best business person in Arkansas. I looked at one of the men, French Hill, an Arkansas congressman, who was my competition, and I just knew he would win. I even congratulated him in advance. When one of the men asked if I had my acceptance speech ready, I replied, "No! If I win I'll just call you up to give it for me." I didn't prepare an acceptance speech. I didn't expect to win, and anyway, I always spoke with no prepared speech.

I was so surprised when my name was called. I jumped up, David jumped up, and we hugged and kissed right there in front of a thousand people. Then I walked up on stage and said my speech: "I wish I could say that starting The Right Solutions was easy, or sexy, but it wasn't; it was just a lot of hard work with a lot of great people." I don't think I've ever been more blessed with a work award. My best friend Jonathan and my banker friend, Art Morris, were there to congratulate me and wish me well. I was just thrilled.

To this day, I don't believe in preparing an acceptance speech; that would be just too much bad karma.

Siloam Springs and Tontitown Day of Proclamation

After I was proclaimed the Arkansas Business Executive of the Year both the town I lived in, Siloam Springs, and the town where I work, Tontitown, both celebrated me with parties. Each had a Mayoral Proclamation naming a day in my honor. Both celebrations included a picture of me that everyone who attended signed. I'm proud to display both in my office.

The job

Words of Wisdom

When your company is experiencing a downturn in sales, most people fire the marketing department, while the exact opposite is what you need to do. The marketing department needs to work overtime getting your name out to potential customers. In a downturn, pour your money into marketing instead of sales.

orders kept decreasing and decreasing. My son-in-law, Taylor was over marketing and they just could not get any orders from the facilities. Most hospitals have endowments that are managed in stock funds. With the stock market tanking, the hospital endowments had less and less value to fund the hospitals. The hospitals were doing what I was doing, which was cutting back on every expense possible and hunkering down, to hold as much as they could financially. This combined with the fact that many construction jobs and other labor positions had been laid off, and the nurses who had been housewives of the now unemployed men, had to return to work in the hospital to support the family. Our job orders had decreased from over 3000 at their highest and were down to 49 at their lowest.

Diana with her award,
a proclamation from Siloam Springs,
Business Woman of the Year

Anita was a recruiter with a healthcare traveler who traveled with many, many things that appeared to have no use, such as multiple toilet seats. He pulled the largest trailer you can pull behind a big truck. It was 40 feet long, full of things he carried around with him on assignment. He traveled with so many things that he never used. He had not been through the trailer in years as he traveled across the US.

TRS humored him by finding a place where he could park his padlocked trailer. He was obsessive about his things. He really put them above most people. Even though he was what other people might term "a hoarder," he was an exceptional nurse. Hospitals begged him to stay for another contract. TRS never

Diana Wright,
Arkansas Business Executive of the Year

heard even one negative comment about him as he performed so well as a nurse.

JCAHO Reviews TRS Again

The Joint Commission was due to come again. They came every year for our first two years and then every two years after that. TRS was always ready for the audit now. JCAHO was sticking to their 45-day window to arrive to audit us. Everything was complete as I could possibly make it. The fourth JCAHO audit scored another 100% again, because of the software for the Audit Screen that printed out the Performance Improvement with a push of a button.

Staffing Industry Analyst Conference

The Staffing Industry Analyst (SIA) is the premiere evaluator of the staffing industry, regardless of what industry is being staffed. SIA also produces the leading magazine in the staffing industry.

The SIA decided in September 2010 to run me on the front cover of their magazine. The article detailed my business and the success I had surviving the downturn. Until the moment that the issue was published, I had been anonymous. Once it was public, I became known throughout the industry. Because I was on the cover that month, I went to Chicago to the Healthcare Staffing Forum. I had previously attended the Executive Staffing Conference where all the owners of the staffing companies were present.

Pauline's Death

I really did not want to leave Pauline to go to the SIA meeting for the Healthcare Forum because she was dying. I went anyway. Two days into the conference David, who was with me, received a call from Pauline's doctor. He said we must return at once she was dying. We immediately got on a plane and returned.

Pauline was in Hospice. I knew she would choose to die in 2010 because there was no tax due that year on any money she had earned in her life. Pauline was a masterful financial wizard at making money. Pauline would say to me," if you make enough

Nurse Story:
The Inmate

I have staffed hospital jails across the United States for years. One day, I was at work when I was called by a news crew from Oklahoma about two TRS nurses that reportedly slept with the same inmate. Inmates cannot give consent to have sex as their bodies belong to the state, so sex with them is always rape. I had never heard of this incident previously, so that is what I told the News Crew. I had to investigate.

First, I looked in the database and sure enough both nurses were placed in the jail hospital. Next, I went to payroll to pull the time sheets to see if the nurses both worked the date of the incident. Glory of glories, only one of the nurses worked for me. The other nurse had quit several months earlier to go to work directly for the jail. Well, the News Crew was half wrong.

I called the jail to discuss the situation. Apparently, the inmate who worked in the Infirmary worked as an aide to both nurses. The jail confirmed that they did employ one of the nurses. The jail had gotten suspicious when the inmate began receiving many outside phone calls from both nurses. Evidently, the inmate had received hundreds of calls in a month. The Infirmary had a camera that recorded everything that occurred there. The camera had recorded confirmation of the sexual activity.

Both nurses were married and had children. The story ran on every media outlet available, also the news and in the papers. This story was very public.

When I asked my nurse what she was thinking, she replied, "he was cute and cool. He had a cute butt."

The jail threatened to press rape charges but never did. I decided that TRS nurse would be better off working for my competitor.

money you don't need to be married." I was married to her son!

Pauline was not saved, even though we had prayed with her endlessly for years. Her daughters, granddaughters, and son all witnessed to her to no avail. When we returned from Chicago on Wednesday, she roused only long enough to tell us that she loved all of us. I knew this was a very bad sign as she never said this to a soul.

On Saturday, September 29th 2010, her daughters Susan, Rosemary, Paula, granddaughters Julia and Angela, and her only daughter-in-law, myself, were present as she passed. Everyone asked my opinion of when she might die. I thought we had several more days.

My youngest, Ali, called to ask if I had called a priest for last rites. I had not. Most priests have Saturday off. I ran to the front desk to ask the nurses for help in finding a priest and then decided to rapidly text a friend for help. As I ran back to the room my sister-in-law, Rosemary, said as she pointed out the hospice French doors in Pauline's bedroom, "is that a priest?" An Episcopal

Nurse Story:

Steve

Steve started to work and travel during his first marriage. His wife quit traveling with him when his daughter was born. Very predictably, they divorced. During his time as a divorced nurse he met and married another travel nurse from TRS while traveling on the job. The new wife now travels with him. They have two small preschool children. When Steve wanted to be placed on assignment in Ohio to be close to his daughter, we were able to place him in the same town that she lived so he could see her every day of the 13 weeks.

priest was getting out of her car. I went running out the French doors to the parking lot, to ask her if she could administer last rites to Pauline. "I would be so honored," she replied.

We cleared off the overbed table and set up for mass. We had an entire mass, complete with songs and Bible readings. As mass ended the communion wafer dipped in wine, was laid on Pauline's tongue. She died at that moment. The Holy Spirit was moving so strongly in the room that it was palpable. We all felt it. It was hard to feel sad for Pauline when she had such a lovely death.

Many people may believe that what we did was not in keeping with the Catholic Church.[19] But God sent the Episcopal priest to Pauline. The Holy Spirit saved Pauline at the last minute. I was so lucky to have been a part of this.

The Fraternity Boy

I hired a chicken manufacturing corporate executive named Jerry, who supervised the nurse recruiters. Arkansas has the largest chicken industry in the U.S. with many chicken processing company headquarters in Northwest Arkansas and Jerry had been the top guy at one of them. Jerry thought he was the most beautiful man on the face of this planet and was used to other women thinking he was also. I personally found him to be repulsive, with his fraternity boy attitude and his sarcastic mouth. I could tolerate him in his position, I just didn't want to spend any of my personal time with him. I did not like talking with him about anything but business. Jerry and I got off to the wrong foot a couple years after he started working for me, when he confronted me about my disinterest in him. He couldn't believe I wasn't attracted to him; I couldn't believe he thought I would be. Both of us were horrified by this revelation.

Soon after his confrontation, he made two fatal decisions. The first mistake was that he decided that my profit margins were way too high and I needed to decrease my profit margins to make money on economy of scale. There is no such thing as making money on economy of scale in the nursing profession. You have to have a clear profit margin on every single nurse you place, and you cannot have a loss leader like they do in the grocery store. There are no other products. Grocery stores have loss leaders, so they get you in the door and you buy everything else in the whole store. We don't sell any other product but the nurses to the hospitals. Jerry could not understand why we couldn't slash the profit all the way down to zero and keep the business running. I tried to explain to him that I still had to pay him, and with zero profit margin there would be no money from a nurse working to pay overhead. While this seemed perfectly crystal clear to me, Jerry didn't get it.

When I wouldn't cut the profit, Jerry lost heart. The second mistake that Jerry made was when he made the decision that no one in the world needed a nurse anymore. He had it in his head that nurses were obsolete, and they had no use in the world. The more he discussed his obsolescence theory, the angrier I grew. Just who did he think was going to hold the hand of a dying hospital patient? No patient wants a machine. They want the touch of a nurse when they are dying or trying to live. Besides, there aren't any type of robotic machines anywhere in the world right now to replace the bedside nurse. To me, this was just the ignorance of the chicken seller who had no experience working in a hospital and no compassion for the people dying there.

David Breaks His Hip

In November, Tracy was pregnant and going to deliver Ava in Shreveport, LA. Melanie was due to deliver at the same time in Tulsa, Oklahoma. Amy, Tracy's sister went with her to deliver while I went with Melanie. Amy experienced an appendix rupture requiring surgery immediately after Ava's birth. Amy spent several days in the hospital. Chad, Amy's husband, called me to ask if I would keep the girls aged two and one. I told him not to leave the car seats as I was going nowhere, this proved to be a big mistake!

David decided to spend that day cutting the limbs off trees at the office. He headed off to cut down the limbs while I babysat. When he got to the back, he leaned the ladder against the dumpster to cut limbs when he lost his balance falling to the paved driveway below, breaking his acetabulum, the socket, the head of the femur fits into. He called me for help. I could tell by the strain in his voice that he was severely hurt. I immediately called for help. I also called for Julia and Taylor to come help me.

David was laying on the ground with his face distorted in such terrible pain that the first responder on the scene who had known him for 15 years didn't recognize him. Our daughter Dana was on the scene of the accident before the ambulance showed up. He was taken by ambulance to Northwest Medical then transferred in the middle of the night to Little Rock, to UAMS. Taylor never left my side while Julia stayed home and babysat Amy's girls. Not having the car seats, I had to wait for Julia to pick up the girls before I could leave.

This was a horrible night. David was in terrible pain. The hospital staff kept him on a back board for hours. This was ridiculous as he was half off the back board. I never left his side. In the morning our friend Jonathan picked us up from UAMS when David was discharged and drove us home.

The Doctor at UAMS said David needed to let everything heal naturally. After he healed the Doctor would reevaluate him. David healed slowly. After several months, I was at my wits end. In desperation, David agreed to stay in a wheelchair on a cruise with cousins Jan and Ron.

Doubling the Company

As 2010 ended, sales were up. This didn't change Jerry's opinions about margins or the nursing profession. My company had reached a highly-anticipated sales goal of doubling the company by early 2011 and we were ecstatic. On January 2nd, 2011, my entire office decided to go on a diet together to celebrate our hard work. My group of employees had worked together for years and were very close. Their reward was a company cruise. My large office is a little bit unusual, as there is a strong sense of fellowship and love for each other. Because of this, many of us choose to do things for group accountability, such as diet together. We all decided to go on a group diet so everybody would look fabulous on the cruise. We worked out a weekly diet fee that would go to the winner of the diet. As a group we all decided to go on the hCG diet, which, in addition to low calorie intake, required that we take pills. That pill would prove to be one of the costliest mistakes I've ever made. Unlike most people, I know exactly the day my cancer started. I bled for 40 days and ended up contracting ovarian cancer. Because of some of my genetic tendencies, the hCG hormone (which women normally produce when they are pregnant) was like feeding gasoline to a fire.

Jerry started fighting with Taylor. They would have screaming matches in front of the employees. The final blow came when I asked Jerry a question in a management meeting in front of all of my Department Heads and he gave a very nasty, sarcastic answer. I did what I always do in a situation like that: I pretended that I didn't notice. I did not call him down in the group. I looked up with daggers in my eyes and sweetly smiled. I then did what I always do when I am going to terminate someone: I looked at every single way that this person could negatively impact my business and closed every single opportunity for them to do so. I was taking the employee trip and I needed Jerry to stay back and

Words of Wisdom

Always terminate when its convenient for you. Never lose your temper and fire somebody without completely thinking through everything that you would have to do yourself if that person was gone. Then choose a date after you've covered all your bases, that works perfectly into your schedule, and let that person go. I recommend not discussing this with other people until after you've completed your research and made your decision.

babysit the remaining half of the employees while I was gone. I also had taxes due by April 15, so I decided to keep Jerry until after I got back from my work trip and my taxes were done.

CEO Training

With Jerry gone, I made the decision to move both Josh and Taylor into my office. But I was in the middle of a credential's software rewrite and the only person that could work with IT for the credentials rewrite was Josh. So, Josh moved into credentials and Taylor moved into my office.

When I first moved Taylor into my office, I was concerned. I didn't know if we would get along or have conflicts. I needn't have worried. The minute Taylor moved into my office, we fit together like hand in glove. One of us would have an idea, and the other would offer improvement to the idea. Neither of us had any difficulty when the other would suggest something that would benefit the employees or the company.

I had a young man in credentials named Caleb, who had been with me for five years. I called Caleb into my office, right

David and Diana, 2010

after I let Jerry go, and told him that I would be taking over Jerry's duties of managing my nurse recruiters. I asked him if he would like to be my assistant manager over the recruiters. I was impressed when Caleb said right away that he would take the promotion and did not have to go home to ask his wife for her permission. I had never asked David for permission to take a promotion in my life! But it seems that everyone else I'd ever asked to take a promotion always had to go home and talk to their spouse about it. I've been impressed with Caleb ever since.

Caleb and I settled into a routine and in about a week, Caleb was doing Jerry's job without me. Taylor was still running marketing out of my office. Caleb and Taylor were about the same age, so they really enjoyed running marketing and recruiting together. The nurse recruiters were happier with Jerry out of the way. The orders were coming back in. Our process improvement had created a submission process that was much superior to what we had had before the recession. We had emphasized with the recruiters for several years that we needed nurses with higher specialty credentials; such as ICU, OR, PACU, and all other intensive care areas. So, when these needs came in, we had the nurses on hand.

Josh was in credentials, so when we booked the nurses to work, we could get the right credentials to the right hospitals in a timely manner. Because everything was going faster and faster, our company was growing larger and larger. During the downturn, the healthcare staffing industry lost, on average, 75% of market share. Many, many of my competitors went out of business. Our company lost 30% of our revenues and our market. In other words, we were 45% better than anybody else.

The market was completely changing, with the vendor management companies taking over almost every facility and demanding a percentage of our profits and a lower rate for the hospitals, while taking a larger share for themselves. The market had shrunk, there was much less competition, and now there were barriers of entry to the healthcare staffing market that prevented new companies from starting up. To do business, a company had to have contracts with the vendor management companies, who would not allow new companies to sign up unless the company had

> **Rule of Thumb**
>
> *When your company is in a market with barriers to entry, it is not the time to sell. It is the time to hold, as the value of your company will continue to accelerate.*

Joint Commission accreditation. The new company couldn't get Joint Commission accreditation without experience, but then the new company couldn't get experience without the accreditation. So new companies were finding it impossible to start up in the healthcare staffing industry.

PART SIX

Cancer Diagnosis

A Terminal Diagnosis

By November 2011, I was so terribly ill over the year and a half leading up to the diagnosis that I was constantly going to all these allopathic doctors. I even had my breast implants removed because I was concerned that they were contributing to the illness. During this time, I did not miss work or any family activity.

But I didn't know all this the day that I started on my hCG diet. I also didn't know that I had a genetic condition that was going to predispose me to cancer, BRCA 1. Within a few days of beginning the hCG, I started hemorrhaging. I would hemorrhage for 40 days until the diet was over. I made an appointment with my oncology gynecologist to find out why I was bleeding. He ordered a pelvic ultrasound, which he pronounced clear unfortunately the radiologist did not agree with that. However, I didn't ask for my test results trusting my doctor. I never knew that until after I was diagnosed with stage IV ovarian cancer, a terminal diagnosis.

Diana and David, 2011

2012

After the breast implants were removed, I felt much better through Christmas that year, but shortly after the new year, I started having severe back pain. My back pain increased, and my doctor's visits increased with no diagnosis. I continued to get multiple x-rays to the back with no resolution and another pelvic ultrasound. Some days I could barely sit at my desk because of the excruciating back pain. But I didn't miss a minute.

Good Friday

Taylor and I continued to grow the company. By the Friday before Palm Sunday, in April 2012, we reached a sales goal that doubled the company from only a year ago. We monitor our statistics very closely, so we were able to predict reaching our goal and planned a surprise celebration party for our employees. Maureen and I ordered decorations and came up with the party theme. We decided our theme would be like the Oscars, complete with Oscar statues, red carpet, a balloon arch, mimosas, breakfast, decorated desks, decorations throughout the company, managers parking employees' cars, lunch out at a restaurant, and a cruise. Taylor interviewed the employees on a microphone.

When the market came back, we were well positioned with trained, experienced employees and we were able to catch the wave and ride to new heights. However, my health had deteriorated and was taking a turn for the worse.

The Metabolic Disturbance

As I progressively got sicker and sicker, I looked for more and more doctors, had more and more tests, and was consistently misdiagnosed. No doctor would figure out I had ovarian cancer. I would have to ask and search for testing until it was finally conclusive. Making one wrong diet decision, I ruined my life forever. Over the next year and a half, I saw 6 different doctors and had 45 visits with failed diagnoses. I was even hospitalized, and that doctor misdiagnosed me too. Doctor number seven.

In April of 2012, my stomach blew up and looked like I was six months pregnant. My husband and I noticed it and worried about my weight, but we didn't think about cancer.

In May 2012, I went to lunch with my assistant, a beautiful, super-efficient lady named Maureen who had worked with me for years. I started having chest pain during lunch but thought it would clear up. It didn't. After lunch, I went to the closest doctor's office: Dr. Jonathan Parker, who immediately gave me a nitroglycerin which provided immediate cardiac relief. I asked for another one and Dr. Parker got nervous. No one ever wants a second nitroglycerin. He immediately sent me to the closest hospital, Washington Regional.

I was admitted to the cardiac ward. Because I was in perfect shape, I was monitored and tested and declared to be cardiac healthy. The hospitalist said that I had "esophageal spasms". Esophageal spasms! Ridiculous! I knew that diagnosis was not accurate but still did not know what was wrong with me. Because my personality is to leave no stone unturned, I made an appointment for an EGD and a colonoscopy even though I was not due for a colonoscopy for three years. Dr. Rogers saw a large ovarian tumor through the colon wall. He took biopsies of the colon wall which were negative of course. I thank God, in his error, he did not reach through the colon wall to rupture the tumor. After two weeks, I was a nervous wreck and still had no definite diagnosis.

The "benign" colon wall biopsies were a gross error, but the doctor did not think he needed to order a CAT Scan. This situation was ridiculous. I had top of the line insurance, money to pay for a CAT Scan if I wanted one but was hassled when I requested that one be performed. I returned to Dr. Parker to request a CAT Scan. Unfortunately, the results of the CAT scan were definitive for ovarian cancer.

The Final Diagnosis

June 28, 2012 was a date that rocked my life and the life of everyone close to me. When you receive a terminal diagnosis it not only affects the life of the person diagnosed, but everyone around them. It rocks the world of everyone in your family, close friends, neighbors, co-workers, church members, and many people you don't even realize care. My diagnosis was like that. People cared. Some people cared a lot.

I would learn that not everyone acts as you would expect when they deal with your illness. I sat up all night sipping cake vodka and crying over facing the end of my life. I had one fantastic pity party. I had worked so hard to come from a terribly abusive child life, overcome a lack of education by obtaining a GED, worked so hard to get a Bachelor of Nursing while working full time as a single mother. I worked day and night, married, taking care of family members who were ill and dying in my twenties and thirties, while having and caring for my own children. I worked hard to get my Master of Business Administration and win every business award I could. To compensate for the mental and physical abuse I endured as a child, I excelled in my work. My goal was that I wasn't ever going to be poor or mistreated again. I had spent the last seventeen years building my dream business, from starting out on my own in the beginning to a multimillion-dollar business with many dear employees who worked very hard. My company had come though the recession with fantastic success while so many other companies had failed, yet under my leadership we had thrived.

As I've always said, "You just do your best and hope it all turns out".

Words of Wisdom

Pray first. Let God guide you. Every decision we make takes us down a path. It is always much better to make a decision than to be swept up by the tide of indecision. Not making a decision is making a decision. Many people do not understand this. They think things "just happen to them" when in actuality their failure to take action and make a decision caused the situation they are experiencing. I was never one to fail to make a decision, in fact, making a right decision and sticking with it is one of my best characteristics.

I alone was in control of my destiny.
I chose. Destiny did not choose for me.

Words of Wisdom

God places things in my path
and it's up to me to figure
out what to do about it and
what actions to take, with
His guidance.

The Wright Family, 2016

Diana's Other Books

Extraordinarily Intentional:
How a Nurse Became an Entrepreneur

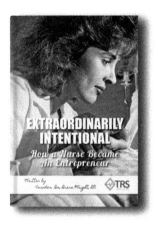

As a single mother and hardworking, experienced nurse, Diana sought to change the nursing industry across the nation. *The Right Solutions*, an intersection of Wright's last name and the right staffing solutions she could provide for hospitals. Diana started the company from the ground up, working the first shifts herself. Ever since the first shift, the team at TRS Healthcare have continually strived to comfort and restore lives nationwide while staying true to their humble roots. From a murder-for-hire scheme and thousands of dollars of embezzlement, to cancer scares and unbelievable nurse stories, Diana shares a unique perspective on the inner workings of TRS Healthcare. She knows one thing for sure: nurses don't just comfort patients and their families, they come home and do it all over again at home. The shift never ends.

More Than Chemotherapy:
How to Survive Advanced Cancer
A QuickStart Guide

In 2012, Diana was diagnosed with stage IV cancer. The tumors were metasizing all over her body and she had to prevent it from growing. After traditional treatments failed, she turned to alternative treatments and natural ways to attacking the beast. Dr. Wright has helped others fight the culprit of cancer and wants to share what she has learned along the way. Cancer patients and their loved ones can use the book as a short reference guide to all things cancer from the processes it thrives in at a celluar level to the supplements and foods that make it shrink. The book is best used as a step-by-step plan to eliminate and prevent any cancerous growth.

~ DrDianaWright.com ~

Diana's Documentary

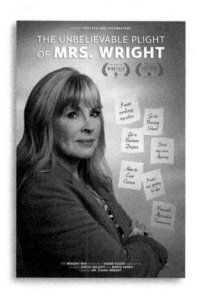

The Unbelievable Plight of Mrs. Wright

The incredible true story of American nurse and entrepreneur, Diana Wright. Overcoming poverty and abuse, Wright built a multi-million dollar business devoted to improving the quality of life for nurses, only to be given a terminal cancer death sentence by the very industry she dedicated her life to. Failed by the American medical system with only eight months to live, Diana takes her health into her own hands, spending her forecasted time in search of the cure for cancer.

Coming Soon to

amazon.com

Visit the Official Movie Site at
www.PlightofMrsWright.com

APPENDIX

Endnotes

1 https://www.webmd.com/sex/birth-control/rhythm-method

2 Dr. Joshua Garren was later my radiation oncologist who treated my brain tumors.

3 Hoppin' John, also known as Carolina peas and rice, is a peas and rice dish served in the Southern United States. It is made with black-eyed peas and rice, chopped onion, and sliced bacon, seasoned with salt.

4 GS11 is the Federal Government Scale of pay for Federal Employees.

5 Edwin Edwards was Governor of Louisiana from 1984-1988 and 1992-1996.

6 We lived on Springlake Drive and in Springlake Subdivision.

7 https://statisticalatlas.com/place/Arkansas/Harrison/Race-and-Ethnicity

8 https://statisticalatlas.com/place/Arkansas/Harrison/Household-Income

9 https://statisticalatlas.com/place/Arkansas/Harrison/Age-and-Sex

10 See page 218 for Kathy's story

11 See appendix for lawsuit.

12 She had a doula who was not qualified trying to override the MD. She was never allowed back into the hospital.

13 Alexander is her oldest. He became my first grandchild.

14 We tried to adopt Jason and were told by DHS we would have to pay $1 million dollars annually for his medical care until we were broke, file bankruptcy, and risk his death while we waited for Medicaid to approve us. I gave him up rather than risk his life. DHS has since changed their policy.

15 Melanie's husband.

16 Dave Ramsey is an American personal finance guru, businessman, and author. Dave Ramsey created Financial Peace University, a nine-lesson, money-management class for getting out of debt, budgeting, and managing your money. Learn more on his website, www.daveramsey.com

17 See appendix for full report.

18 Rick Steves is an American travel writer, author, activist and television personality.

19 This was disapproved by the existing clergy in the Catholic Church. I was a Youth Leader and a Eucharistic Minister. But the Priest from the Catholic Church never came. Pauline's soul would have been lost. I thank God he sent us someone to save Pauline, even if she was Episcopal.

20 I have both the BRCA 1 del 4 and MTHFR genes that predispose you to cancer.

21 Jan would save my life in 2012. She found Doctor Kleef and the treatment I needed.

1975

The Fontenots and Thibodeauex Family Feud
From https://noperfectplaces.jcink.net/index.php?showtopic=1672

There's a rupture to the structure of this house that we built TW: Death of a parent, death of a child, alcoholism, prostitution, infertility/birthing complications etc. Chapter I: A Not-So-Brief Family History Even with today's technology and an endless array of magical means, the origins of the Thibodeaux family remain largely shrouded in mystery. Their bloodline can be traced back to the 19th century, but peculiarly, there seems to be no record of them prior to 1846. They have tried just about everything, including tracing their family by maternal surnames. But what's even more peculiar is that the history of every name that holds a strong familial connection to the Thibodeauxes seems to completely disappear past 1846 as well. Because of this, it can only be assumed that they derive from Acadian exiles who settled in southern Louisiana in the 18th century. No one can know for sure, as there isn't a single scrap of evidence to provide them with any answers. Many assume that this has something to do with Le Garçon Cunja (roughly translated in English to "The Boy Curse"). The story of Le Garçon Cunja derives from the earliest Thibodeauxes on record; Etienne and Aurelie (nee Fontenot). It is said that the couple had six stunningly beautiful daughters together, and men of every age, background, and socioeconomic status from across Acadia wished to court them. Etienne, however, did not take the idea of marrying his daughters off lightly.

He grew desperate to conceive a son in effort to keep his family name alive; so much so, that when it was discovered that Aurelie could no longer bear children, he turned to a bonne a rienne (a good-for-nothing or promiscuous woman) named Violette for help. On January 1st, 1846, Etienne was given a son out-of-wedlock, who would be raised by his mother until he came of age. Aurelie didn't discover her husband's secret until after his death, when the second cholera pandemic took his life, as well as the lives of their daughters. The same home Aurelie raised her family in would go to her late husband's only heir; a young boy by the name of Aristide Thibodeaux. It is said that Etienne's betrayal was so potent that Aurelie made a deal with a demon, so that when she died, the Thibodeaux bloodline became tainted with Le Garçon Cunja. Etienne desired a son and so sons were what his descendants would have. For the generations that followed, there would be heartbreak, complications, miscarriages; while every boy would grow to be strong and healthy, every girl was born still, or too small or sickly to survive. It wasn't until 1994, when the Thibodeaux and Fontenot bloodlines entangled once more, that Le Garçon Cunja began to crumble for good. It took two dreadful years and two consecutive miscarriages, but finally, in 1997, the curse was lifted altogether with the arrival of a set of multiples (as it began with six children, it would end with six children); the last of which was a strong and healthy daughter, no less. But as is the way with every form of magic, there was still a price to be paid. On April 22nd, 2004, James Thibodeaux dropped dead like a ton of bricks, and for the life of them, none of the local authorities could understand why. From what they all gathered, the man was 29 years old, as fit as a fiddle, and didn't partake in anything that would've compromised his health; no smoking, drinking, narcotics, nothing.

His family, on the other hand, know full well what really happened to him. His children have been hearing the legend of Le Garçon Cunja since they were little, and as for the older generations, it's just about the only thing they like discussing. James might've done them all a truckload of good by marrying a Fontenot, but the fact remains that the cycle had to be completed. Where there is life, death is sure to follow, and in an eerily similar fashion to his infamous ancestor, he had to conceive six beautiful children before his untimely death, thus putting an end to the curse once and for all. Of course, the whole thing's nothing more than a story. No one can know for sure. Officially, James suffered a massive heart attack while he was out on his morning jog; the autopsy has proven that much. And as for the Thibodeaux kids, the only factual history they know of is their grandparents' relocation from Savannah, Georgia to Waverly, Louisiana in the early 70s, where they had a son, James, and his two younger brothers. The Fontenots, on their mother's side, are the ones that have been in Waverly since… well, since as far back as anyone can trace them. 1846. But aside from their mother and grandmother, they don't have the slightest notion as to where any other living relatives are. It's as if the whole family just up and disappeared one day. Aunts, uncles, cousins; all of them gone without a trace. Chapter II: The Infamous Fontenot Women Legend has it that after Aurelie left Arcadia, she was drawn to Waverly, where she married another witch by the name of Braxton and found herself capable of bearing children once more. But because she refused to make the same mistake twice, Aurelie initiated the tradition of embracing a matriarchal lineage; spouses and children would take on the Fontenot surname, and anyone who attempted otherwise would be completely expunged from the family. And if one wished to marry or bear children, they would have to do so with a human; fornicating with another witch family was no longer acceptable. Such laws were drilled into Aurelie's children, as well as her children's children.

For the multiple generations that followed, the Fontenot bloodline became known for producing incredibly strong witches. Their daughters were known for being exceptionally beautiful, shrewd, and cunning, and their sons were known for breaking hearts and taking names when necessary. The girls tended to be stronger than the boys when it came to magic, but they were also subjected to a stricter lifestyle, as they were seen as the primary caregivers of the future bloodline. This continued well into the 1990s, until one of the Fontenot women fell in love with an outsider at the tender age of sixteen. James Thibodeaux was everything she imagined he would be and more. The problem was that it became a lot more difficult for them to hide their relationship when she found out she was pregnant with his child. Her great aunt, who was head of the Fontenot coven at the time, demanded that she get an abortion and never speak to James again. This initiated a gigantic fight between her great aunt and her mother, which started a feud that would last for decades. Officially, it was her mother and herself who were permanently excommunicated, but because her great aunt secretly feared the wrath of her mother, rather than having the two of them leave, the rest of the coven migrated to the Bas-Saint-Laurent region of Quebec. Neither of them has spoken to another Fontenot family member since then, which explains why the Thibodeaux kids have their father's last name rather than their mother's. Nowadays, the glorious Fontenot family is little more than another mystery, to the citizens of Waverly as well as the Thibodeaux kids. Their grandmother is the last person in the state to bear the Fontenot surname and she's definitely not considered "glorious" to most. She's a surly old woman who lives in a surly old cabin out near the woods, of which she built with her own two hands after her husband died. She has plenty of knowledge pertaining to magic and spells dating back to the late 1800s, but she would much rather spend her time sitting in the rocking chair on her front porch, refilling her mason jar with some good ole Jack Daniels. As far as she's concerned, she's old and she doesn't have enough shit left in her body to give for anything more than the protection symbols carved into the doorways and windows of her rundown home. Provided you're her daughter, a grandchild, or of the very few percentages of people she doesn't want to shoot in the face with her sawed-off, there are times when she'll impart some wisdom on a wandering soul, but it's not without brutal honesty, grouchiness, and a fair share of insults. Chapter III: Sons and Daughters it's been fourteen years since the death of James Thibodeaux, and what remains of his family is more akin to a tragedy than a success. Unable to keep a steady job due to her own family history serving as the root of much local stigma (Every family in Waverly that's been around for generations knows that befriending a Fontenot woman equals a lifetime of bad luck and misfortune), his wife took to a lifestyle of con artistry and prostitution to provide for their children.

Which, truth be told, meant leaving them in motel rooms to fend for themselves once they reached six or seven years old, while she was gone for days at a time. Or worse, leaving them with their grandmother, who wouldn't let them go to school or play with other kids in the area and always reeked like whiskey after ten o'clock. Now twenty-one years of age, the Thibodeaux kids have long since learned that they can only really depend on themselves and one another. Because when the going gets tough, Angela Thibodeaux gets going. That's how it's always been and probably how it will continue to be for the rest of their lives, so most of them have long since stopped attempting to contact her altogether. Last they heard, she was off somewhere in the mountains of Arkansas with some werewolf, so truthfully, she's still pretty damn useless to them, as a mother and as anything else. Aside from the occasional errand Angela sent them on as kids (which typically included going to her various nefarious sources to obtain pig's blood, chicken feet, the heart of a virgin etc.), I imagine that all of the magic they know, they learned by reading a weather-beaten copy of the Fontenot family grimoire from their grandmother's library and teaching themselves anything they needed to know after making their deal. Which, according to Fontenot family tradition, is done at the age of eighteen. Emma hasn't made hers yet, but I imagine that most, if not all, of the boys have embraced this tradition, seeing as it's been taught to them by their grandmother that that's what they're meant to do. Some of the siblings might have went to university, others might not have. I like to think that they all rent a shot-gun house together because adulting is hard and they're horribly co-dependent on one another at this point, primarily since they served as each other's lifelines growing up, especially after their mother left for good and they needed to survive on their own for the most part. But we can always discuss alternative living situations (roommates, lovers, or maybe one of them just found a way to make bank and can afford their own place idk). All in all, their characters as individuals are entirely UTP! The only thing I'm going to be adamant about are the face claims. Otherwise, go with whatever and we'll figure the rest out later! first thibodeaux21, choleric/utp, nick robinson 2, open first-born Thibodeaux son and eldest of the quadruplets. witchy embodiment of chaotic neutral. likes to refer to himself as the evil twin, even though he's fiercely loyal and not a bad person... deep down. think along the lines of nick jones (house of wax), s1 dean Winchester (spn), and loki (mcu)

Infamous Fontenot Women Legend has it that after Aurelie left Arcadia, she was drawn to Waverly, where she married another witch by the name of Braxton and found herself capable of bearing children once more. But because she refused to make the same mistake twice, Aurelie initiated the tradition of embracing a matriarchal lineage; spouses and children would take on the Fontenot surname, and anyone who attempted otherwise would be completely expunged from the family. And if one wished to marry or bear children, they would have to do so with a human; fornicating with another witch family was no longer acceptable. Such laws were drilled into Aurelie's children, as well as her children's children.

Jimmy Wingo
CHRISTMAS MORNING 1982

It was Christmas 1982. The Browns were killed in their bedroom, and their children found them on Christmas morning. There had been a roadblock in Dixie Inn on Christmas Eve night, but the law enforcement people did not tell them about two convicts who had escaped. The Browns did not know of the danger -- may have never known what happened to them. He was the brother of the late contractor L. T. Brown. Mrs. Newton Brown may have been named "Earlene," but that has not been verified. We think the convicts were caught around New Years' Day, tried, convicted, and eventually executed, there was no motive established.

Newt was Clyde's brother. Another brother was Edgar Brown, killed himself a year after the murder because he was despondent over the death of Newt.

Wingo and Glass had just escaped from prison and were "on the run" Law enforcement were looking for them and knew immediately who had killed the Brown's. These escapee's were on the run and may have needed money. They didn't catch them and Wingo's girlfriend until January 6, 1983.

JIMMY GLASS AND JIMMY WINGO
Mr. Glass, the dad of Jimmy worked at Arizona Chemical. He was an instrument repairman. The company had a policy of hiring employees children as temporary summer laborers.

1983

Dorothy Gipson
Dorothy Hallie Gipson

Dorothy
Hallie Gipson
SHREVEPORT
Services for Miss Dorothy Hallie Gipson, 25, of Shreveport, will be held Wednesday, April 13 at 2 p.m. at Rose-Neath's Marshall Street Chapel. The Rev. Dr. Donald Webb, president of Centenary College, will officiate.
Miss Gipson, a native of Long Island, N.Y., died April 10, 1983 at her residence. She had resided in Shreveport since 1969. She was an employee of B. Dalton and the L.S.U. Medical Center Library. She was a graduate of Byrd High School and was a senior at L.S.U. Shreveport majoring in English. She was a member of the Methodist church.
She was survived by her parents, Lt. Col. Ret. Guy Gipson and Asenath Snyder Gipson of Shreveport; and four brothers, Patrick Gipson of San Francisco, Robert Gipson and Eric Gipson, both of Shreveport, and Ralph Gipson of New Orleans.
Pallbearers will be Loftin Greer, Kevin Greer, David Egan, Steve Aymond, Patrick Montague, and Bill Trippe.

Birth   17 Oct 1957
Death 10 Apr 1983 (aged 25)
Burial Forest Park East Cemetery
Shreveport, Caddo Parish, Louisiana,
USA
Photo requests are not allowed for this memorial.

Murder victim in Shreveport, LA. She was killed at her garage apartment on Kings Highway, about where the southwest corner of Julie Anne's Bakery is now. She was employed at B Dalton Bookseller at Mall St. Vincent and at the LSU Medical Center Library. Her murder has never been solved. People with information on this slaying should call Shreveport Police detectives, the Caddo Parish district attorney or call Crime Stoppers at (318) 673-7373.

416

Both Jimmy's were in the Minden jail when they escaped. It seems they escaped and went to a shed of some sort at the Brown's residence. We were told they got into the house while the Brown's were not at home. When the Brown couple came home, they shot them. They both denied doing the shooting and blamed it on each other so they were both executed.

Murderer of a Couple Executed in Louisiana
Published: June 13, 1987

LEAD: A swaggering inmate who said he would ''rather be fishing'' was executed in the electric chair early today for the shooting deaths of a bound and gagged couple in 1982.

A swaggering inmate who said he would ''rather be fishing'' was executed in the electric chair early today for the shooting deaths of a bound and gagged couple in 1982.

Jimmy Glass, the third Louisiana inmate executed in five days, was pronounced dead at 12:14 A.M., Corrections Commissioner C. Hall Phelps said.

The 25-year-old high school dropout went to his death after the United States Supreme Court rejected an appeal without comment Thursday evening. The High Court also refused to stop Louisiana executions on Sunday and Tuesday.

Mr. Glass grinned as he was strapped into the electric chair. A short time earlier he was asked if he had a final statement and he said, ''Yeah, I think I'd rather be fishing.''

Mr. Glass was condemned for killing Newt and Erlene Brown on Christmas Eve five years ago at their home in Dixie Inn.

He contended that Jimmy Wingo, a cellmate who escaped with him from the Webster Parish jail the night of the murders, had held a shotgun to his head and made him kill the Browns after he called Wingo by name.

Mr. Wingo, 35, is scheduled to die next Tuesday for the killings. He said he had nothing to do with them.

Ralph Moss, PHD, LINK BETWEEN TROPHO-BLASTS AND CANCER CORROBORATED, 1997, http://www.ralphmoss.com/html/cach377.shtml

"Cancer and pregnancy share a number of characteristics, one of which is an altered immune system. In pregnancy, the embryo which is biologically distinct from the mother, must find a way to avoid being attacked as a foreign or non-self-mother's immune system. HCG appears to have a role in making the embryo invisible to the mother's immune system, and may play a similar role in cancer too, disguising the immunologically foreign characteristics of the tumor in such a way as to prevent the immune system from recognizing and challenging the abnormal cells."

My grandpa's backpack and helmet

About Kharis Publishing

Kharis Publishing is an independent, traditional publishing house with a core mission to publish impactful books, and channel proceeds into establishing mini-libraries or resource centers for orphanages in developing countries, so these kids will learn to read, dream, and grow. Every time you purchase a book from Kharis Publishing or partner as an author, you are helping give these kids an amazing opportunity to read, dream, and grow. Kharis Publishing is an imprint of Kharis Media LLC.

Learn more at https://www.kharispublishing.com